U-BOAT
COMMANDERS
AND CREWS
1935-45

U-BOAT
COMMANDERS AND CREWS 1935-45

Jak P. Mallmann Showell

The Crowood Press

First published in 1998 by
The Crowood Press Ltd
Ramsbury, Marlborough
Wiltshire SN8 2HR

British Library Cataloguing-in-Publication Data
A catalogue record for this book is available
from the British Library

ISBN 1 86126 192 6

Printed and bound by The Bath Press, Bath

Contents

Preface and Acknowledgements 6

Glossary and Abbreviations.. 7

Chapter 1: Enlistment and Training.. 9
Joining the Navy. Initial training and the Naval Commands. Initial training regiments and units; main naval schools at the outbreak of war. Non-commissioned officer training. The officer "crew". Deck and specialist officer education. Specialist training.

Chapter 2: The U-boat Crew.. 18
Trades and ranks. Composition of a representative crew, 1943.
Uniforms and protective clothing Insignia and decorations. Unofficial boat badges.. 20

Chapter 3: The U-boats Go to War... 37
From the building yard to the front; getting boats ready for action. Early operational restrictions; propaganda and morale. Conditions of life at sea. Early mechanical failures. The first rewards. Living arrangements in harbour.

Chapter 4: The U-boat Crew in Battle... 50
Alarm - diving and submerging. Action stations: submerged attack; surface attack. Anti-aircraft defence. Gunnery.

Chapter 5: The U-boat Commander.. 57
A commander type? Relative contribution to overall success by small number of individuals. The "aces" - correlation of operational successes against age and experience. Young commanders and unexpected commands. Older commanders. Unusual circumstances of death and loss of command. Ill-treatment of U-boat men in captivity. Excessive discipline suffered by U-boat men ashore. Combat fatigue. An unsuccessful volunteer for U-boat service. U-boat families. Difficult command decisions. Collisions, and "friendly fire".

Chapter 6: The Changing Face of the U-boat War... 68
Low initial morale but growing confidence. The "Happy Time". Summarised logs of U48's second operational cruise, autumn 1939, and eighth cruise in autumn 1940. The end of the Happy Time, March 1941; the changing balance of the Battle of the Atlantic, 1941-43. Autumn 1943: return to the convoy routes with improved equipment - radar detectors and acoustic torpedoes. The Leuthen Wolf Pack. Summarised log of U377's twelfth operational cruise. Comparative analysis of the three summarised cruises. Analysis of torpedo launches and hits by U48.

Chapter 7: Some Untypical Operations.. 88
The Mediterranean interlude. Landings on hostile shores.

Appendix 1: Operational U-boat types - basic data................................... 95
Appendix 2: Register of commanders and their U-boats 98
Appendix 3: Register of U-boats and their commanders.............................. 113
Appendix 4: Chart of service life of individual U-boats 125

Bibliography.. 142

Preface

Close to the U-boat Archive in Cuxhaven-Altenbruch stand some cold stones. Written on their sides are the names of people who died during two World Wars. When one tries reading these names, one finds that the words could just as well be a secret code - hieroglyphics, or columns of a meaningless language; but they are not. They are lists of real people who once lived and who are now dead.

Who were these people? Why and how did they die? What did they die for? Why are their names written on these stones? Are they the last memories of a meaningless past which is now better forgotten? Is there also a message for our future? When one asks these questions, the stones remain solemnly silent.

Inside the U-boat Archive one can find pictures of the dead. Here one can see that they were real people, with personalities and feelings; one can read about the events of their lives, and their behaviour; one can find out how they lived, and how and why they died. Inside such archives one finds that the dead are still alive.

Sadly, many of the people who have helped to write this book have now also died, but their names will never appear on stone war memorials because they were survivors - even though the war took the best years of their lives, and sometimes left its harsh marks on their bodies. They are the forgotten survivors.

Hopefully this book will surpass the silent stones, to stand as a memorial to everyone who was unfortunate enough to have lived through those horrific war years.

Acknowledgements

Much of the information in this book is based on material collected by Horst Bredow of the German U-boat Archive, and I am most grateful for the support which he has given me. I should also like to express a public vote of thanks to him for having devoted so much of his life to preserving the memories of history. The U-boat Archive stands as a magnificent monument to a dreadful past which must not be forgotten; and those rooms, which Horst has filled with life, are far more poignant than any collection of dead stones. Anyone stepping inside the archive will quickly realise that guns only give a temporary illusion of power and that wars can never truly have winners; it is simply a case of one side losing less than the other. It is a sad reflection on mankind that men still have not realised this.

I should also like to thank the late Professor Gus Britton DSO, MBE, and Commander Richard Compton-Hall MBE of the Royal Navy's Submarine Museum at *Dolphin* for allowing me to rummage through their records. It would have been impossible to have started this project without their support. I am especially grateful to these two archives for allowing me to literally brush shoulders with people who have helped to make history.

Because it is difficult to list everybody who has contributed I should like to express my sincerest thanks to all who have helped. I am especially grateful to the following for providing information or documents. My research started during the 1970s, and I apologise if the passing of time has led me unwittingly to omit anyone from the following list:

Franz Albert, KS Kurt Baberg, KS "Ajax" Bleichrodt, Heinrich Böhm, George Clark OBE, Wayne Colwell of Parks Canada, Rudi Conrad, Mike Coverdale, KS Peter Cremer, Naomi Desiderio, KS Kurt Diggins, Grand Admiral Karl Dönitz, Hans-Wilhelm von Dresky, Ralph Erskine, Col. Keith Farnes, Victor Felton, Ursula von Friedeburg, Sepp Fürlinger, Ernst-August "Jumbo" Gerke, Viktor Gernhard, Capt. Otto Giese, Konteradmiral Eberhard Godt, Janice and John Hansford, KS Robert Hering of Crew 37a, Wolfgang Hirschfeld, Georg Högel, Rudolf Hoffmann of Crew 36, Harry Hutson, Walter Illig, Frank Jackson, Geoff Jones, Karl Keller, Fritz Kiemle, Fritz Köhl, KS Otto Köhler and Dr. Erika Köhler, Dr. Heinz Konrad, KS Claus Korth, the late Fltadm. Otto Kretschmer, Albert Lebasch (French Division of the German U-boat Archive), David Lees (German Navy Interest Group of the World Ship Society), Elizabeth Lochner, Wes Loney (ex-RAAF), Christopher Lowe, Kevin Mathews, Edward McLaughlin, KS Hans Meckel, Heinrich Mueller, Dr. Timothy Mulligan, Jim Nelson of the World Ship Society, Axel Niestle, KS Karl-Heinz Nitschke, FK Albert Nitzschke and Deutscher Marinebund, Hermann Patzke, Oskar Pfannschmidt, Paul Preuss, Ray Priddey, FK Georg von Rabenau, Allan Ransome, Gerhard Reichard, Werner Reinke, Prof. Dr. Jürgen Rohwer, Edward Rumpf, Klaus Schäle, Franz Selinger, Knut Sivertsen of the Trondheim Defence Museum, Eveline Stock, Siebrand Voss, Karl Wahnig, Charles Walker, Gordon Williamson, Elaine Womack, George Young.

Glossary of Terms and Abbreviations

For many official terms I have tried to use meaningful translations instead of British or American naval equivalents. It is important to remember that the names refer to specifically German institutions, and the translations should do more than conjure up visions of Allied systems in different uniforms.

aD / ausser Dienst: Retired or withdrawn from service
abt / Abteilung: Department or detachment
Abzeichen: Badge
2.AdN / 2. Admiral der Nordsee: 2nd Admiral of the North Sea
2.AdO / 2. Admiral der Ostsee: 2nd Admiral of the Baltic
AGRU Front / Ausbildungsgruppe Front: A technical branch whose personnel reported on the operational readiness of new boats and crews
AO / Artillerieoffizier: Artillery officer
Asto / Admiralstabsoffizier: Admiral's staff officer
Auszeichnung: Award or medal
Bat / Batl / Bataillon: Battalion
BdU / Befehlshaber der Unterseeboote: Commander-in-Chief for U-boats. This title was used from October 1939 until the end of the war (earlier known as FdU)
Boot: Boat - a warship whose commander is not a staff grade officer and which does not have a First Officer, the second-in-command usually being known as First Watch Officer
BRT: See GRT
Bundesmarine: Name used for the German Navy between 1848 and 1852 and again after 1956
Crew: A German term meaning the annual intake or class of naval officer candidates
Dienst: Duty
Dienstgrad: Rank
Dienststelle: Headquarters or place of work
EK / Eisernes Kreuz: Iron Cross
EKK / Erprobungskommando für Schiffneubauten: Command which conducted trials with new vessels
FdU / Führer der Unterseeboote: Flag Officer for U-boats, meaning the most senior officer commanding U-boats - term used from late 1935 or early 1936 until October 1939 when the post became known as BdU. After this regional commanders were given the title FdU, but these only had operational control in their immediate coastal waters. Operational control of U-boats at sea remained with the U-boat Command.
Feindfahrt: War patrol or cruise against the enemy
Fl / Flotille: Flotilla
Freiherr von: Baron of - a title of nobility
FT / Funktelegraphie: Radio telegraphy
FTO / Funkoffizier: Radio Officer
Graf von: Count or earl of - a title of nobility
GRT: Gross Registered Tonnage
iD / in Dienst gestellt: Commissioned
Ing / Ingenieur: Engineer
IWO / 1. Wachoffizier: 1st Watch Officer (pronounced Eins W-O, "One W-O")
IIWO / 2. Wachoffizier: 2nd Watch Officer (pronounced Zwei W-O, "Two W-O")
IIIWO / 3. Wachoffizier: 3rd Watch Officer - this position was usually only filled in large boats and for long voyages
Kaiserliche Marine: Imperial Navy - the term used until shortly after the end of the First World War
Kaleu / Kaleunt / Kapitänleutnant: Lieutenant Commander - the usual form of address was "Herr Kaleu"
Kalipatrone: A container of potash to absorb carbon dioxide, used as a breathing aid when having to remain submerged for long periods; worn by individuals early in the war, but later - when prolonged dives became more common - these air purification devices were attached to the inside of the hull.
Kdo / Kommando: Command
KM / Kriegsmarine: The German Navy from 1935 to 1945
Komdt / Kommandant: Commanding officer of a vessel
Kommandeur: Commanding officer of a land-based unit
KTB / Kriegstagebuch: War diary
KuK / Kaiserliche und Königliche Marine: The Austro-Hungarian Imperial Navy
LI / Leitender Ingenieur: Engineering Officer
Lord: Seaman usually of lowest rank or new officer recruit
Lt / Leiter: Leader, although this could also mean "ladder"
Lt / Ltn / L / Leutnant: Lieutenant. In the Navy the term zur See (for the sea) was added after the rank
M / Marine: Navy. The Kriegsmarine called itself Marine more often than Kriegsmarine, and the official abbreviation was M, not K
MA / Marineartillerie: Naval artillery
MAA / Marineartillerieabteilung: Naval artillery detachment
MArs / Marinearsenal: Naval arsenal
MFlaA / Marineflakabteilung: Naval anti-aircraft detachment or unit - Flak is short for Flugzeugabwehrkanone
MFlaR: See above - Naval flak regiment
Mixer: Nickname for torpedo mechanic
MLA / Marinelehrabteilung: Naval school for warrant officers
MNHA / Marinenachrichtenhelferinnenausbildungsabteilung: School for female naval assistants
MNO / Marinenachrichtenoffizier, Marinenavigationsoffizier: Naval intelligence officer, or navigation officer
MOK / Marineoberkommando: A group command responsible for specific operational areas. Not to be confused with Oberkommando der Marine
Moses: The youngest member of the warship's company
MOV / Marine-Offizier-Vereinigung: Naval Officers' Association
MVD / Marineverbindungsoffizier: Liaison officer
NavS: Navigation school
NO: Navigation officer
ObdM / OdM / Oberbefehlshaber der Marine: Supreme Commander-in-Chief of the Navy
Obersteuermann: Coxswain, a senior warrant officer responsible for navigation
OKM / Oberkommando der Marine: Supreme Naval Command
Rangliste: Rank and seniority list, published annually
Rgt: Regiment
RK / Ritterkreuz: Knight's Cross of the Iron Cross. Although there was also a Knight's Cross for the Kriegsverdienstkreuz or War Service Cross, the term Ritterkreuz used alone applied only to the Order of the Iron Cross
RM / Reichsmarine: The German Navy between the dissolution of the Imperial Navy in 1919 and the change of title to Kriegsmarine in 1935
See: Sea
Schaltung Küste: Radio frequency for coastal waters; and name of the journal of the German Submariners' Association
SKL / Seekriegsleitung: Naval War Staff or Supreme Naval Command

Sm / Seemeile: Nautical mile

Smating: The most senior Oberbootsmann

Smut: Cook

SStA / Schiffsstammabteilung: A detachment for training new recruits

SSS / Segelschulschiff: Sail training ship

Stm / Strm / Steuermann: Could mean helmsman, but in U-boats the term Rudergänger was used for the helmsman; coxswain would be a better translation. In U-boats he was usually responsible for navigation and also held the position of IIIWO

TO: Torpedo officer

UAA / Unterseebootsausbildungsabteilung: A personnel pool for men who had completed their training but who had not yet been allocated to a boat

UAK / Unterseebootsabwehrschule: Submarine defence school. Set up prior to 1935 as a cover to train submariners at a time when the possession of U-boats by Germany was still banned

UA / U-Ausland: A submarine built for Turkey shortly before the beginning of the war, but not handed over and later commissioned by the Kriegsmarine as UA

UB: A U-boat class during the First World War; and identification for HM Submarine *Seal* after capture by the Germans

UC: A First World War U-boat class; later, submarines captured in Norway and commissioned by the Kriegsmarine

UD: Capturerd Dutch U-boats commissioned by the Kriegsmarine

UF: French U-boats commissioned by the Kriegsmarine

UIT: Italian U-boats under German control

Uboot / Unterseeboot: Submarine. The form Uboot, without a hyphen, has now become an accepted word in the German language

UFl / Unterseebootsflottille: U-boat flotilla

UJ / Unterseebootsjäger: Submarine chaser

Upper deck: The top, outside deck of a U-boat

USFl / Unterseebootsschulflottille: U-boat training flotilla

Verb / Verband: Unit

Verband Deutscher Ubootfahrer: German Submariners' Association

Chapter 1: **Enlistment and Training**

In the 1930s volunteers to join the German Navy had to be over 17 years of age and under 23 (unless they wished to join a coastal unit, in which case the upper age limit was 25). Under regulations introduced in 1937 they also had to meet the following requirements: to be physically and mentally fit for national service; to hold German nationality, and to be of Aryan origin; to hold a satisfactory school leaving certificate; to be unmarried; not to have a criminal record; to have completed their service with the Reichsarbeitsdienst (National Labour Service); to have completed an apprenticeship; to hold written permission from their parents, if under the age of 21; and to have sound teeth. The Navy emphasised that it was especially keen to employ mechanics, fitters, technicians, plumbers, electricians (and musicians), of a high physical standard as proved by sporting activities. After the years of hyperinflation and mass unemployment the secure prospects and social prestige made enlistment in the regular armed forces attractive, and very few unskilled men were considered.

Men meeting these basic criteria were eligible to apply to the Second Admiral for the North Sea or the Baltic one year before they wished to enlist. There were no application forms; instead, each applicant had to submit a hand-written letter giving at least the following information: full name, address, date and place of birth; religion; body weight and measurements; any injuries; details of schooling and further education; qualifications and employment; periods of unemployment; service with the National Labour Service; sporting achievements; membership of the Hitler Youth and other Party organisations; sailing experience; driving qualifications; any technical knowledge, or foreign languages spoken. The letter had to be accompanied by a Volunteer's Certificate with two passport photos of the applicant in civilian clothing. This document, obtainable only from the police, was used as confirmation that the person did not have a

Naval basic training included frequent infantry drill and rifle training on the range. These recruits wear the field grey naval uniform worn for shore duties; note that in 1932 the Nazi eagle emblem is not yet worn on the cap and right breast. The joke seems to be the unflattering sit of their naval caps on heads which have just been shaved.

criminal record and that his statements, such as date and place of birth, were supported by the necessary documentation.

The period of waiting following the posting of the application very rarely ended with a refusal. The vast majority of men then received a questionnaire and instructions to attend a medical, usually with a doctor close to the applicant's home. The next step was to receive a Volunteer's Acceptance Form, with which it was necessary to report to the local military office, where arrangements were made for another medical and for joining up. These offices were located in major towns throughout Germany and catered for entry to any of the armed forces.

If successful, the enrolment obligations were to serve for four years plus a period of not more than 12 months of training. Men wishing to become non-commissioned officers had to sign up for 12 years service. However, candidates could not choose a trade; instead, they underwent short tests to determine a suitable posting. In 1937, the main trades requiring special qualifications were as follows:

Mechanic (Mechaniker): At least three years apprenticeship as fitter, plumber, electrical technician or mechanic. Anyone wishing to join this branch had to undergo a further period of special naval training.

Radio Operator (Funkmeister): Good hearing with good comprehension, clear and fast handwriting, plus a basic knowledge of electronics.

Signalman (Signalmeister): Excellent sight with quick recognition and clear, fast handwriting.

Musician (Musikmeister): Auditions assured that only professional musicians were accepted. Especially talented men were offered an opportunity to attend a three-year course at the National Music Academy in Berlin.

Telex Operator (Fernschreiber): Technical training as mechanic or instrument-maker. The majority of telex operators were employed only on land.

1932: the Schiffsstammdivision der Nordsee at Wihelmshaven. These men have just joined the Navy and are photographed during the first phase of their initial training, wearing blue naval jumper uniforms with the early uniform jacket worn as service and walking-out dress. The Matrosenobergefreiter in the centre is one of their instructors; he wears the plainer dark blue "pea jacket" with blue collar patches.

Officer Candidates

In addition to being physically and mentally fit, officer candidates also had to prove that they had the necessary competence and knowledge to lead others. A grammar school education was essential and substitutes for this were not accepted, not even an excellent report from a technical high school. By 1937, swastikas adorned almost everything in Germany; and thus it goes without saying that the requirements included phrases such as "being in full support of the Führer and the National Socialist state". In addition to the political overtones there was the usual wording, found in almost every other country, saying that officer candidates had to be willing to put all their energy into the activities and well-being of the armed forces and state. It is interesting to note that the Führer und Vaterland flavour appears not to have made much of an impression on the men. Although there was a rule saying the education system had to include political instruction, today no one seems to remember what was actually taught during these compulsory lectures.

The basic conditions for officer applicants were similar to those for other ranks, although the rules were more stringent. Applicants were expected to be over 17 and under 21 years of age; they had to submit four passport photos showing front and side views. In addition to general qualifications officer candidates required financial support during their three-year training period; the Navy suggested at least 25 Reichsmark per month plus RM20 for a uniform allowance.

Letters of application had to be hand-written in German script. Although this had already been replaced by Latin-style handwrit-ing long before the war, German script continued to be taught in many schools until the latter half of the 1950s; the requirement to write a letter in what might appear to be an incredibly difficult script was not, in fact, a great hurdle. (It is interesting to note that German script was prohibited by the Allies after the war, because it was believed to make it too easy for Germans to pass information in secret.)

The letter of application had to contain considerable details, such as full name, date and place of birth; mother's maiden name; father's occupation; family details with parents' addresses, and information about both sets of grandparents, brothers and sisters; reasons for wanting to join the Navy as an officer; educational history, listing schools attended and qualifications gained; sporting achievements; any foreign languages spoken; names and addresses of three referees. (The head of the applicant's school was not admissable, as he would always be consulted anyway; and women were not eligible as referees.)

Wolfgang Hirschfeld wearing field grey naval uniform (now adorned with a golden-yellow National Socialist eagle and swastika on the breast) and steel helmet while a student at I.MLA, the non-commissioned officers' school at Friedrichsort, during winter 1938/39. Time on the drill square was supposed to teach the future Unteroffizier confidence in the giving of orders.

Basic training concluded with a swearing-in ceremony, here by the Schiffsstammdivision at Wilhelmshaven before the war; note that ranks of local **SA** men parade behind the sailors. The ratings will continue their practical education elsewhere; before the re-intro-duction of national conscription this usually meant joining a coal-fired minesweeper - an exceptionally filthy job, but an ideal posting for learning about the behaviour of small ships at sea.

Members of Crew 34 pictured at a formal function at the Naval Officers' School, Mürwik; at every stage a sense of loyalty between classmates was encouraged, and when free from their duties good fellowship lubricated with plentiful alcohol was the norm - as it is today, at Crew reunions. The cadets wear mess dress with the narrow silver shoulder cords of Fähnrich status, and department emblems above their ringless cuffs.

The letter had to be accompanied by the father's written permission to join; swimming certificates; birth certificate; the usual Volunteer's Certificate from the local police (mentioned above); and a family tree going back at least three generations, the latter requirement introduced by the National Socialist government in pursuit of the policy of excluding non-Aryans from public service. The family tree had to be certified by registrars or clergy.

Initial Training and the Naval Commands

Two Naval Commands, one for the Baltic and the other for the North Sea, were responsible for coastal administration, defence, and for the supply of an adequate number of well-trained men. These commands were later known as Marineoberkommandos; they should not be confused with the Supreme Naval Command in Berlin, which was known as the Oberkommando der Marine.

Following the re-organisation after the First World War, initial military training came under the jurisdiction of the two divisions, known as the Schiffsstammdivision der Ostsee (Baltic) or Nordsee (North Sea); in 1934 their commanding officers became known as Second Admiral for the Baltic or North Sea. Later, when the increase in personnel demanded that training facilities be enlarged, the two divisions were subdivided into six regiments, each identified by a number. The odd numbers belonged to the Baltic Command and the even numbers to the North Sea. These regiments were, in turn, divided into a number of detachments known as Schiffsstammabteilungen. Their function was to accept new recruits, take them through a selection process, and then give them three to six months of initial training.

All recruits, including officer candidates, had to undergo this basic training process, which was virtually identical for all trades, although men had already been partly segregated according to their chosen career. For example, the Schiffsstammabteilung at Stralsund specialised in the training of officer cadets. It was also possible to go through the initial training with a naval artillery unit, but this was unusual for sea-going personnel and such a path was considerably longer, lasting up to 12 months. Exactly what happened after basic training depended on the nature of the chosen career, but for the majority there followed a spell in a training ship, before going on to a specialists' school.

Initial Training Regiments

(Division/command - Unit number - location)

B 1 Stralsund, specialising in officers' training.
NS 2 Wesermünde (now Bremerhaven). Disbanded at the
  end of 1939; refounded at Beverloo (Belgium) in October 1943.
B 3 Libau. Founded early 1943 and shortly afterwards moved
  to Epinal, France. Disbanded April 1944.
NS 4 Groningen, later Steenwijk (Holland). Founded late 1943.
B 5 Pillau. Only operational for 12 months towards the end of the
  war.
NS 6 Belfort (France). Operational for about nine months in 1944.

Initial Training Detachments

B 1 Kiel. Renamed 1st Naval Reserve Detachment in January
  1944.
NS 2 Wilhelmshaven. Moved to Norden in 1941 and renamed 8th
  Naval Reserve Detachment in 1944.
B 3 Kiel, then Eckernförde, then Waren, then Müritz. Renamed 9th
  Naval Reserve Detachment.
NS 4 Wilhelmshaven. Renamed 4th Naval Reserve
  Detachment.
B 5 Eckernförde, the Libau, then Epinal (France).
NS 6 Wilhelmshaven, then Gotenhafen. Renamed
  16th Training Detachment in 1940 and moved to
  Steenwijk, then Wazep (Holland).
B7 Stralsund. Renamed 1st Training Detachment in 1944 and
  moved to Epinal, then to Fort Schiesseck near Bitsch.
NS 8 Leer. Renamed 28th Naval Reserve Detachment in 1944.
B 9 Stralsund. Renamed 3rd NCO Training Detachment in 1944.
NS 10 Wesermünde. Renamed 4th NCO Training Detachment in
  1944.
B 11 Stralsund. Renamed 3rd NCO Training Detachment
  in 1944.
NS 12 Brake. Later renamed 6th NCO Training Detachment.
B 13 Sassnitz, then Libau, then Pillau, then Epinal.
NS 14 Glückstadt, then Breda (Holland).
B 15 Beverloo (Belgium), then near Copenhagen (Denmark).
  Renamed 15th NCO Training Detachment in 1944.
NS 16 Bergen op Zoom (Holland), then Gotenhafen.
B 17 Memel
NS 18 Buxtehude near Hamburg, then Husum, then Belfort
  (France). Handed over to Army jurisdiction in 1944.

B 19 Diedenhofen, then Beverloo (Belgium), then Hansted (Denmark).

NS 20 Norden, then Arnhem (Holland), then Harkamm (or Harham?). Founded in 1941.

B 21 Leba, then Copenhagen.

NS 22 Beverloo, then Almelo (Holland).

B 23 Deutsch-Krone. Before 1944 this was known as 3rd Naval Artillery Reserve Detachment.

NS 24 Groningen (Holland). Formed from the 6th Naval Artillery Reserve Detachment.

B 25 Pillau. Formed from the 5th Naval Artillery Reserve Detachment.

NS 26 Wazep, then Helchteren.

B 27 Ollerup (Denmark). Formed from the 7th Naval Artillery Reserve Detachment.

NS 28 Sennheim. Operational for one year from October 1943 to specialise in the training of non-German naval volunteers.

B29 Not operational.

NS 30 Wittmund.

B 31 Windau.

NS 32 Stralsund.

(Not all the above detachments were operational for the whole war; some existed only for brief periods.)

Main Naval Schools at the Outbreak of the Second World War

Anti-Aircraft and Coastal Artillery School, Swinemünde
Coxswains' School (Navigators' School), Mürwik
Experimental Institution of Chemistry and Physics, Kiel
Naval Academy, Kiel
Naval Defence School (Sperrschule), Kiel
Naval Gas Protection School, Kiel
Naval Medical School, Kiel
Naval Officers' School, Mürwik
Naval School, Kiel and Wesermünde
Naval School for Air Force Matters, Kiel
Naval Telecommunications School, Mürwik and Aurich
Naval Sport School, Mürwik
Naval Workshops (Training), Kiel and Wilhelmshaven
Non-Commissioned Officers' School, Plön and Wesermünde
Ships' Artillery School, Kiel
Torpedo School, Mürwik
U-boat School, Neustadt

Non-commissioned Officers

By the end of 1920 the Imperial Navy had been whittled down to the limitations imposed by the Versailles diktat; and the beginning of 1921 saw a new navy emerge under the name of Reichsmarine. Germany was still in considerable turmoil, and the lack of political direction made itself felt in the naval education system, resulting in makeshift training schedules. At first warrant officers were taught at Mürwik, in the same school as commissioned officers. Despite these distractions it quickly became clear that the men of the small Reichsmarine would have to be of exceptional calibre if they were to get the best out of the old remaining weapons and to make maximum use of new technologies.

The lack of specialised training for non-commissioned officers was recognised as having caused major problems for the Imperial Navy, and many of the failures of the Great War were attributed to men not being abreast of the latest technical developments. This lack of knowledge led to the issuing of equivocal orders by warrant and petty officers. Towards the end of the war it was recognised that NCOs required an excellent specialist grasp of their own field, a good general understanding of naval matters, and the dual ability to both inspire and command men. The process of promoting such vital members of ships' companies from lower ranks, as had frequently been done during the war, was recognised as having been highly unsatisfactory. One of the first steps taken by the new Reichsmarine administration was to remedy this fault; it was decided that NCOs would have to become a body of professional men with a commitment to a minimum of 12 years service.

Although the Reichsmarine administration recognised the important new role that NCOs would have to play, no immediate attempt was made to establish exactly how they should be educated. Three years passed, and it was the winter of 1924/25 before KL Werner Lindenau concluded a detailed study resulting in a thesis on NCO training. The main point of his findings was that NCOs required special professional education instead of the *ad hoc* general training they had received in the past. Lindenau stated that it was most important to give this group a sense of identity and a strong *esprit de corps*. He pronounced the training

Officer candidates of Crew 31 practising their knots aboard the sail training ship *Niobe*; looking towards the camera in the left background is Otto Köhler, who later became commander of U377 and who afterwards led the Acoustic Torpedo School. Heinrich Lehmann-Willenbrock, who would later command U96 and U256 and subsequently the 9th U-Flotilla at Brest, is second from right in this photo. On 26 July 1932 the *Niobe* would go down, taking nearly 70 men of Crew 32 to their deaths.

Before the war officer cadets participated in at least one training cruise to foreign waters. For Crew 31 this was a 12-month voyage, commencing in December 1931, aboard the light cruiser *Karlsruhe* (KS Erwin Wassner). Their arrival in South American ports aroused great interest. Here the first officer leads the ship's company and officer cadets on a parade through Callau in 1932 following a reception by the state president of Peru. The flag they are carrying is the old ensign of the Reichmarine, which was superseded by the swastika flag a year after this photo was taken.

system worse than archaic and, by analysing subjects which might be taught in the future, he made suggestions for improvements.

Lindenau's recommendations were based on the firm belief that NCOs needed the combination of technical expertise and first class leadership qualities. To this end, he suggested that the education system should follow a similar pattern to the way in which ships' boys had been brought up under the Imperial regime. The employment of ships' boys (volunteers between the ages of 14 and 16) had been abolished with the coming of the First World War; and numerous stories of rough treatment originate from earlier days, when these youngest members of ships' companies must have led a difficult existence. Kaiser Wilhelm II had already recognised these lads as being a vital spark for the Navy's future, and he imposed stricter rules governing the handling of this vulnerable group. He made the maltreatment of ships' boys a punishable offence and prohibited their employment on dirty and menial duties. Despite these improvements a drop-out rate of about 35% was still recorded, caused largely by homesickness.

Erich Raeder (Chief-of-Staff of the Education System and later Supreme Commander-in-Chief of the Navy) received Lindenau's thesis with great enthusiasm, and acted upon it virtually before the ink had dried. Recognising NCOs as the vital link between the higher command structure and the men, Raeder recommended that the majority of Lindenau's suggestions be put into immediate effect. Because the Versailles diktat reduced the Navy to 15,000 men, and most of the buildings from the Imperial era had remained intact, it was possible to accommodate Lindenau's proposals without embarking on a large-scale construction programme; and what place could have been better than the old ships' boys school at Friedrichsort near Kiel? The building was modernised, accommodation improved, recreational facilities provided, and in less than a year it was ready to accept its first intake of NCO candidates.

On 1 November 1926 the school for NCOs was officially opened by its first commanding officer, KK Robert Witthoeft-Emden. He had received his double-barrelled name from the Kaiser, who initially failed to recognise the impressive war service provided by the light cruiser *Emden*. The Naval Command had not appreciated the sacrifices made by the men who manned her and, instead of decorating her commander, FK Karl Müller, they threatened him with court martial for losing his ship. This attitude led to a scandal of considerable proportions, resulting in the Naval Command acknowledging that *Emden* had probably contributed more to the war than any other ship. The Kaiser later reacted by instructing the members of the cruiser's crew to add *Emden* after their family names.

Robert Witthoeft-Emden went on become the Naval Attaché at the German embassy in Washington, where he served from 1933 until the end of 1941. He was an ideal choice to get the new project at Friedrichsort off the ground. His ability to improvise was put to good use when it came to acquiring those items not provided by the usual channels, and it did not take long before he could boast that his school was one of the best equipped of them all.

Unlike the applicants for commissioned officer rank, men could not join the Navy as warrant officer candidates. Instead entrants to the school were specially selected after having served a number of years in lower ranks, thus ensuring that they all had the discipline and ambition to make the most of the opportunity. They had already gone through initial training with a Schiffstammabteilung or a naval artillery unit, and had served from two to four years aboard ship. Only men of the right calibre were then selected for another three to ten months at a trade school before going to Friedrichsort. By the time they arrived they were in a unique position, having had more experience than even officer candidates.

Although the emphasis of the training varied slightly with each new commanding officer, the overall objectives of the school remained the same. The basic aim was to teach the men the appropriate skills to master their professional environment, making them self-sufficient, reliable and capable of handling the machinery around them. The curriculum was broken down into four main disciplines: schooling, infantry training, nautical studies and sport; regular written, oral and practical examinations were held.

NCOs were not only expected to command men, but to command with confidence. Hence there was strong emphasis on drill and the giving of precise orders. The high quality of the training was emphasised by the fact that many visiting dignitaries who witnessed demonstrations went away convinced that they had seen a special naval display team rather than an ordinary class of NCO candidates.

Hitler's proclamation and re-introduction of national conscription on 16 March 1935 led to major organisational problems at Friedrichsort, since the facilities there just could not cope with such a large increase in numbers. As a result NCO training was divided between the two naval Commands, and a new school was established in Bremerhaven (then called Wesermünde). The name was also changed, from Marineschule to 1.Marineunteroffizierlehrabteilung (1.MLA) at Friedrichsort and 2.MLA at Wesermünde. It was not only the increase in numbers, but also the growing complexity of the training which made it necessary to improve

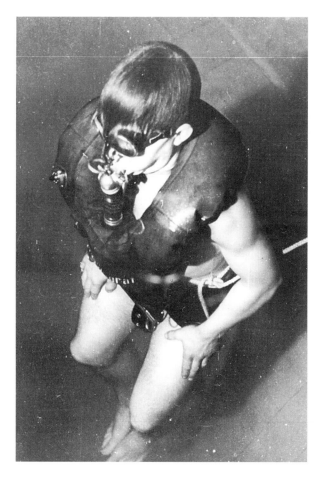

A trainee at the U-boat School at Pillau practising with the "Dräger lung" escape apparatus in the diving tank. These air purifying devices functioned in a similar manner to the British Davis submarine escape apparatus. The rubber bag contained an oxygen cylinder and a filter for removing carbon dioxide which made it possible to use the lung as a closed-circuit breathing system for about sixty minutes. Once on the surface the bag could be inflated and used as a lifejacket.

 8: Weapon training - five months
 9: Service with the Fleet - six months
10: Promotion to Oberfähnrich zur See
11: After three years service, promotion to Leutnant zur See

Engineering officers:
(Engineering officers had the suffix *Ing* for Ingenieur after their rank; they were identified by a cogwheel badge above their sleeve rings.)
1: Initial training - five months
2: Workshop training - four months
3: Promotion to Engineering Cadet
4: Training ship - nine months
5: Examinations; if successful, promotion to Fähnrich zur See (Ing)
6: Home leave - 15 days
7: Naval Officers' School, Mürwik - seven months
8: Engineering Examinations
9: Workshop Training - five months
10: Service with the Fleet - six months
11: Promotion as for sea officer

Weapons officers:
(Weapons officers sometimes had the suffix *W* after their rank, although this was frequently omitted except in the official Rangliste; their badge above the sleeve rings showed either a mine or crossed gun barrels.)
1: Initial training - five months
2: Workshop training - four months
3: Promotion to Cadet (W)
4: Training ship - nine months
5: Examination; if successful, promotion to Fähnrich zur See (W)
6: Home leave - 15 days
(At this stage weapon training was split into gunnery or mine warfare, as follows:)
Gunnery officers:
7: Ships' artillery school - six months
8: Training at naval shipyards - six months
Mining officers:
7: Workshop training - two months
8: Mine warfare school - four months
9: Training at naval shipyards - six months
(Thereafter:)
Naval Officers' School, Mürwik - seven months
Special weapons courses - five months
Service with the Fleet - six months
Promotion as for sea officer

In addition to the categories listed above, there were also Administration and Medical officer categories. The former did not serve in U-boats, and doctors only in long-range boats in the latter years of the war when injuries - especially from air attacks - became more frequent. The majority of naval doctors went through medical school before embarking on their officer training.

*   *   *

The naval life of an aspiring officer began in front of the railway station at the small Baltic port of Stralsund. Lying due north of Berlin, it was situated on the mainland side of a narrow strip of water which made Rügen Germany's largest island. A bus took

the facilities at the schools. In 1938 a purpose-built school for NCO training opened at Plön, where it has remained to this day, although the facilities were not used between 1945 and the re-introduction of national service in the mid-1950s.

The Officer Crew

The word "Crew" is used in German as a term to describe an annual intake of officer cadets. There was considerable emphasis on forging such groups into efficient teams, and individuals continued to identify with their Crew long after the training was complete - just as do, e.g., the former members of a year's Class at the US Naval Academy at Annapolis. (Only recently a few members of a pre-war German intake felt that they could not organise a regional reunion without first obtaining permission from the eldest survivor of their Crew.)

The exact nature of the educational process between joining the Navy and promotion to the most junior sea officer rank of Leutnant zur See varied according to the year of joining and the career selected. In 1938 the pattern was as follows:
Sea or deck officers:
(Sea or deck officers were identified by a star above the gold lace rank rings around their jacket cuffs.)
1: Initial training - five months
2: Sail training ship - four months
3: Promotion to Sea Cadet
4: Training ship, usually with a tour in foreign waters - nine months
5: Examinations; if successful, promotion to Fähnrich zur See (probationary officer candidate, midshipman)
6: Home leave - 15 days
 7: Naval Officers' School, Mürwik - seven months

the assembled company over the Rügendamm and on to the small island of Dänholm, home of the Schiffsstammabteilung specialising in officer training. Up to this point the candidates had only gone through medicals and short interviews, and the first hurdle of getting into naval uniform was to pass a selection test lasting about two days. This test was dominated by hard physical activities and intensive interviews, and weeded out about 25% of the applicants. Those incapable of doing everything at running pace were sent home, although promising younger boys were often told to join a sports' club or the Hitler Youth and to re-apply later when they had built themselves up. The NCOs responsible for the physical activities were fully aware that one day they might end up under command of the men they were training; they had no intention of allowing mediocrity into the system.

Those men who survived the two days in their civilian sports gear were allocated a bunk and a training company before being kitted out with a blue naval uniform, a field grey uniform and working denims. Only then were they greeted by the commanding officer as "sailors", and by that time none of them had any remaining illusions about living a comfortable officer life.

The 1936 Crew had assembled at Stralsund railway station on 1 April, and it was exactly one month later when they paraded on the school's playing field to be sworn in as sailors of the Kriegsmarine. Two-and-a-half weeks after that everybody was eagerly looking forward to packing their kitbags and going on to the next stage of training. This entailed taking a train to Kiel, where a barge took them the short distance from the station to the Blücher Brücke (pier). Today most of this shoreline is open as a right of way, only the Sweden and Oslo Quays being fenced off. In the prewar era most of this area was a military zone with limited public access.

Hopes of furthering friendships already established at Stralsund were frustrated by the Navy's policy of not allowing cliques to develop. Training schedules dictated that all members of the Crew should work with as many men as possible and, while lined up by the side of their first ship, the Crew was randomly divided into two groups. Although the initial training process had been fairly consistent throughout the prewar years, this next step saw considerable changes. In 1932 it was still possible to fit the

entire Crew into one training ship; but the increase in numbers, together with the sinking of the only sail training ship, demanded a new approach.

The Reichsmarine training ship *Niobe* had been launched in 1913 as a Danish four-masted gaff schooner named *Marten Jansen*. In 1923, following extensive conversion and modification, she was commissioned into the German Navy. Despite one of the masts having been removed a top-heavy tendency remained; and on 26 July 1932 a freak summer storm turned *Niobe* over and sank her in a matter of minutes. Only a few men on or near the upper deck survived; almost 70 officer candidates and 30 of her permanent crew lost their lives. Lying in shallow waters off Fehmarn Island, *Niobe* was raised for recovery of the dead, and almost exactly a year later she was sunk a second time while serving as a target for new torpedoes. Meanwhile, a controversy about the role of sail training ships raged throughout Germany.

Politicians and the ill-informed public called for an end to what they considered the outdated extravagance of sail training. However, the Navy held firm to the principle that every sailor's worst enemies will always be the sea and the weather, and that a sailing vessel is the best place of all to learn their ways. The Navy made plans to build better and safer sailing ships.

Following the deaths of almost the entire Crew 32, Admiral Erich Raeder (Supreme Commander-in-Chief of the Navy) wrote to Germany's leading commercial shipping lines asking for their best officers to come forward as replacements. The later U-boat commanders Günter Prien and Heinrich Bleichrodt were among the 15 "merchant boatmen" to join in 1933, but their previous experience earned them places in Crew 31; these men are often recorded as Crew 31/33.

By 1936 only one sailing ship, *Gorch Fock*, had been launched and only part of Crew 36 could be accommodated. Therefore it was decided to place those men who had volunteered to undergo additional training for the Naval Air Arm into the sailing ship, while the rest of the Crew boarded the old battleship *Schleswig Holstein*. Although the new ship was considerably safer, sail training was not without its casualties. It was common for at least one or two men to be dismissed because they did not have heads for heights, and Fritz Neumann of Crew 37 was killed as a result of falling from the rigging. The sail training experience involved con-

Loading practice torpedoes into **U35 (KL Lott)** - the large white boat numbers on the conning tower would be removed at the outbreak of war. These training torpedoes were more or less identical to operational weapons, but did not contain an explosive charge and were usually collected after firing for re-use. The nose was painted red and white for high visibility, and in this case bears the name of 2.U-Flotille "Salzwedel"; some of them even had a small lamp mounted so that their progress could be tracked after dark.

siderable exercises in Kiel and usually a voyage into foreign waters.

The next step of the training process was a long cruise to foreign parts in a cruiser or battleship. A variety of ships were used for this purpose. Crew 31 went in the light cruiser *Karlsruhe* and Crew 37 in the battleships *Schlesien* and *Schleswig Holstein* and the light cruiser *Emden*. The last-mentioned had been deployed a year earlier to the Spanish Civil War and, since cadets could not board in Kiel, they were brought south by the freighter *August Schultze*. Whilst these tours were hard work, veterans give the impression that they were generally enjoyed. It was certainly an experience of a lifetime at a time when only the very rich could afford to travel abroad. On returning to Germany, the prospect of having to sit an examination was made easier to bear by the knowledge that it would be followed by promotion and two weeks' home leave. For almost all cadets this was the first opportunity to go home since joining the navy 18 months earlier; for many of them this homecoming was like being the centre of attention at a state visit, with family, friends and neighbours crowding round to admire the uniform and to hear the stories.

Officer education

Officer education can be traced back to the foundation of the Prussian Naval Academy at Stettin in 1851. The academy had a somewhat nomadic existence, but in 1888, 16 years after the foundation of the Imperial German Navy, it moved to a new building at Düsternbrook in Kiel, which is now occupied by the administrative offices of the Schleswig-Holstein government. It was not until after the move to Düsternbrook that the introduction of steam propulsion and other new technologies, together with the influence of Kaiser Wilhelm II, brought a truly professional outlook to the field of officer's education.

Twelve years after moving to Düsternbrook and shortly after the turn of the century, Wilhelm II gave the go-ahead for a team of architects under Walter Kelm to build a new officers' school at Mürwik near Flensburg. The main reason for moving the considerable distance north was that land near the major ports was

Members of Class No.64 at the Commander's School at Memel on the Baltic in February 1944; these courses, at various bases, lasted from three to four months depending on experience and progress. (Left to right) Ernst-August Gerke (U382, U673, U3035), Dr.Karl-Heinz Frischke (U881), Prosper Ohlsen (U855) and Albert Kneip (U1223). Gerke and Kniep were both only 22 years old in February 1944, but their badges and decorations show that both had previous seagoing experience as watch officers; both survived the war. Frischke and Ohlsen did not; the latter was killed five days after taking U855 out for the first time in September 1944.

becoming scarcer and the site at Mürwik had already been donated to the Navy. On 21 November 1910 the Kaiser officially opened the grand red-brick school. The building is most impressive, and its strong Gothic style led to it becoming known as the "Sea Castle" long before the "Lords of Mürwik" made their presence felt. Wilhelm II's strong belief that Germany's future would be determined by sea trade was encapsulated in a unique presentation of his coat of arms painted on the wooden ceiling of the school's great hall: he insisted that the head of the eagle be painted the wrong way round, so that it looked out over the water rather than inland.

The first Crew to go through the portals of Mürwik had hardly been promoted to Leutnant zur See when the First World War broke out. Five years later, in 1919, the British Army of Occupation moved in to use the building for troop accommodation. The period immediately after the war was so turbulent for the German Navy that a considerable effort had to be made to retain autonomy and to prevent the maritime forces being placed under Army jurisdiction. Finally, by early 1920, when the Navy had succeeded in re-establishing itself under the new title of Reichsmarine, the splendid Sea Castle was returned to be used again as a school, although this time it accommodated both commissioned and non-commissioned officer candidates.

The naval administration was just as unpredictable as the new national government, with the consequence that the educational system restarted with a number of violent jerks and without any clear direction. This was largely due to the naval leadership recognising the failures of the command system during the Great War, but being unsure as to how improvements should be made. Some admirals suggested that it might be best to adopt the British or American systems; but in the end Paul Behncke (Commander- in-Chief of the Navy) insisted that nothing be changed until the results of a detailed study into the role of officers during the First World War became available.

The findings of this study were shattering for the more traditionally minded officers. Much of the old education system was condemned, and the report suggested a completely new approach. One of the most negative points was that officers had been isolated in their commands and, consequently, were often out of touch with reality. The study stated that the majority of officers had too little understanding of how the ordinary people of Europe lived, and almost all of them were utterly ignorant about the men they commanded. To remedy this it was suggested that all officer candidates should serve for at least one year in the ranks before being creamed off for special training. As if this were not a sufficiently demeaning prospect for a class which expected to lead by right of birth, the study went on to recommend an entry examination to select men on the basis of ability rather than financial or social status. This was a most revolutionary concept at the time; as late as 1922 the commanding officer of the Naval Officers' School (FK Werner Tillessen) is reputed to have written in an official report that "men cannot be educated to become officers, they have to be born to such a role".

Tillessen's attitude prevailed into the latter half of the 1920s; and in addition, Mürwik started the beginning of that decade with considerable problems of discipline. The majority of students were promising men who had risen through the ranks during the turbulent years of the Great War, and many of them were former members of the Naval Brigades which had been involved in the internecine turmoil of the immediate postwar period. Although they were now serving the Weimar Republic many still held to the traditional attitudes of the old Empire. During the 1920s many naval officers considered themselves to be Prussians, Bavarians, Saxons, etc., rather than Germans. To make matters worse for the instructors, many of the men had been promoted because they had shown the initiative to adapt to the rapidly changing demands of war; this hardly made for a docile student body.

In 1922 unruly behaviour resulted in more than 50 major incidents of indiscipline, with 49 men being sent to detention. Of the 120-strong Crew, 23 were discharged, several committed suicide, and one vanished never to be heard of again. Naval inspectors delving into the activities of the officers' school were left in no doubt that the youngsters were not in harmony with their government in Berlin and, despite their war experience, their own performance was far from praiseworthy. Many senior officers complained about the low quality of the new intake, and many were openly asking how the Navy could allow some of these characters into the officer ranks. In 1925 the disquiet voiced by senior officers led to the appointment of an Inspector of Naval Training, but another five years would pass before drastic changes were made to the system.

The first inspector, Admiral Hosemann, voiced deep concern over the aims and objectives of the Naval Officers' School, saying that the students knew too little about too much. This led to several major changes in the general curriculum and a strong emphasis on strict scientific principles, with seamanship, navigation, practical mathematics and English being put higher up the ladder of priorities. However, this new curriculum had hardly been introduced when external pressures forced the curtailment of the lengthy education process. The four-and-a-half years of training for Crew 30 was whittled down to three years, meaning that the period at Mürwik was reduced from a year to seven months. Some critics stated that this later had a profound effect on officers' education in subjects such as electronics, mathematics and languages where a solid theoretical basis was required.

During the Second World War these cuts resulted in tensions within U-boat crews; even some of the better officers failed to understand the technical limitations of their equipment, and blamed any shortcomings on the supposed incompetence of the operators. For example, Ajax Bleichrodt admitted long after the war that he did not understand the effects of temperature changes and variations of salinity on his sound detection gear; as a result there were times when he surfaced confidently because the microphones did not detect any noises, only to find a ship close by.

The results of the final examination at Mürwik helped to determine candidates' first postings. Before the war a summary of these figures was published in the Rangliste; and it has often been said that an officer's future depended on his results in more than one way - the majority of potential mothers-in-law were reputed to sleep with copies of the book under their pillows...

*   *   *

Although all U-boat men are now often assumed to have been volunteers, a good number did not actually make the choice to join entirely by themselves; instead they were gently nudged into the service. Whoever made the decision, upon arrival at U-boat School men went through a medical to establish whether they were fit for the rigorous service in submarines. The next step was to go through a process of initial submarine training, which was common to all candidates and involved a general education, including the use of escape apparatus. Following this there came a special course with one of the four numbered Submarine Training Divisions (1.-4. Unterseeboots-Lehrdivision, ULD) which involved working with simulators. For the majority of men, this took the form of practical activities in a training boat for half the day and lectures for the other half. Following this, some of the better men were posted to operational boats without further formal training, although the majority continued studying specific subjects applicable to their trade.

Potential commanders, watch officers and engineering officers participated in technical training with one of the specialised instruction flotillas. (It should be emphasised that a German Navy "flotilla" was a shore-based administrative headquarters, not a tactical unit of the fleet.) This usually involved practising submerged attacks during the day and surface attacks at night, although before the war the emphasis was on the first-mentioned. In peacetime much of the programme progressed at a fairly leisurely pace, with ample opportunities for long evening discussions of the day's events over a few bottles of wine or beer.

On completion of the course, men were shunted into one of three possible routes. They were posted either directly to a operational boat; or to a U-boat attached to a training flotilla; or to the Unterseeboots-Ausbildungsabteilung (U-Boat Education Detachment, UAA), which had nothing at all to do with training or study. Instead it was a personnel pool from which qualified men were distributed to fill vacancies. On the whole the Navy tried to avoid sending men straight from submarine school to operational boats, and the majority were allocated to a boat which first went through an operational training flotilla. At the time many men sent to training units considered themselves hard done by, and were frequently envious of those who posted straight to "front boats". Today, however, the survivors have to acknowledge that this lucky posting probably saved their lives.

It gave them the opportunity to really learn and practice the intricacies of service in submarines while not yet receiving the attentions of a determined enemy. Men arriving on a "front boat" direct from U- Boat School or ULD often found themselves regarded as mobile ballast, and even those with specialist qualifications complained of being treated like little apprentices - only allowed to watch and clear up after the experienced men. Of course, later on in the war there were no longer any experienced men aboard the majority of new boats...

Chapter 2: **The U-Boat Crew**

Trades

The creation of the Reichsmarine after the First World War led to the introduction of a new rank system. At the same time commissioned officer branches were reduced from nine to five, while the number of trades under which ratings were classified were drastically reduced to 15 main types. The following NCO trades were represented in U-boats, although not all of them were found in every boat:

Seaman *(Bootsmann)*
Engineer, Diesel *(Maschinist, Diesel)*
Engineer, Electrical *(Maschinist, Elektro)*
Coxswain/Navigator *(Steuermann[1])*
Radio Operator *(Funkmechaniker)*
Paramedic *(Sanitäter)*
Torpedo Mechanic *(Torpedomechniker[2])*
Mine Mechanic *(Sperrmechaniker[2])*
Gunnery Specialist *(Feuerwerker [1],[2])*
Artillery Mechanic *(Artilleriemechaniker [3])*
Signalman *(Signalmeister)*
Radar Operator *(Funkmessmeister [4])*

(1) The lowest rank in these trades was Maat.
(2) Introduced in 1938 as part of the Seaman Division.
(3) There were opportunities for men to attend special courses. The majority of U-boat gun crews were made up from personnel of other trades.
(4) Introduced in 1944. Earlier these posts were filled by radio operators with special training.

Ranks:
Seamen

On joining the Navy men held the rank of Matrose; officer candidates were distinguished by *Offiziersanwärter* (Officer Candidate) in brackets after their title. During the early days of the Reichsmarine an attempt was made to distinguish between seamen and engineering trades by using the term *Heizer* (Stoker) instead of *Matrose*. The Kriegsmarine adopted terms such as *Matrosen-Gefreiter* for Able Seamen and *Maschinen-Gefreiter* for the same rate in engineering branches. (In German the titles would have been written as a single word; we hyphenate them here for clarity.) Before the war there were four rates for seamen:
Ordinary Seaman *(Matrose)*
Able Seaman *(Matrosen-Gefreiter)*
Leading Seaman *(Matrosen-Obergefreiter)*
Leading Seaman after 4.5 years service *(Matrosen-Hauptgefreiter)*

Ranks were indicated by a chevron on the left sleeve under a trade badge. The Ordinary Seaman had a plain trade badge without chevron, an Able Seaman one chevron and Leading Seamen two or three chevrons depending on length of service. This system was changed in 1938 and again in late 1939. As a result, seamen who passed NCO entry examinations wore a more elaborate single chevron of plaited pattern with a smaller one underneath until they passed their final tests and were promoted out of the seamen grades. After six years of service in his rate the Leading Seaman received a new badge consisting of a single plaited chevron surmounted by a star. The rank of Matrosen-Stabsgefreiter was added in 1939, marked by a double plaited chevron and star.

Friedrich Kiemle wearing the Uberzeiher or pea jacket with cornflower blue collar patches, as worn by ranks from Matrose to Matrosenstabsobergefreiter. His rank of Maat is indicated by the single lace bars on the patches; these were silver until December 1939, gold thereafter. His junior petty officer rate and the engineering branch are also identified by the yellow metal cog and anchor badge pinned to the left sleeve.

Petty Officers

This category was termed in German *Unteroffiziere ohne Portepee*, i.e. non-commissioned officers not authorised to wear a ceremonial sidearm with appropriate orders of dress. There were two ranks, Petty Officer *(—maat)* and Chief Petty Officer *(Ober — maat)*, the man's trade being inserted where we show dashes: e.g. *Bootsmannsmaat* (Seaman PO), *Funkmaat, Maschinenmaat, Obersteuermannsmaat* (Coxswain CPO), *Obermaschinenmaat*.

Warrant Officers

These were termed *Unteroffiziere mit Portepee*, i.e. non-commissioned officers authorised to wear the naval dagger with appropriate orders of dress. Initially there were two ranks, Boatswain

(*Bootsmann*) and Chief Boatswain (*Oberbootsmann*); during the war the senior rank of *Stabsoberbootsmann* was added.

Again, the term Bootsmann applied only to seamen, and the man's trade was incorpated in the title to give, for instance:

Maschinist	*Obermaschinist*	*Stabsobermaschinist*
Funkmeister	*Oberfunkmeister*	*Stabsoberfunkmeister*
Steuermann	*Obersteuermann*	*Stabsobersteuermann*
Signalmeister	*Obersignalmeister*	*Stabsobersignalmeister*

Officer Candidates

Seaman / Officer Candidate (*Matrose Offiziersanwärter*)
Cadet / Midshipman (*Kadett*)
Senior Cadet / Midshipman (*Fähnrich zur See*)
Sub-Lieutenant (*Oberfähnrich zur See*)

Commissioned Officers

Commissioned officer ranks were as follows; the most senior rank normally seen on a U-boat was Commander, and some boats were commanded by a Senior Lieutenant:

Lieutenant, Junior *Leutnant zur See (LT)*
Lieutenant, Senior *Oberleutnant zur See (OL)*
Lieutenant Commander *Kapitänleutnant (KL)*
Commander *Korvettenkapitän (KK)*
Captain, Junior *Fregattenkapitän (FK)*
Captain, Senior *Kapitän zur See (KS)*
Rear Admiral *Konteradmiral (KA)*
Vice Admiral *Vizeadmiral (VA)*

Matrosenobergefreiter Alfred Schultze in 1942, wearing the pea jacket as service and walking out dress. His rank is indicated by the double gold left sleeve chevrons, and the engineering branch by the cogwheel above them. The ribbon of the Iron Cross 2nd Class is worn in the buttonhole, and on his left breast the U-Boat War Badge and the National Sports Badge. Before the outbreak of war a vast range of cap tallies identified a man's ship, unit or establishment, but these were quickly replaced for security reasons with this general issue *Kriegsmarine* tally.

Admiral *Generaladmiral*
Admiral of the Fleet *Grandadmiral*

Commissioned officer ranks were suffixed as follows:
Sea/deck officer: none
Engineering officer: (Ing) = *Ingenieur*
Administration officer: (V) = *Verwaltungsoffizier*
Weapons officer: (W) = *Waffenoffizier*
The rank sequence for medical officers was different; e.g. *Marineassisstenarzt* was equivalent to LT, *Marine-oberassistenarzt* equivalent to OL, *Marinestabarzt* equivalent to KL, and so forth.

* * *

To give a representative idea of the ranks and trades comprising a typical U-boat's company, we duplicate here the crew of a Type VIIC boat, U377, as recorded before putting to sea on her twelfth operational cruise in autumn 1943:

Commander OL Gerhard Kluth
Watch officers LT Ernst-August Gerke, and either LT Wolfgang
  Herpich or LT Kurt Menger
Engineering officers LT(Ing) Karl-Heinz Nitschke with trainee
  LT(Ing) Erich Altesellmeier
Obersteuermann Martin Weidmann
Stabsobermaschinist Jak Mallmann
Obermaschinist Willi Schulz
Maschinenobermaat Herbert Dorn, Kurt Göllnitz
Maschinenmaat Willi Hiess, Johannes Hilbert, Helmut Hofstede,
  Paul Jaguttis, Arthur Allenstein
Maschinenobergefreiter Helmut Bachmann, Heinz Badstüber, Karl
  Guth, Arthur Kobs, Norbert Pampusch, Hans Pfeiffer, Herbert
  Richter, Gerhard Sikorski, Alfred Schultze, Kurt Schulz, Paul
  Ziwiski
Maschinengefreiter Wolfgang Blümel, Peter Fehlhaber,
  Otto Fröhlich, Heinz Hannecke, Hermann Stehning
Funkobermaat Siebrand Voss, Paul Czinczoll, Heinz Neugebauer
Funkobergefreiter Helmut Schaar
Funkgefreiter Artur Meiser, Heinz Panning
Oberbootsmaat Hermann Patzke, Albert Jungclaus

The collar patches for Obermaat bore two bars, as shown in this fine posed prewar portrait; as a chief petty officer he also sports gold collar braid (Tresse). The pea jacket is worn over the blue jumper uniform and "Nelson" collar.

Bootsmaat Erich Köhler, Otto Schnell
Matrosenobergefreiter Otto Diening, Harry Eydam, Bruno Merkel,
  Horst Michel, Horst Ober, Richard Reissner, Otto Sommerer
Matrosengefreiter Kurt Dams, Stefan Istvanitz, Wilhelm
  Wiederhold
Obermechniker Heinrich Böhm
Mechanikersmaat Werner Reinicke, Jakob Möhl
Mechanikersobergefreiter Karl-Heinz Schütt
Mechanikersgefreiter Erich Weinert
Sanitätsobermaat Bruno Günther
(Total: Five officers, 52 men)

UNIFORMS & PROTECTIVE CLOTHING

Rather than duplicate here the detailed descriptions of the
Kriegsmarine's general orders of dress which are available elsewhere, we limit ourselves in this chapter largely to photographs
of the various types of dress worn by U-boat officers and their
crews on operational service.

   After 1935 there were two basic regulation uniforms in the
German Navy, although contemporary photographs reveal many
instances of men wearing permutations not mentioned in official
orders. The two main types were:

Field Grey
Easy to mistake in monochrome photographs for Army uniform,
this comprised a four-pocket tunic and straight trousers worn
with marching boots; it differed from Army issue most obviously
in the design and colour of insignia. It was worn for a number of
aspects of basic training, or for prolonged shore-based duties.
Many "beached" naval personnel were ordered into the field to
fight on land towards the end of the war, which explains photographs showing infantry-style uniforms bearing naval War
Badges such as the U-boat and E-boat Badges.

Navy Blue
In 1935 there were eight different official versions of the blue
uniform, although the majority of these were not worn in U-
boats. The basic rating's uniform was the flat seaman's cap; dark
blue jumper with detachable linen "Nelson" collar and black scarf;

**The gold-laced blue shoulder boards with crossed anchors and two
silver stars identify the Obersteurmann or coxswain - the senior
warrant officer responsible for navigation, who was sometimes
appointed as a boat's Third Watch Officer. The boat commander
at left, wearing the white cap cover, appears to be KL Adalbert Schnee,
which would place this photograph aboard U201 in mid-1942. "Adi"
Schnee was 22nd in the list of the war's most successful U-boat
commanders in terms of Allied tonnage sunk.**

and dark blue trousers. A white version of this uniform was
issued for summer and tropical wear and for some other occasions; parts of the blue and white jumper uniforms were also seen
worn together in various combinations.   Over the jumper uniforms could be worn a rather elaborate short-cut uniform jacket
with two rows of decorative buttons; the Nelson collar was displayed outside. This "monkey jacket" is seen in some prewar photos of U-boat personnel in harbour, but its issue ceased on the
outbreak of war. Most commonly worn over the jumper uniform
by ratings and petty officers was a longer double-breasted "pea
jacket", the Überzieher, with a deep collar bearing cornflower
blue patches - either plain, or barred with silver or (from 1940)
gold lace, according to rank.   The flat cap was also set aside very
early in the war, in favour of a Bordmütze or sidecap which was
much more practical in the confines of a submarine. From 1943
khaki tropical dress was also issued; this consisted of sidecap,
jacket, shirt, shorts and long trousers, but was of general armed
forces design rather than being essentially naval in character.

   Warrant and commissioned officers both had a dark blue
"square rig" uniform: peaked cap (Schirmmütze), double-breasted
"reefer" jacket worn over a white shirt and black tie, and trousers.
A gold-piped Bordmütze was also available for commissioned officers. Photos do show officers wearing reefer jackets when on
board, and particularly when coming into harbour after a patrol;
but normally the conditions dictated that only the oldest and
most battered uniform jacket would be worn at sea. The same
applied to the Schirmmütze; the cap was often retained as the
only visible mark of warrant or commissioned rank, but many submariners seemed to take a pride in its battered condition.

Specialist Clothing

Seagoing U-boat personnel were issued with (normally grey) leather outfits consisting of jackets and trousers. The seaman branch had double-breasted jackets with large collars and lapels, for maximum protection when exposed to the weather; technical personnel, whose duties kept them inside the boat, wore shorter single-breasted jackets without lapels and only very narrow collar bands, to avoid snagging on machinery.

The modifications of naval clothing for use in submarines were imposed by the limited storage space, the dirty working conditions, and the length of time boats remained at sea. Although blue uniform items are occasionally seen in wartime photos, after 1940, when longer voyages became more frequent, all ranks of boats' companies concentrated on wearing comfortable and practical attire. The Navy's prewar brown "dirty working" suit - a single-breasted open collar jacket with skirt pockets, and straight trousers - was used at sea to some extent. In the quest for functional gear the Navy pushed a variety of cast-offs towards U-boat men, apparently because they could not practically be worn by other services; these included French sailors' striped undershirts, and checkered shirts. It is well known that after the fall of France in June 1940 fairly large captured stocks of British Army khaki-brown denim battledress were immediately issued to several U-boats as working dress. With its short blouse, loose cut and plentiful pockets it proved a very practical outfit; photos show it worn by, e.g., the crew of Otto Kretschmer's U99 as early as August 1940.

By at least spring 1941 a very similar German version of the denim battledress was on issue, in a grey-green herringbone twill material, and this became the most widely worn seagoing dress for U-boat personnel. With the leathers, these overalls became the trademark of the submariner. An almost limitless variety of sweaters, shirts, jackets, seaboots, canvas and rubber shoes, gloves, scarves, and other issue or privately acquired items are seen in photos of U-boats on patrol; personal preference and practicality were given much more weight than regulations, and often the only identifiable item is the oily, crumpled Bordmütze.

Boat-issue items

A number of items of clothing and equipment were issued as boat stores rather than to individuals, being handed out as necessary.

Foul weather clothing was available in small quantities and had to be shared. Since a number of makers received contracts a variety of different styles were issued; most appear to have been of black rubberised cloth. Outfits varied from trousers, long coat and sou'wester, to trousers attached to waders worn with a large coat, often with a huge hood. Men referred to the foul weather clothing as "big seal" or "little seal".

Lifebelts are seen carried on the outside of the conning tower before the war, but were discarded shortly after the outbreak of hostilities. Various lifejackets continued to be carried for situations when men had to work on the upper deck; however, photographs suggest that Dräger lungs became more popular as the war progressed, presumably because of their versatility. They could be used for escaping from submerged boats, as emergency breathing apparatus inside a boat, and as life jackets. Produced by Dräger of Lübeck (a firm whose emergency breathing apparatus had also been supplied to the British coal mining industry), this equipment consisted of a large inflatable bag worn around the neck and on the chest, usually of an orange-brown coloured rubberised fabric. Inside was a small cylinder containing enough oxygen for about one hour's breathing via a closed circuit system which absorbed carbon dioxide. Once on the surface the bag could be fully inflated, either by allowing oxygen from the cylinder to fill it or by blowing into a mouthpiece. Each boat usually carried enough escape apparatus to allow for one set per man.

In addition to the Dräger lung boats carried a supply of so-called Kalipatronen for use when having to remain submerged for long periods. This had a mouthpiece connected by a tube to a tin

Jak Mallmann, the author's father, on his first home leave in 1933, wearing a white jumper with the uniform jacket, cap and trousers of the blue naval uniform. This striking, many-buttoned jacket was somewhat impractical, and issue ceased at the outbreak of war. The mechanics' trade badge can just be seen on the left sleeve, and one of the several grades of plaited marksman's lanyard is worn from the right shoulder.

filled with a chemical which absorbed carbon dioxide as it was breathed out. Although these were quite efficient, the rather cumbersome container worn in front of the chest restricted activity and in later years, when prolonged dives became the order of the day, boats were fitted with similar air purification apparatus attached to the inside of the boat itself.

Binoculars were also taken only in small quantities. The commander, watch officers and coxswain usually had their own, while the duty look-outs used boat issue. German binoculars differed from their British and American equivalents in that they did not contain any special filters. Instead U-boats carried a variety of special goggle-like glasses for different climatic conditions, such as direct sunlight or bright overcast days. These were especially designed for binocular eyepieces to butt onto. (Although it has been thought that men obliged to wear spectacles were accepted for service in U-boats during the late part of the war, this appears to be untrue; recent research has turned up only one exceptional engineering officer who required spectacles - photos of men wearing glasses on U-boat conning towers in fact show these special filter sets.) They had the advantage over light-filtering systems fitted inside binoculars that the light intensity remained roughly the same when the binoculars were removed from the eyes for cleaning - something which had to be done relatively frequently. British Naval Intelligence calculated that during a four-hour long spell on look-out men would devote a total of 30 minutes to wiping their lenses.

Insignia and Decorations

Only two official badges were unique to the U-boat arm: the famous oval U-Boat War Badge, and the U-Boat Combat Clasp introduced much later.

The former had originally been created by order of Kaiser Wilhelm II during the Great War. It was re-introduced on 13 October 1939 - the day when U47 (KL Günter Prien) was lying on the bed of the North Sea waiting for darkness to cover the break-in to the Royal Navy's anchorage at Scapa Flow. Paul Casberg based his design on the First World War badge, changing only the

Matrose Otto Giese walking out in blue jumper uniform during the summer of 1942 while serving as senior rating in the bow torpedo room of U405. Beneath the oval U-Boat War Badge on his left breast is a somewhat rare circular Blockade Runners' Badge. Giese had been an officer aboard the blockade runner *Anneliese Essberger*, but when he joined the U-boat arm on 22 December 1941 he had to start again at the bottom. However, after a brief spell in U405 he became an officer in U181 for a voyage to the Far East, where his merchant ship experience in foreign waters was of great value.

Matrose Wolfgang Hirschfeld pictured shortly after joining the Navy. The knot in his silk scarf required considerable practice, and many runs ashore were frustrated at the last moment because duty petty officers would not pass sailors with slovenly knots. The German Navy copied the broad detachable "Nelson" overcollar from the Royal Navy, its three white stripes supposedly referring to the hero's three great victories at the Nile, Copenhagen and Trafalgar.

Imperial crown for an eagle with swastika and substituting a more modern looking submarine motif. The first examples, made variously from gilt-washed bronze, brass, German silver and tombak alloy by Schwerin & Sohn of Berlin, were delivered towards the middle of November. As demand later increased a number of other manufacturers were brought in; consequently a variety of slightly differing designs appeared. There was also an embroidered cloth version.

The U-Boat War Badge (U-Boots-Kriegsabzeichen) was awarded to men who had participated in two operational patrols, although this criterion was waived if the recipient had shown exceptional bravery or was injured by enemy action. Later during the war Admiral Dönitz introduced a special gold-plated silver version with nine small diamonds set in the swastika; this was for presentation to submariners who had already been decorated with the Oakleaves to the Knight's Cross and who had earned further distinction. Only 29 of these were presented.

The U-Boat Combat Clasp (U-Boots-Frontspange) was introduced on 15 May 1944 for men who had already been awarded the U-Boat War Badge. The long gap between the introduction of the two badges might suggest it was partly awarded as a morale booster at a time when the original criteria for the Knight's Cross were becoming increasingly difficult to meet. There were no special rules for awarding the clasp, other than a recommendation endorsed by a flotilla chief; each recommendation had to be approved personally by Admiral Dönitz. Demand for the clasp grew steadily, and a silver version was added before the end of 1944, the original clasp having been cast from zinc with a copper plating and olive-bronze wash.

Both U-boat War Badge and Combat Clasp were worn on the left breast, the first-mentioned low down below any award of the Iron Cross 1st Class, and the clasp positioned just below the rim of the breast pocket.

(It could be argued that there was actually a third U-boat-related badge. A small lapel pin showing a U-boat sailing through a cogwheel with the national eagle above, this Achievement Badge for Shipyard Workers (Werftleistungsabzeichen) was awarded to civilian dockyard or office workers who had helped with the building, repair, fitting-out or replenishing of warships - it did not matter whether they worked on U-boats or surface ships. Since the badge was introduced as late as 1944, however, the majority of people who received it must have worked with U-boats, since there were very few surface ships left.)

The Iron Cross

Although the various grades of this decoration were awarded to all the armed services, it would perhaps be perverse to omit it from a discussion of U-boat commanders and their crews, because a considerable number of them were decorated with this prestigious award. In 1939, when the Iron Cross was re-introduced for the Second World War, it appeared in three grades, each of which could only be awarded to men who had already received the next lowest grade: the Iron Cross Second Class, Iron Cross First Class, and Knight's Cross of the Iron Cross. (The later Grand Cross was invented specially for award to Hermann Göring, and is irrelevant to any discussion of combat decorations.)

Although there was also a Knight's Cross grade of the War Merit Cross (Kriegsverdienstkreuz), in German the term Ritterkreuz was and is usually understood to refer to the Knight's

Cross of the Iron Cross. The Knight's Cross itself was awarded in four progressive grades: Knight's Cross, Knight's Cross with Oakleaves, Knight's Cross with Oakleaves and Swords, and Knight's Cross with Oakleaves, Swords and Diamonds.

Over 2,300,000 Iron Crosses Second Class were awarded throughout the war, but only about 300,000 First Class, marking a considerable difference between the two awards. Although it is sometimes said that they were handed out like rations towards the end of the war, Knight's Crosses remained considerably rarer, with only some 318 awarded to naval personnel throughout the whole war; of these about 145 were awarded to U-boat men, so a Knight's Cross was indeed a mark of outstanding bravery or achievement.

Although originally conceived as a decoration only for commanders, circumstances later persuaded the Naval High Command to award Knight's Crosses to lower ranks. The first one of these went to Gerd Suhren (Engineering Officer of U37 under KL Victor Oehrn) on 21 October 1940, for outstanding performance. Just a couple of weeks later, on 3 November, his brother Reinhard (better known as "Teddy") also received a Knight's Cross as First Watch Officer of U48. This came about after his commander, KL "Ajax" Bleichrodt, caused a considerable fuss at U-boat Headquarters.

Following a signal from Dönitz informing him that U48 had been awarded a Knight's Cross, Bleichrodt queried the message: "Who gets the Knight's Cross?" The Commander-in-Chief, with his usual impatience at apparently stupid questions, answered: "Knight's Crosses are awarded only to commanders". Later, when the boat arrived in port, the battle continued verbally; Bleichrodt pointed out that Suhren had sunk more ships than anyone else, and insisted that he should have a Knight's Cross as well. Dönitz dismissed the matter, but a day later he phoned Bleichrodt and asked him to put the request in writing. Consequently Suhren became the first Watch Officer to receive the Ritterkreuz. (It is interesting to add that Gerd Suhren was the first of fourteen Engineering Officers who were decorated with the award, but only one other Watch Officer received it. This was Hans Limbach of U181, who received his at Penang, Malaya, on 6 February 1945.)

Throughout the entire war only seven U-boat warrant officers were awarded Knight's Crosses. The first of these was Stabsobersteuermann Heinrich Petersen (U99, KL Otto Kretschmer) and the last Obersteuermann Jäckel (U29, U160 & U907), who received his on 28 May 1945 - a number of days after the Dönitz government had been arrested. Despite being without a government the Navy still awarded one more Knight's Cross on 8 June 19345, to KL Hans Lehmann of U997.

Instead of second awards of the Knight's Cross, from June 1940 small silver Oakleaves were added to the top of the decoration; only 881 were awarded during the war. Those qualifying for a third award received, from June 1941, silver crossed swords below the Oakleaves; only 159 such awards were made. The following month Hitler instituted the Knight's Cross with Diamonds; of 27 German officers to receive this enormously prestigious decoration two were awarded in the Navy - the first to KK Wolfgang Lüth (U181) in 1943, and the other to KK Albrecht Brandi (U967) in 1944. The Swords were awarded to five commanders - apart from Lüth and Brandi, to KK Otto Kretschmer (U99), KK Erich Topp (U552) and KL "Teddy" Suhren (U564).

Knight's Crosses were awarded for outstanding bravery or achievement and never through favouritism, although some U-boat men claim that they were also handed out for grossly over-estimating the sizes of the ships which had been sunk. Dönitz's son-in-law did not receive a Knight's Cross, although he was more than eligible for one, until Grand Admiral Erich Raeder (Supreme Commander-in-Chief of the Navy) sent a terse memorandum to Dönitz: "If the Commander-in-Chief for U-boats fails to award a Knight's Cross to KL Hessler, then I will award it personally". Dönitz's determination not to show favour to his family and close friends went as far as allowing his son, Peter, to go to sea as Watch Officer in U954 (KL Odo Loewe) despite his suffering from injuries serious enough to exclude anyone else from active service.

Hans Kalo of U145 wearing the more elaborate version of petty officer's insignia introduced in December 1939. His rank of Maat is indicated by the single gold bar across the cornflower blue collar patch, his status as a petty officer by the gold braid collar edging. Note that he is wearing the blue jumper complete with "Nelson" collar underneath the jacket.

Left: U35 (KL Werner Lott) under way during the Spanish Civil War. The national colours of black, white and red are painted the full height of the front of the conning tower for easier identification; the super-imposed national badge is presumably gold or yellow picked out with black. The seamen seem to wear the four-button single-breasted jacket of the prewar brown working denims, with leather trousers and dark blue fall-collar sweaters; and note that the flat seaman's cap is still worn by all ratings.

Opposite top left: The commissioned and warrant officers' "square rig" uniform, here walking-out dress with ceremonial dagger slung from attachments under the jacket. KK Rolf Hopman of U405 is awarding an Iron Cross Second Class to his watch officer. Commissioned officer ranks can be distinguished by the "piston rings" on their sleeves and their branch by the small badge above them; they also had gilt wire borders or oakleaves on the peaks of their caps. The warrant officer in the centre displays his rank on shoulder boards, and has an untrimmed cap peak (his dagger knot is also in silver rather than gold metallic thread). He wears a Minesweeper's War Badge under his U-boat badge, marking previous service.

Opposite top right: Oberleutnant zur See Helmut Kandzior in full dress uniform; the silver and white brocade belt was worn only for official functions, and the decorations on the boat suggest that this picture was taken on 15 May 1943 at the commissioning ceremony of U743. Two "piston rings" mark his rank, and the star above them a deck officer. On the left breast he displays the pin-on Iron Cross First Class, and war badges for both U-Boat and Minesweeper service. On the right breast is the gold national eagle with swastika; the Iron Cross Second Class ribbon is worn in the buttonhole.

Grand Admiral Karl Dönitz inspecting U-boat men. In cold weather both commissioned and warrant officers could wear this long blue greatcoat with the dress dagger. The coats did not have sleeve rings, and rank was displayed by both categories on shoulder straps. These coats were normally worn buttoned to the throat; admirals wore theirs open at the neck to reveal cornflower blue lapel facings.

The officer second from right appears to be OL Dietrich von der Esch (U583); he transferred to aircrew training after graduating as a naval officer, and was serving with the Luftwaffe at the beginning of the war - hence the Operational Mission Clasp for reconnaissance and air-sea rescue units above his left breast pocket, and the Observer's Badge below his Iron Cross First Class.

Above: **OL Heinz Nagel, IWO of U586**, wears a battered seagoing **Schirmmütze** and reefer jacket. Commissioned officers' gold wire cap peak trim was in this scalloped pattern for ranks up to **Kapitänleutnant**; a single row of oakleaves identified **Korvettenkapitän, Fregattenkapitän** and **Kapitän zur See**, and **Admirals** wore a double row. The checked shirts seen in so many photos of U-boat men are often captioned as privately purchased civilian items, but were in fact official issue for wear at sea - a large number of them started appearing around the time of the invasion of Denmark and Norway in 1940. Shortage of water while at sea meant that virtually all submariners grew beards while on war cruises.

Above right: Obersteuermann **Willi Kronenbitter of U48** wearing issue sun goggles, one of the variety designed for wearing when using binoculars in different weather conditions. Kronenbitter is wearing a reefer jacket which will obviously never again pass muster on a parade ground, and his rank and trade are indicated by the warrant officers' gold-laced blue shoulder boards.

Right: **Hannes Limbach, Obersteuermann** and **IIIWO of U181**, who became one of only two watch officers to be awarded the Knight's Cross. He seems to have some sort of home-made trim added to his cap peak; this kind of thing was not uncommon at sea.

Right: Three warrant officers and a visitor from the **Luftwaffe**, one of an aircrew who were rescued at sea, aboard U405 in Norway during summer 1942. In harbour the U-boat men have neatened themselves up, wearing standard issue white shirts with black ties under the grey-green working overalls which were based on the design of British battledress.

Below: Admiral Rolf Carls is greeted aboard U405 by KK Rolf Hopman after the battle for Convoy PQ18. The battle-dress-style U-boat overalls were worn by all ranks. After the outbreak of war it became a fashion for the boat commander alone to wear a white-covered cap, although some commanders felt it unnecessarily ostentatious.

Crewmen on board U181 wearing the Bordmütze or "little ship" sidecap, and the deep-collared, double-breasted grey leather coat issued for seaman trades. The leather coats and trousers were heavily lined with a rough blanket material, and were treated to make them more or less impermeable to water.

Engineers aboard a boat of 7th U-Flotilla in autumn 1940. Their Iron Crosses Second Class have probably just been awarded; the decoration was usually worn only on the day of presentation or on parade uniforms, and only its ribbon, through a buttonhole, at other times. Their collarless, single-breasted leathers identify them as members of their crew's engineer division; under the jackets they wear the issue dark blue sweater with a three-button front and a fall collar.

Bootsmaat Eduard Maureschat of U109 wearing cold weather gear, including a fur-lined leather cap commonly worn in polar regions. A wide variety of practical headgear was seen on board boats on operational cruises.

Below left: A one-piece leather cold weather suit worn by a look-out on U405, searching for convoys in northern waters. Note also the swastica finial on the jack staff at the rear of the anti-aircraft gun platform or "winter garden".

Below: U181 in 1943 while on its way to the Far East; note the doubled shoulder yoke of the saeamen's leather coat, and the stitched-in rear half-belt. Several different types of binoculars were used on U-boats, the type seen here having thick rubber protection.

Above left; The Navy issue dark blue knitted woollen watch cap worn by men of U405, enjoying a visit to the "winter garden" for some fresh air and a rare smoke.

Left: A wet watch aboard an Atlantic boat in winter 1942-43. The petty officer wears the black rubberised cloth sou'wester and the trousers of the black oilskins with his grey leather coat. On the coat collar he has stitched light metal L-shapes to simulate rank braid; this was unusual on leathers, but was often see on working overalls, improvised in various materials.

Above right: Look-outs at sea; safety rails have been clipped between the periscope support and the conning tower wall, but it obviously is not rough enough for the men to be wearing full safety harness. They wear the so-called "small seal" version of foul weather gear consisting of rubberised trousers, coat and sou'wester; substitution of a large caped hood covering the shoulders and upper arms turned it into the "big seal" outfit.

Opposite above:
Carl Emmermann of U172 wearing an uninflated Dräger lung (Tauchretter) as a life-jacket, although this breathing apparatus was intended primarily for escaping from sunken submarines. The black knob of the oxygen cylinder inside the rubber bladder can be seen just to the right of the binoculars; this could be used to inflate it. Usually after falling into the water and waiting for the boat to go through "man overboard" procedure the submariner was expected to use the mouthpiece for inflating the lifejacket. The Knight's Cross at Emmermann's throat seems to be suspended from Oakleaves, which he was awarded in July 1943.

Right: It seems likely that this is U103 in June 1941, shortly after the radio signal that KK Victor Schütze had been awarded the Oakleaves to his Knight's Cross - note the crude painting of a cross surrounded by oakleaves on the conning tower. The pennants on the raised periscope represent U103's total sum of ships sunk to date. The men on the upper deck are not wearing Dräger escape apparatus with its single bladder, but lifejackets with two separate bladders laced together at the front, which appear to be Luftwaffe single-seat fighter issue. Most commanders insisted that lifejackets of some sort be worn when men were out on the casing while the boat was under way. Schütze's successor, KL "Reddel" Winter, gained another Knight's Cross for U103. Towards the end of the war the boat served as an emergency electricity generator at Finkenwerder on the south bank of the river Elbe in Hamburg.

Above left: Oberleutnant zur See Otto Giese of U181 at Penang, Malaya, wearing a short-sleeved khaki tropical shirt; note the gilt pin-on version of the national eagle and swastika badge on his right breast. Decorations and war badges are also displayed, but no apparent rank insignia. The uniform was completed by khaki shorts, short socks and lace-up brown canvas and black rubber deck shoes; a naval version of the peaked khaki field cap of Afrika Korps type was also sometimes seen. Items of this uniform were also worn in warm weather in the South Atlantic.

Left: KK Kurt Freiwald awarding the Iron Cross First Class to Radio Petty Officer Michalski, who wears a white version of the Bordmütze with bright blue national insignia. On the right breast of the khaki shirt is a yellow embroidered national badge on its triangular backing.

Above, top: An original U-Boat War Badge in gilt-washed finish; only this single class existed

Above, centre: When at sea submariners often used to make up insignia to present to shipmates whose awards had been announced by radio. This heavy copy of a U-Boat War Badge was made by the author's father aboard U377 after the radio brought the news that the commander would receive the award when the boat returned to harbour. KL Otto Köhler later kept the badge, in its boat-made wooden presentation box, at his home in Dresden. When he returned after the great air raid on the city in the last weeks of the war he found his home destroyed and his daughter dead. Although the box was charred almost beyond recognition, and the solder holding the pin had melted, the badge itself survived.

Above, bottom: An original U-Boat Combat Clasp by Peekhaus, in bronze finish.

Unofficial boat badges

The German U-boat arm spawned a vast number of unofficial boat insignia during the Second World War, many of which were painted on the sides or front of conning towers. Since this started as a pure fad - probably in 1939 - it is now somewhat difficult to determine which insignia were the first. There is photographic evidence showing U48 coming home from her first operational war mission with a painted conning tower showing tonnage sunk and probably also the famous black cat. However, it is also possible that Georg Högel had already by that time decorated the conning tower of U30 with a drawing of a dog. Whilst decorated boats were tolerated by the U-boat Command, there were instructions not to carry identification marks at sea, but this order appears to have been largely ignored in later years. Some boats carried a variety of different badges, making them useful for the identification and dating of old photographs.

U-boat men also produced a large variety of unofficial badges, worn mainly on caps. Many of them were similar to the large emblem painted on the conning tower and their quality varied from crude boat-made pieces to specially commissioned works of art.

The origins of the motifs are as varied as the designs and some cannot be determined without a detailed knowledge of the boat's history. For example, after sinking in Norway, men from U64 (KL Wilhelm Schulz) were rescued by Army Alpine troops wearing their famous Edelweiss badge. The majority of the survivors remained together and when they commissioned their next boat (U124), they invited their rescuers to the ceremony and painted the alpine emblem onto their conning tower. U99 (KL Otto Kretschmer) sported horseshoes on the conning tower because at one time two of them had become entangled with the chain while weighing anchor in Kiel. U69's design also had a most unusual beginning. On joining the 7th U-Flotilla in France, KL Jost Metzler ordered the flotilla's emblem to be painted on the conning tower. This was U47's Snorting Bull of Scapa Flow, which had

Above: The combination of the two badges on the conning tower, that of an Edelweiss and a frog, suggest that this is U124, the fourth most successful boat of the war. The man standing up high in front of the raised periscope looks like KL Wilhelm Schultz, the boat's first commander; he is probably bringing her into the 2nd U-Flotilla's base at Lorient, France, in the winter of 1940. The commander's jack staff to the right of the periscope could be removed when not required.

Left: A Japanese radio reporter in Europe interviewing KK Manhard von Manstein, who was later lost while attacking Convoy HX237. The bunch of flowers in his hand suggests he has just come back from an operational cruise. Note U753's unofficial death's-head badge on the side of his cap.

33

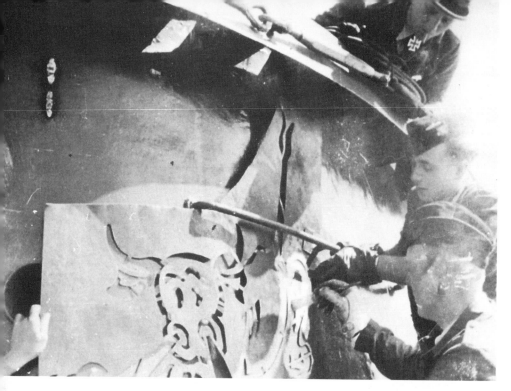

Left: **Painting the Snorting Bull of Scapa Flow on to the side of U567. This boat was commissioned by KL Theodor Fahr and later commanded by KL Engelbert Endrass, who had been watch officer on Prien's U47 during the famous break-in at Scapa Flow. U47's emblem had been adopted thereafter by all boats of the 7th U-Flotilla; getting such a complicated work of art right was not easy, so a template was used.**

Below: **The white bull as it appeared on 7th U-Flotilla conning towers.**

been adopted by the whole flotilla. Unfortunately there was no artistic talent among U69's crew and the problem was solved by copying a picture of a laughing cow from a packet of French cheese - the trademark of the popular 'La Vache Qui Rit' brand. Using this the men attempted to change it into a snorting bull, but didn't quite succeed. Consequently U69 became known as 'The Laughing Cow'.

Drawings of badges painted on conning towers reproduced in this book have been taken either from the first edition of *U-boats under the Swastika* (Ian Allan Ltd. 1973) or they were drawn by Georg Högel, an ex-U-boat radio operator who has made a life-long study of this fascinating topic. Georg Högel's drawings have now been published in an excellent book, *Embleme Wappen Malings deutscher U-boote 1939- 1945* (Koehlers Verlagsgesellschaft MBH, Herford).

Right: **Leutnant zur See Meyring of U586, wearing new U-boat overalls with shoulder straps of rank, and his boat's badge of an armoured fist pinned on the side of his gold-piped Bordmütze. The badge was chosen because during a depth charge attack someone remarked that it sounded like an iron fist banging on the hull.**

Below: The emblem of a Viking longship's prow suggests that this is **U404** under **KK Otto von Bülow**, although the insignia was later adopted by the 6th U-Flotilla at St Nazaire. The hump at the front of the conning tower housed a magnetic compass as well as fuel, oil or water inlets. The helmsman sat in the central control room, immediately below the hump so that he could see the illuminated magnetic compass through a special periscope, although most of the time he would have used the more stable giro compass for steering. The lip at the top of the tower was called the "wind deflector" or "swallows' nest", and the one half way up the "spray deflector". One of the radio aerials attached to the forward jumping wire can be seen entering the conning tower at the front, just above the spray deflector. The partly raised attack periscope can also be seen.

Right: **KL Otto von Bülow** with the Viking prow badge clearly visible pinned to the left side of the band of his cap.
His shipmate also wears it, as well as a second badge possibly identifying his previous boat.

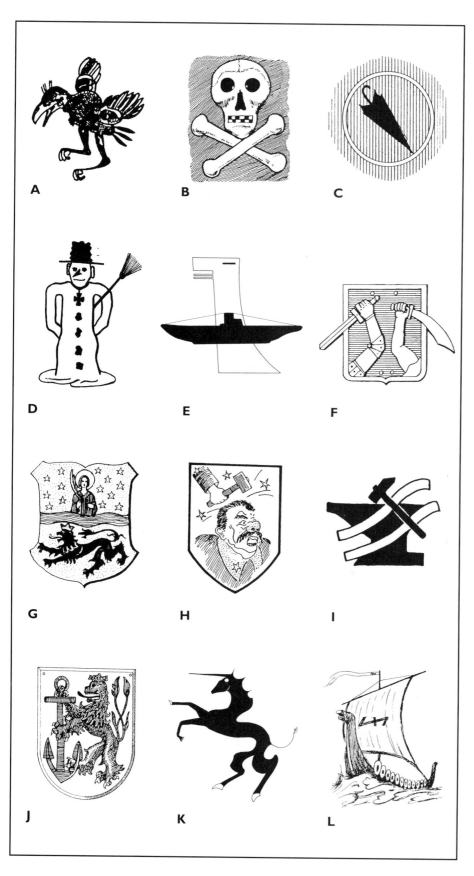

A small selection of unofficial boat badges: (A) U34 (B) U40, front of conning tower; (C) U40, left and right of conning tower (D) U201, KK Adalbert Schnee (E) U270, front of tower (F) U370, arms of Karelia (G) U371, arms of München-Gladbach (H) U481 (I) U481, cap badge (J) U475, arms of Düsseldorf (K) U763 in 1944 (L) U857. The colours of most badges are unknown; black and white were probably the most common, but some emblems, such as city and state arms, seem to have been painted in full colours. Weathering damage would have meant that badges had to be re-painted from time to time, which would have introduced some variations.

Chapter 3: **The U-boats Go to War**

Crews for new boats were usually assembled at the building yard, where the men had an opportunity to get to know one another while participating in lectures and practical work with construction engineers. The crew were frequently chased around the incomplete boat, being told to crawl into the deepest corners while the characteristic showers of red sparks from welding torches still cascaded over the untidy maze of steel. During the final stages of completion stores, documents and portable equipment started arriving for the harassed officers and crew to deal with.

Once ready, the new U-boats were commissioned in or close to the building yard. It had been general practice for ships built at naval yards to be commissioned before going on trials, but those constructed by private firms went on their trials before being commissioned. However, during the war this rule was not maintained because the yards did not have the specialised personnel for testing submarines. Instead, the crew took the new boat to the U-boat Acceptance Command (Unterseebootsabnahmekommando), where all machinery was thoroughly tested.

Boats launched from yards on the Baltic coast had the relatively easy option of travelling only the short distance into the open sea for their trials. Those built in Hamburg or Bremen first had to face the daunting task of travelling through rivers, dangerous coastal waters and the Kiel Canal before acceptance trials could begin. Although crews were left to negotiate open coastal waters on their own, many took river and canal pilots for the more prob-lematic stretches. Despite the fact that relatively short distances were involved, it took six to nine hours to negotiate the river Elbe and slog through the Kiel Canal, and the journey required taking on board three pilots for different stages of the waterway. Commanders who knew the waterway were allowed to travel on their own without pilots, although many took on the additional help anyway - they preferred to keep a watchful eye on the overall performance of men and machinery rather than having to concentrate on conning their boats.

Following trials with the U-boat Acceptance Command, boats were degaussed, the magnetic compass was compensated, and speed trials were conducted over the measured mile in Eckernförde Bay. Another vital hurdle was to get past a submarine listening station near Rönne on the Island of Bornholm; here boats cruised at varying speeds past a series of microphones to check that the machinery was running smoothly enough to escape detection by the enemy. Weapons were tested, the deck and anti-aircraft guns being fired while the calibrations on the aiming gear were checked for accuracy. By this stage the majority of boats had already been back in dock for a number of minor repairs and modifications. The time taken over all these preparations varied from a number of weeks to several months, depend-

At last, when all the graft of training was over, came the commissioning of the new boat. This shows U333 (OL Werner Schwaff) being formally handed over to the Navy in October 1942.

ing on how much work needed to be done.

Once all its machinery was functioning satisfactorily the boat moved on to an operational training course. This started with a shooting range atmosphere - the pressure was high, and the crew found themselves short of drinking time in the evenings. The boat progressed in no particular order from one to another of the specialised training flotillas; there were too many of these, and they moved their bases too often, for a full list to be justified here. For instance, the 20th U-Flotilla at Pillau and the 27th at Gotenhafen specialised in tactical training; the 23rd at Danzig concentrated on submerged torpedo attacks, and the 25th on gunnery; and the 19th at Pillau taught look-outs, and boat handling. Submerged torpedo trials were practised during the day and surface attacks at night. These activities usually required a boat to be out at sea until late in the evening. On returning the commander, watch officers and engineering officer were faced with a detailed debriefing and, if they were lucky, a short sleep before leaving for the next practice.

This training culminated with a spell at the AGRU-Front (Ausbildungsgruppe-Front, or Final Operational Training Group), where everything was repeated under simulated war conditions. A number of instructors came on board to designate various pieces of machinery as having broken down, leaving officers and men to cope as best they could without them. Eventually, when the boat returned from a small-scale war game, the crew were classified as "Frontreif" - ready to face the enemy. They then proceeded to the 4th U-Flotilla at Stettin or the 5th at Kiel, which specialised in final fitting out and supply of new boats. From here the crew soon afterwards took their boat to sea on their first operational cruise; on their homeward journey they would be directed by BdU to one of the operational flotilla bases. (Again, it should be stressed that the flotilla was not a tactical unit, simply a home base, and exerted no operational control

4 September 1941: the commissioning party in the bow torpedo room of U586 (KL Dietrich von der Esch). Representatives from the building yard and sometimes veterans from the boat's First World War predecessor were often invited.

once a boat was at sea. "Wolf packs" would be assembled by BdU from available boats of a number of flotillas.)

Claus Korth recalled the unpleasantness of being an instructor with the AGRU-Front. Although boats were at sea for several days on end, a good proportion of commanders did not think it necessary to provide a bunk for their AGRU-Front instructors; indeed, many made it plain that they considered their presence on board as an additional annoyance rather than a help. They were keen to face the enemy, and did not see the necessity for this extension of training. Korth's reaction was to fail the best and the people he liked most. That way, with prolonged practice, they stood a slightly better chance of not being sunk during their first or second operational patrols.

The preparation process of getting boats to the front has hardly been analysed, yet this must have been one of the most important periods in any submarine crew's service. Karl Dönitz put great emphasis on good training, and towards the beginning of the war his diary is full of comments to the effect that the good results achieved by U-boats could be attributed directly to excellent pre-war training. In 1940 he stated that all results achieved at sea would always be determined by the ability of the commander. Yet, as time went on and the battles along the Atlantic convoy lanes became more difficult, training schedules became shorter and shorter. A sample of 20 boats chosen at random shows one to have gone to the front after four months of training, and the longest period spent in the Baltic to have been nine months - incredibly short periods of time, especially when one considers that finishing-off work at the shipyards also had to be fitted into

Loading boats for action. The wide deck indicates that these are larger, long range boats and the 105mm quick-firing gun suggests the photograph was taken before the summer of 1943. Men are obviously loading torpedoes and stores. The bollards holding the cable in the foreground were retractable into the deck casing when at sea. The horseshoe-shaped objects on the sides of the conning towers are lifebelts, which would have been taken inside once the boat was clear of harbour, but were not there for decoration - working on the upper deck was quite tricky, especially when the wooden planking used in later years became permanently slippery through prolonged soaking. Note how little clearance the working party have for manoeuvring the torpedo through the forward hatch.

Bottom right: A petty officer doing some laundry, and enjoying the unusual freedom to smoke his cigar, on the upper deck of U405 (KL Rolf-Heinrich Hopman) during a break in a Norwegian harbour.

this programme. The exact nature of the training needs more detailed study, and the following are only a few points which must be considered when making an evaluation.

Was too much emphasis in training placed on crews achieving bare technical competence in the handling of machinery, without sufficient practice under war conditions? It is debatable whether a few weeks of sailing around the Baltic gave young and inexperienced crews the necessary background to tackle the vastness of the Atlantic, haunted from at least spring 1943 by strong, determined and increasingly well equipped enemies both on the surface and in the air. One simple example was the challenge of submerged operations while "schnorkelling". Until 1943 boats spent as much time as possible on the surface running on the diesel engines, which also recharged the batteries for the electric engines on which they ran when submerged. After about 24 hours submerged they were forced to surface and run the diesels to recharge batteries. In 1943 the schnorkel or air mast was introduced: a periscopic pipe with automatic cut-off valves at the top, which could be extended to the surface as an intake and exhaust pipe allowing the diesels to run underwater. Its operation was tricky and hazardous: if the valves were shut off by a wave the diesels would almost instantly suck all the air out of the boat, creating a painful and debilitating near-vacuum.

The procedure was practised during training, and the crews were presumed to have got the hang of it and grasped the implications of its use before they sailed into the Atlantic. But out there vastly different sea conditions prevailed; the threat from enemy aircraft was constant; and war cruises might require unrelieved periods of submerged operation and repeated three-hour schnorkelling sessions over several days or even weeks. In these unnatural conditions the men had to come to terms not only with the discomforts and hazards of the schnorkelling process itself, but also with the squalid stink and accumulating rubbish inside

U181 (KS Kurt Freiwald) on its way to the Far East. The upper deck of this very long range Type IXD2 boat is much wider than a Type VII; this contributed to a longer diving time, and later in the war, when air attacks became a constant threat, the upper decks of some long-range boats were modified for faster diving by making the front section much narrower. Working on deck in anything but the calmest sea was always potentially dangerous; the men were supposed to wear safety harness, but it was awkwardly confining and not particularly strong. These two are not wearing lifejackets.

Bottom left: A member of the crew of U382; note the rear of the Dräger lung, and the safety belt with its line clipped to the jumping wire.

the long-submerged boat - and at the same time to maintain their alertness and operational efficiency on this merciless battlefield where the approach of unseen enemies must always be suspected.

The aims and objectives of training in the Baltic are also rather suspect and in need of further analysis. For example, during the winter of 1944/45 training logs show boats to have been practising wolf-pack attacks; yet for the past 18 months conditions at the front had prevented anyone from getting close to a convoy. Dönitz shrugged off some of the later failures; he wrote in his diary that the U- Boat Command must constantly send advice to young commanders at sea because the few months of training did not allow for everything to be learnt which had previously been drilled in over a period of several years. This raises the question of whether the catastrophic losses might have been less if the men had been better prepared for the task they had to face. Using that wonderful illuminator called hindsight, one wonders whether the eagerness to get boats out into the theatre of war was exploited by the governing commanding officers to condemn Germany's youth to avoidable death.

Once arrived at their operational base, getting boats ready for war was the responsibility of flotilla chiefs, who were supported by Flag Officers for Submarines (Führer der Unterseeboote - FdU). Initially this title of Flag Officer was used for the Commanding Officer for U-Boats, but in October 1939 Karl Dönitz was promoted to Commander-in-Chief (Befehlshaber der Unterseeboote - BdU); thereafter there were regional posts of FdU West, East, Mediterranean and Norway. Flotilla chiefs had virtually no operational control, and the jurisdiction of flag officers stopped at the limits of coastal waters; the control of the entire U-Boat Arm at sea was wielded by the surprisingly small operations staff at BdU.

*   *   *

From mid-August 1939 onwards Germany's 40 or so available operational U-boats were prepared for war, and by the end of that month a number had taken up waiting positions around the British Isles. This was nothing new; the U-Boat Arm had been put on a war footing during previous periods when tensions in Europe were expected to reach the point of hostilities. However, this time things were slightly different. The boredom of remaining unseen at sea was aggravated by an acute shortage of information about what was going on. Not only were the boats enforcing radio silence, but it appeared as if the High Command was starving them of essential instructions for assessing possible developments around them.

A further unsettling factor during this waiting period was a continuous and determined flow of inflammatory comments from German radio stations about alleged atrocities committed by the Poles. KL Herbert Schultze wrote that this rabble-rousing over the airwaves was rather transparent, making everybody aboard U48 thoroughly depressed and cynical; the men even started joking with the radio operator by asking "How many children's hands have the Poles chopped off today?" Schultze stated that Germany was now issuing the same ludicrous propaganda with which Britain had inflamed Europe before the beginning of the First World War, but German leaders seemed to have forgotten that the world was now much better informed. At the same time he praised British propaganda, saying that the BBC news and the way in which it was presented was excellent. In his view it would have been far better for Germany to publish the exact reasons for wanting back its eastern territories, which the Allies had taken away after the First World War.

(Throughout the war warships had permission to monitor foreign broadcasts, although in Germany the tuning in to broadcasting stations from other countries was prohibited. The BBC even made matters difficult for clandestine listeners by their choice of introductory signal to announce the start of broadcasts for their friends in Europe; the deep drumbeats of the Morse signal V - three dots and a dash - easily penetrated windows, doors and even brick walls, making it fairly easy to overhear.)

Early operational restrictions

Once war operations commenced these annoyances paled into insignificance as U-boat commanders found themselves faced with the task of grappling with the Prize Ordinance Regulations. These were a set of highly complicated rules of engagement drawn up in London during 1936, and considered important enough for Germany to have written a special handbook informing officers how they were to be applied. This summary was still too difficult for operational use. Men with seagoing experience found the details beyond comprehension even when reading them within the confines of a quiet room ashore; at sea, under battle conditions, they were a hopeless guide. Something much simpler was required; and consequently the German Navy actually produced a circular type of slide rule on which commanders could dial in various conditions and then read off what action they should take.

The basic purpose of Prize Ordinance Regulations was to try to prevent merchant ships from being sunk without warning; however, the rules were conceived by politicians with little knowledge of the reality of sea warfare. Under these provisions U-boats were expected to surface on sighting a possible target; to stop the ship, and search it for possible war contraband; then, if any were

found, the ship could only be sunk after the attackers had seen to the safety of the crew. Seeing the merchant seamen into their lifeboats was regarded as an insufficient presumption of their safety when on the high seas; but the protocol did not suggest what submariners should do with them. Anyone who had ever set foot inside a submarine would have known that it was impossible to accommodate prisoners, so U-boat men were left in an unexplained quandary.

The other senseless point was that, as far as Dönitz understood the rules, the submarine was expected to follow this protocol even if the merchant ship was armed. U-boats were apparently expected to surface under the gun muzzles, ask the ship to heave to, and then put men aboard to search it. The only merchantmen excluded from the protection of this protocol were those escorted by men-of-war or aircraft; ships which were participating in aggressive action; or those which resisted. Troop transports could also be attacked without warning, but there was no indication how a submarine commander should determine the difference between an ordinary passenger ship and one carrying soldiers.

After the passage of the years it is now generally accepted - and attested by numerous Allied witnesses - that towards the beginning of the war there were many instances of humane behaviour by U-boat commanders. For example, having sunk the British freighter *Royal Sceptre*, Herbert Schultze (U48) stopped his next victim and ordered the master to pick up the survivors

There were times when U-boats passed through "safe" areas and the men could allow themselves the luxury of imitating cruise ship passengers. Not only could men sleep on the bridge, but often afternoon coffee was served out there was well. Looking astern from the "winter garden" accomodating the single 20mm anti-aircraft gun we see two "jumping wires" running aft from the conning tower; a single wire led forward from the tower to the prow - originally, so as not to unnecessarily restrict the arc of fire of the deck gun. (Later, when radar was fitted to the fronts of conning towers, some boats also had two jumping wires to the bow.) The use of these wires predated the First World War, when they had been intended to help a submerged submarine slide under defensive nets; in 1935 net cutters were fitted to some boats. Although very few U-boats ever became entangled with nets the jumping wires were retained; they also served as radio aerials, and as an attachment point for the safety belts of men working on deck in rough weather.

These so-called "success pennants" were usually flown from the top of the extended periscope when returning to harbour to indicate the number of ships which had been sunk. The numbers on them show the Gross Register Tonnage of the victims.

from his first target. KL Hans-Wilhelm von Dresky (U33) torpedoed the 4060GRT freighter *Olivegrove* during the mid-afternoon of 7 September 1939, causing her to go down in a matter of minutes. Von Dresky then towed the lifeboats with 17 survivors for several hours closer to land. Leaving them at first light of the following day, he returned shortly before nightfall, and later even fired his own distress flares to attract the attention of a passing neutral ship.

These, and many other examples of strikingly decent behaviour during the first months of the war were partly due to commanders trying to enforce this almost impossible set of regulations. The German High Command did not give permission for unrestricted sea warfare until February 1940, and then only for two limited areas: along the western edge of the North Sea, and areas close to the British Atlantic ports. The seas around the Bay of Biscay were opened for unrestricted warfare in May 1940, but the zone to the west of the British Isles was not included until August of that year. The conclusion - supported by much other evidence - can only be that Hitler was indeed still hoping to conclude a negotiated peace with Britain.

Living conditions at sea

Prize Ordinance Regulations hardly concerned the rank and file in U-boats, and for them the political rantings over the radio were frequently considered as a bit of a joke. For the vast majority it was a case of carrying out boringly routine jobs while being confined in incredibly cramped and uncomfortable surroundings. These physical problems began even before the boat went to sea.

Accommodating some 20 tons of food inside a U-boat was a far greater problem than filling fuel, oil and water tanks or loading ammunition. Until the late arrival of the Type XXI "electro-boats" there were no special facilities for storing food, and things had to be stowed wherever there was room - and in the reverse order to that in which they were going to be required. To make things more difficult, when loading the boat for sea everything had to pass through a circular hatch of about 50cm (20in) diameter located in the boat's "ceiling". The only consolation for U-boat men as they struggled to pass sacks, crates and kegs along the

human chain and stuff them into impossible crannies - or when they later got knocked off their feet by a heavy net of provisions swinging wildly from the deckhead in choppy weather - was that the quality of the rations they received was very high. U-boat crews enjoyed foods which civilians, and indeed men in other branches of the armed services, never even saw. (Even towards the end of the war, when the population of Germany was suffering extreme scarcities and shortages, U-boat men had special passes attached to their travel warrants allowing them the privilege of two or three eggs per week.) There were occasional problems, of course. In U30 (KL Fritz-Julius Lemp) they discovered that the tinned bread had been incorrectly labelled; the tins actually contained condensed milk - reputedly nutritious, but hardly suitable for keeping a boatload of sailors fit in mind and body.

However good the rations, especially in the early stages of a patrol when fresh stuff was still available, the difficulty of moving about in the cramped conditions at sea meant that many men suffered from such chronic indigestion that they could hardly enjoy their food. Some tall men could not stand up properly for lack of headroom inside the compartments where they lived and worked, or stretch out full length in their alloted bedspace. Even moving about the interior was a major problem. Permission was needed before a man walked from one part of the boat to another, and most of the time the crew were confined to their dark and increasingly noisome quarters or workspace.

Accommodation inside the boat was extremely basic. The higher ranks slept in bunks, but only the commander, and later the cook, had their own: otherwise the boats operated a "hot bunk" system under whereby a man coming off duty would clamber into the bunk vacated by a shipmate going on duty. The lower ranks had hammocks, and some had no proper bedding at all; instead they slept on thin mats covering metal floor plates. The bow torpedo room, where the majority of the junior ranks were accommodated, was often the scene of great activity, and the servicing of equipment took priority over men wishing to rest. Comforts there were few, and privacy nonexistent.

Even washing was virtually impossible and usually the men had

One of the "Grey Wolves" returns to a massive reinforced concrete U-boat pen in one of the Atlantic ports - probably St Nazaire, home of the 6th and 7th U-Flotillas. The roofs were originally made 3m-5m (10-16ft) thick; after air raids by Lancasters of No.617 Sqn.RAF with "Blockbuster" bombs a programme began to increase their protection to 8m (26ft) of overhead concrete.

Bottom left: **U471 (KL Friedrich Kloevekorn)** sliding into a double pen of the massive bunker in Brest, base for the 1st and 9th U-Flotillas. Getting the boat into position was relatively easy because marks were pained onto the concrete walls with which the commander could line up the conning tower. Once berthed, the boat was usually identified by a shield with its number hung on the conning tower.

to content themselves with a rag soaked in eau-de-cologne. There were washing water tanks on board, but the difference between these and the drinking water was that one was filled from a tap and the other from a fire hydrant - the water itself was usually the same. The conservation of drinking water, which could determine how long a boat could remain at sea, had priority over washing. The crew knew that things were becoming really problematic when the commander ordered the handles to be removed from the taps because supplies were running so low. Thirst was usually accompanied by high temperatures; cold regions were closer to home and boats did not operate there for very long periods. Thirst made life almost unbearable - it was not unknown for the interior of a boat to reach a temperature of over 50 degrees C (122 F) - as hot as a moderately cool cooking oven. In fact the schnorkel, which became a life-saver towards the end of the war, was first conceived by Commander J.J.Wichers of the Royal Netherlands Navy specifically as a means of overcoming the intense tropical heat by cruising submerged with diesel engines running.

Going to the toilet was also a procedure fraught with difficulties, the first being simply to get in. Although the larger U-boats had two of them one was usually used as an extra larder space, meaning that about 50 men had to share a single facility. Towards the beginning of the war it could only be used when the boat was on the surface or dived at shallow depths. High pressure lavatories - fearsome devices, hard to master, which directly caused the loss of at least one boat - were only installed later, when prolonged dives at deep depths became the order of the day. Empty tins always served as makeshift receptacles when men could not get into the tiny compartment. All this, together with rotting garbage which could not always be thrown overboard, 50 long-unwashed and sweating bodies, and the stink produced by oil and machinery, added up to a characteristic stench which the men could only endure while they developed an indifference to it.

Going up for a smoke while running on the surface was usually the only way men could sometimes leave the claustrophobic confines of the hull. Quite a number of them started smoking simply because it offered the only chance of an occasional breather outside. The submarines' batteries were of the lead/acid variety - similar to those used in cars but very much bigger - which gave off a highly explosive mixture of oxygen and hydrogen. Consequently the battery space was fitted with a special ventilation system; but it was still difficult to determine whether any of these gases had collected inside the boat, and so smoking was always prohibited even when made fast in port. The engine room, where flames sometimes shot out of vents when they were opened for clearing the fuel or exhaust pipes, was closed off from the electrical system and the diesels occupied the entire space at the bottom of the boat, without the layer of batteries which were installed underneath the other compartments.

Smoking on top of the conning tower at night was usually banned because the glow of cigarettes could be seen from a surprisingly long way off; so men were only allowed on to the conning tower for a smoke during the day, or at night in very safe waters. Some commanders allowed a couple of men to smoke inside the conning tower when the boat was travelling on the surface, since the tiny space there was then well ventilated.

Look-outs generally got rather a lot of fresh air, but the natural ventilation on top of the conning tower was often also rather damp, making their four-hour duty spell quite an ordeal. The exact number of look-outs varied from boat to boat and from area to area. When aircraft might be encountered the duty watch consisted of a watch officer, three look-outs sweeping the sea and two further look-outs concentrating on the sky. In some boats they had to stand their turn almost as if on a parade ground, being forbidden to speak, eat or smoke even during hours of daylight. The more successful commanders found that discipline and efficiency improved if the men were allowed to lean against the periscope support and chat with one another while sweeping the horizon with binoculars.

Mechanical failures

Even before Britain and France declared war on Germany, mechanical uncertainties had started making the idea of fighting a war ludicrous in the eyes of some submariners. A number of engine mounts were rather on the weak side, making some men joke that they might as well prepare for swimming home or hitching a lift in a merchant ship. On top of this, every U-boat soon compiled a list of other mechanical disasters. U48, for example, itemised the following towards the beginning of September 1939: the navigation periscope was completely out of action; the conning tower hatch did not seat properly and leaked, as did one of the exhaust valves; the compressor was blasting air too strongly and creating excessive pressure inside the boat; the main reflector inside the attack periscope needed to be constantly cleaned and dried; and the periscope raising gear malfunctioned (though this was repaired). U48's periscope was the main cause for allowing the 5475GRT freighter *Jamaica Progress* to escape. When KL Schultze first spotted her through the milky haze of the periscope just before dawn, he identified the blurred image as a possible warship and decided it would be best not to surface. By the time it got lighter and the periscope produced a clearer picture the target was too far away and moving too fast for the 88mm gun. After several misses due to heavy seas and the long range Schultze gave up gracefully and ordered the gun crew back below decks. (*Jamaica Progress* was sunk almost a year later, on 31 July 1940, by U99 under KL Otto Kretschmer.)

By far the most disturbing problem to emerge during the first few weeks of war was the chilling discovery that torpedoes did not seem to work properly. Many U-boat men heard their "eels" strike the target without detonating. At first Dönitz put this down to the crew not following the correct launch procedure, but the problems persisted throughout the autumn of 1939 and well into the beginning of 1940. The reasons for these malfunctions are well known today - basically the use of unreliable con-

In the early war years at least, a boat returning from a successful cruise could expect a rousing welcome complete with bands, flowers, champagne, and a round-up of the best-looking members of the female auxiliary personnel. Admiral Dönitz insisted that his men should receive their medals and badges as soon as they tied up; note that this commander has the Knight's Cross suspension ribbon round his neck. From mid-1943 onwards the homecoming celebrations became rather more muted.

tact detonators rather than magnetic pistol detonators - but at the time when they were happening they represented more than just bitter disappointments for men who were risking their lives to carry out the attacks. None of them knew that the torpedoes were malfunctioning, and the comments floating through boats about the poor performance by commanders and first watch officers would have made the most ardent dockers blush. The situation did nothing for morale or discipline. Many crews would go a long way and do some tricky things for their officers, but no one was keen on passengers who couldn't do their jobs properly. In their turn, commanders had the natural tendency to bite back and blame the torpedo mechanics for the failures; thus the persistent torpedo failures soured relationships in already strained circumstances.

This is not to say that everything at the beginning of the war was doom and gloom. The propaganda system made sure that the news media did not run out of an adequate supply of heroes. The first U-boat commander to rock Germany and Britain alike was KL Günter Prien in U47, who succeeded in breaking through the defences of the Royal Navy's huge anchorage at Scapa Flow to sink the battleship *Royal Oak* during the night 13/14 October 1939. The attack took quite some time because the first bow salvo, followed by a single shot from the stern tube, had no effect. One of the torpedoes exploded, but luckily for U47 it failed to bring any effective response. After reloading, the second salvo sent the battleship to the bottom in less than 15 minutes. On returning home the entire crew were flown to Berlin to be presented with Iron Crosses; Prien became the first man in the Navy to receive a Knight's Cross, and his name became a household word.

Later it became apparent that just sinking a large warship was not going to be good enough for a Knight's Cross. Otto Schuhart (U29), who sank the aircraft carrier *Courageous* in the Western Approaches, did not get his Knight's Cross until he had chalked up sufficient tonnage sunk in May 1940. The second naval Knight's Cross went to Herbert Schultze in March 1940, the third to Karl Dönitz in April; a good number then followed during the next few months. During this period names such as Kretschmer, Rollmann, Lemp and Liebe were starting to become nationally famous, with the news media assuring that their exploits received maximum coverage. Dramatically emotional fanfares, crackling through valve-operated radios, interrupted normal programmes with the announcements: "The Supreme Command of the Armed Forces wishes to announce that ...". Heroes were appearing in ever-increasing numbers, and ordinary men in uniform found themselves becoming celebrities.

Life in harbour

Readers who have seen Wolfgang Petersen's memorable film *Das Boot* will no doubt recall the scene in which a group of sailors on shore leave are seen merrily urinating from a roadside bank onto their commander's passing car, and another in which U-boat officers enjoy an impressive party. When the present author asked U-boat men whether this depiction was accurate their answers were interesting. Half of them agreed with what they had seen in the film, while the other half were adamant that such wild activities never took place. This clearly shows that one needs more than memories when reconstructing the events of the war years. Yet, although there are very few records of what submariners did in their spare time, the U-boat Archive was fortunate enough to secure a pile of documents left by Margret Wiese. The letters she wrote home to her mother are probably one of the most authentic surviving records of social life in foreign U-boat bases.

At the beginning of the war Margret Wiese was employed as a civilian secretary at the Naval Dockyard in Wilhelmshaven, and in 1940, when the facilities were moved to Brest, she was ordered to France. Civilian employees had no choice in these matters; they too came under the jurisdiction of military law, and were informed that any breaches of the rules would be dealt with by court martial rather than the civil authorities. The Germans have a long history of being fond of law and order, and the move to France was no exception. The dockyard director in Brest, Admiral Hans-Herbert Stobwasser, ensured there was a plentiful supply of printed matter dealing with all aspects of general rules and regulations relating to behaviour in foreign countries.

Despite the creation of regulations to cover every conceivable occurrence, female employees seem to have given some cause for concern; and as early as September 1941 the admiral himself was forced to remind them that the rules of behaviour had been created as a guide to make life more comfortable for everybody. At the same time he felt it necessary to threaten a variety of punishments for persistent offenders. The biggest problem seems to have been the keeping of curfew and the vacating of common rooms by 23.30 hours. On top of this the admiral was worried by the number of people who failed to turn up for work in the mornings; he reminded everybody that it was intolerable for individuals to decide for themselves whether they were fit for work - if anyone felt they were too ill to turn up then they must see a doctor straight away. The admiral pointed out again that the rules had been created for everybody's benefit, and that he couldn't understand why some people looked upon them as a curtailment of their individual freedom.

All in all, the admiral's complaints suggest that his employees

Karl Dönitz, Commander-in-Chief for U-boats, seen greeting a U-boat crew after his promotion to Supreme Commander-in-Chief of the Navy. Although still in their motley seagoing gear these officers look remarkably clean for submariners who have been at sea for any length of time; it seems likely that they have had an opportunity for a quick brush-up before being presented to the BdU.

were enjoying a fairly vigorous nightlife, and this impression is reinforced by examining the printed sheets which he circulated outlining the punishments which employees could expect. He emphasised the seriousness with which he regarded drunkenness on or off duty; failing to return punctually from leave; not turning up for work; leaving work early; impropriety against superiors; failing to salute or greet according to the law. Any one of these offences carried a maximum of four weeks in jail. However, the admiral also understood the importance of rewards in his battle for the efficient running of his dockyard, and promised that workers who behaved themselves and did their duty well would be placed at the top of the list for leave.

Although Margret Wiese suffered quite considerably from serious illness which kept her off work for several weeks, she seems to have enjoyed a full and interesting social life in France, with ample opportunities for going to the theatre and concerts. (It is interesting to note that in February 1942 the main theatre in Brest, catering for a German audience, put on a German adaptation of Shakespeare's *A Midsummer Night's Dream*.) However, being out in town at night was not a recommended pastime for a young lady. In one letter Margret told her mother that the French were generally very correct and polite towards Germans, and that none of the girls had anything to fear from Frenchmen. The behaviour of some Germans, however, and especially that of wild

U-boat crews, left much to be desired. One had to make a conscious effort to avoid them; their language was foul, the majority of them were too drunk to stand up on their own, and they were likely to take the wildest of liberties if they cornered female employees.

Marget Wiese, who worked in an office dealing with U-boat supplies, was one of the very few German women not to be evacuated back to Germany when the Allied armies threatened the French bases. Remaining on duty, she was eventually taken prisoner by an army which did not have facilities for coping with women. Consequently the few female prisoners suffered more than the men, often being confined in squalid conditions for long periods.

* * *

The first U-boats to run into French ports were supplied very quickly and many of them were back at sea within a week or so. Later, when better repair facilities could be provided, the length of the periods spent in port increased. Towards the middle of 1941 the average period a boat would spend in port between patrols was about 37 days. This usually meant that some men would get travel warrants for home leave. The skeleton crew remaining in France - often as few as half a dozen men - were usually accommodated in a variety of hostels; it was only very rarely that men had to sleep on board the U-boats while in port. Generally the accommodation and the standard of food in the hostels, which were often local hotels, were extremely good. One factor which did not work in favour of the boozing, basking U-boat men was the superior performance of French dockyard

23 March 1942 in St. Nazaire: men from KL "Recke" Lehmann-Willenbrock's U96 come ashore. This shows the thickness of the bunker walls on the landward side.

Lagona near Brest: impressive premises taken over as a hostel to accommodate U-boat crews on shore leave.

workers. They proved able to achieve much more than their German counterparts, and consequently boats were being turned around ready for sea faster than in Germany. (Few submariners would have had any way of making direct comparisons, and no doubt this statistical information was kept from them.)

Unlike Britain, Germany did not put its industrial output on full war production until 1944, and until then a wide variety of unnecessary consumer goods were still being produced. Even so, the shortages of the Depression before the war had never completely disappeared. In addition to this many Germans had grudgingly accepted Reichsmarschall Göring's words that it would be better for everybody's protection to have tanks and aircraft in preference to butter, so Germans were used to general shortages. In France the consumer boom continued until almost the very end of the German occupation, and U-boat men could buy and bring home luxuries unheard of in Germany.

When the Royal Air Force started making life uncomfortable by bombing the French ports, the Germans at first responded by moving their accommodation away from target areas and, at the same time, they started building the massive bunkers some of which remain standing to this day. The main purpose of these "U-boat pens" was to provide secure anchorage and dry dock facilities for U-boats, but there were others which included comfortable underground hotel accomodation for the men.

It is rather curious that both British and American interrogation reports and other Intelligence documents seem to devote considerable space to the subject of prostitution. Not only do the documents list brothels, but they even give details on how many girls worked there, what they charged and how long they were on call. Prostitution has always been part of life, and Germany has taken the view that it is better to keep such activities in the open than to drive them underground. There was an adequate supply of brothels, although initially in some places officers and men had to share the same facilities. Stories of the German Navy sending German prostitutes into France to educate their French counterparts in the entertainment of U-boat men seem rather far-fetched. One concern of the German authorities was the well-being of very young men who under normal circumstances would still be under the wing of their parents (this was, we must recall, half a century ago). The authorities were not so much concerned with the boys' moral protection as with their physical health: having part of a U-boat crew laid up in hospital with a sexually transmitted disease did nothing for the war effort. The idea of a deliberate conspiracy to infect U-boat personnel does seem to have crossed some minds on both sides, but it is doubtful whether it ever got off the ground.

Above: More typical of the submariners' shore accomodation - from the vegetation, perhaps near the 12th **U-Flotilla**'s base at **Bordeaux**?

Below: Warrant officer enjoying peace and quiet; after the stinking metal cell of a boat at sea nobody objected to sharing double rooms.

Left & below: The real business of shore leave gets under way - drinks, tobacco, sunshine and shop-talk.

Below: Once the first edge had been taken off, a spell in port gave men the opportunity of wearing more civilised clothing, like the white summer undress tunics sported here at La Baule by (from left to right) Erich Zürn, Friedrich Guggenberger, Heinrich Schonder, Helmut Rosenbaum, Fritz Frauenheim and Hans-Werner Kraus, all members of the 7th U-Flotilla based at Brest.

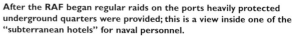

After the RAF began regular raids on the ports heavily protected underground quarters were provided; this is a view inside one of the "subterranean hotels" for naval personnel.

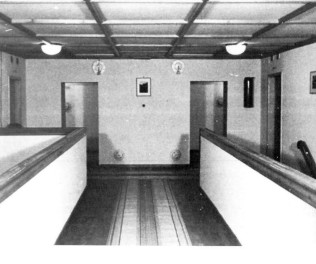

Below & right: March 1944: The returning crew of U989 (OL Hardo Rodler von Roithberg) pose in front of the 9th U-Flotilla headquarters in Brest, under the flotilla's famous swordfish emblem; and OL von Roithberg photographed with his flotilla commander Heinrich Lehmann-Willenbrock.

Bottom: Not all accommodation between patrols was luxurious. Far from the soft life of the French ports, two Type VIIC boats are made fast alongside the repair ship *Kamerun* at Narvik in Norway.

Chapter 4: **The U-boat Crew in Battle**

Alarm!

U-boat crews could be spurred into instant activity by the orders "Alarm" or "Action Stations". The first was the more nerve-racking of the two because it was usually followed by an attack on the boat, and survival depended on everybody's quick reactions.

Fast alarm dives became increasingly important as the war progressed and as aircraft started playing an ever greater role in the battles of the Atlantic. According to prewar regulations, vents and hatch had to be shut before tanks could be flooded for diving. (Under battle conditions at sea, only the main conning tower hatch would be used.) A plane circling out of range of a U-boat's anti-aircraft guns required about ten seconds more than the boat's fastest diving time to run in and drop depth charges. Later in the war, U-boat men themselves revised the diving procedure in the hope of gaining a slight advantage in this critical "battle of seconds". The diving process was frequently started at the same time as the alarm button was pressed, and it was necessary to rely on the efficiency of the crew to shut vents and hatch before they were engulfed by water. It will never be known how many boats were sunk because tired men did not react fast enough, but there are a few cases of boats surviving a dive with a partly-open hatch or with open vents.

For example, in the hurry to get below after ordering "Alarm" Leutnant zur See Bruno Langenberg (WO of U377) failed to notice that the large clip of his safety harness had got stuck between the deck planking on the outside of the boat. The other end of the cable being firmly secured around his body, it was impossible to close the hatch. Leutnant zur See (Ing.) Karl-Heinz Nitschke, the LI, who already had enough patrols to his credit to be well versed in the routine of standing by the bottom of the ladder keeping one eye on the hatch and the other on the controls, decided upon a reversal of the diving process as soon as the sea began to pour in the jammed hatch. This in itself was no easy matter; there was no automatic order to achieve what he wanted, and he had to issue the correct commands in the right sequence to men who were expecting to do something completely different. At the same time he closed the hatch between the central control room and the commander's attack position in the conning tower. After water had been pumped out of the conning tower again, Langenberg was found to have survived; but U377 was extremely lucky that she did not come under attack at that critical moment.

Quick diving was achieved by pushing the boat to a fast speed. Since the diesel engines had to be shut off before vents were closed, this burst of speed was usually maintained by using the less powerful electric motors. While this was going on, all spare hands would run to the front torpedo compartment to make the boat bow-heavy. Then, when ready, the diving tanks were flooded and the hydroplanes set on dive. (Since most of these procedures were performed without a great number of specific commands, it is understandable that film-makers have invented urgent dialogue to make their audience appreciate what is happening; the clever remonstrative commentary in scenes from the film *Das Boot* is a little unrealistic.)

The duty petty officer in the electro-engine control room and stern torpedo compartment; we are looking forwards and to the port side. Beyond the Maschinenmaat (note trim on the overall collar) is the door to the diesel engine room.

Since a number of other fanciful ideas have crept into technical textbooks, it might be useful to consider the technology of diving and surfacing.

U-boats had two types of tanks for this purpose: trim tanks and diving tanks. The idea was to balance the boat and to adjust its weight with the trim tanks. After leaving port a boat would go down so that the engineering officer could adjust the trim by allowing just the right amount of water into these tanks. They were located inside the pressure hull at both ends of the boat, and water could be pumped from one end to the other. German submarines had two independent tanks at each end, connected by two pipes. One tank in the system was pumped up with compressed air while the corresponding tank at the other end remained at normal pressure. Opening a tap in the central control room would the permit water to be blown out of the high pressure tank to the other end of the boat. The other pair of tanks obviously worked in the reverse direction. This system had the advantage of being virtually noiseless because there was no need to run an electric pump. Although this trimming process was silent, adjusting the trim during battle conditions was usually done by moving men around the interior. The least experienced usually found themselves being used for this purpose, which

worked much faster than water flowing from one end to the other.

Since it is virtually impossible to achieve a perfect trim so that a submerged submarine goes neither up nor down, the Germans usually adjusted their boats to be slightly heavy, meaning the boat would sink slowly. Correct depth was then maintained with the hydroplanes, which have a similar function to elevators on an aircraft. Since rudder and hydroplanes only worked as long as the boat was moving through the water, depth could only be maintained as long as there was enough power in the batteries to turn the propellers.

Once trim had been adjusted, the diving tanks could be used to keep the boat on the surface or to make it dive. The idea was that when these tanks were full of air there would be sufficient buoyancy to prevent the submarine from sinking, and when they were filled with water the boat would go down. Many science books suggest that air was blown into the diving tanks to bring a submerged submarine to the surface, which is not quite correct. Diving tanks need to be open to the sea, and water pressure decreases as the boat rises. Therefore the volume of air in the diving tanks expands as the boat rises, which will produce an uncontrollable upward acceleration.

To prevent the boat from coming to the surface in a mass of bubbles like a champagne cork released under water, a careful surfacing procedure had to be maintained, and this usually did not involve the pumping of air into diving tanks. In fact, the opposite usually happens: water is pumped out of the tanks as the boat rises to allow for the expanding hull. The rate varies, but generally about 1 ton per 100 metres should give an approximate figure.

Before surfacing it was necessary to determine whether it was

safe to do so. This was done by sweeping around with sensitive sound detection gear which could detect propeller noises of ships at greater distances than they could be spotted by a lookout on the conning tower. Waves washing against the hull and the boat's own engine noises made it impossible to use this equipment on the surface, however. The next step was to engage the hydroplanes to steer the boat to periscope depth, and then to the surface. The trim would have allowed the upper deck of the casing to come roughly level with the surface of the water, but the boat would have been too heavy to get much higher. At this stage the conning tower, with the ends of the ventilation shafts on the top, was clear of the sea, making it possible to start the diesel engines and to use exhaust fumes for blowing water out of the diving tanks. This had the advantage of saving compressed air.

Large vents at the bottoms of the diving tanks were always open to the sea. Other vents at the top could be opened or shut. When open, air would be allowed out of the tank for it to fill with water so that it could eventually take the boat down again. Once shut, the air or exhaust gasses trapped inside the tanks acted like water wings to keep the boat afloat. It would have been most difficult to allow just the right amount of compressed air or exhaust fumes into the diving tanks to surface the boat, especially as the short distance from periscope depth to the surface still presented a considerable difference in water pressure. Consequently boats often appeared on the surface in a great mass of bubbles and foam.

U570 (KL Hans Rahmlow) surfaced in such a fashion right underneath a Hudson aircraft piloted by RAF Sqn.Ldr.James Thompson, who lost no time in attacking. The rest of the story is well known: U570 surrendered to the Royal Air Force. Cases of aircraft being right above surfacing submarines, in their periscope's blind spot, were very rare, however, and only a few Coastal Command pilots witnessed a boat actually breaking the surface. More often they saw one vanish below the waves before they could reach it.

If damaged while diving, a boat might keep on going down without responding to hydroplane controls until it was eventually crushed by the pressure of the water, or hit the sea bottom. A slow downwards movement might be corrected by reversing the propellers, but if all else failed there was a chance of returning to the surface by blowing the tanks. However, this would have resulted in an uncontrollable upward movement and usually, if an enemy were waiting, ended in the boat having to be abandoned before it plunged down again for the last time. (Such an incident had resulted in Karl Dönitz becoming a prisoner during the First World War.)

Boats stuck on the seabed had several options even if blowing the diving tanks failed to lift them. The trim tanks could also be blown, fuel could be pumped out and torpedoes jettisoned to lighten the boat. Of course, all this depended on there being enough compressed air and electricity to work the machinery; and it must be remembered that the volume of air depended on the water pressure outside the boat. The deeper it was, the more the air in the diving tanks would be compressed, thus filling a smaller space than when nearer the surface. In shallow water it was also possible to use one of the several ballast pumps to push water out of the interior.

The influence of the weight of torpedoes was considerable, and torpedo tanks were fitted under the tubes to compensate for the loss of weight after they were fired - this was especially critical when they were launched when submerged. There were several cases of U-boats accidentally surfacing before the torpedo tanks could be filled with water to maintain the correct trim. One torpedo weighed about 1.5 tons, so when a salvo of three were fired the front end of the boat suddenly became 4.5 tons

Maschinenobergefreiter Gerhard Fischer of U376 (KL Friedrich-Karl Marks) on duty in the diesel engine room.

Basic layout of a Type VII U-boat, as used in the Atlantic.

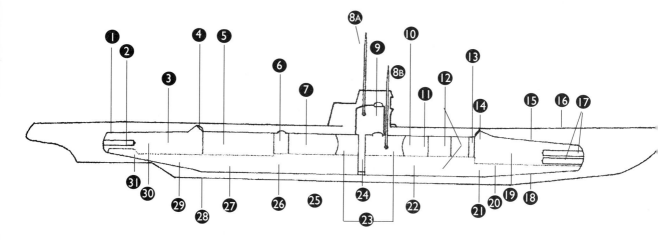

(1) Space between top of pressure hull and upper deck, which was free-flooding when dived. There was just enough crawl space to admit a man. (2) Stern torpedo tube. (3) Electric engine controls. (4) Torpedo loading hatch. (5) Diesel engine room. (6) Galley, with hatch. (7) Warrant officer accomodation. (8a) Attack periscope. (8b) Navigation periscope. (9) Commander's control room, with main hatches. (10) Commander's accomodation - port side; radio room - starboard. (11) Sound detection gear - starboard. (12) Officer accomodation - batteries under floor plates. (13) Toilet. (14) Torpedo loading hatch. (15) Top of pressure hull. (16) Upper deck. (17) Bow torpedo tubes. (18) Bottom of pressure hull. (19) Bow torpedo room and crew accomodation. (20) Dotted line indicates floor level inside boat. (21) In underfloor space are trimming tanks, torpedo tanks, spare torpedo stowage. (22) Munition storage. (23) Central control room - diving tank under floor. (24) Periscope well. (25) Batteries under floor - there was just enough space for a small man to slide between the top of the batteries banks and the floor plates above. (26) Fresh water and dirty water tanks. (27) Various oil tanks. (28) Solid keel. (29) Electric engines. (30) Crew accomodation. (31) Trimming tanks and torpedo tanks.

lighter. Since a single man walking from one end to the other could upset the trim, it is clear that such a great differential required some skill to compensate.

Action Stations:

The order "Action Stations" was often given in less urgent circumstances than "Alarm", and was followed by a more leisurely sequence of activity, although the air was always thick with anticipation. There were no universal regulations for procedures to be followed when attacking, and commanders were free to make their own rules; considerable variations existed, and the following should only be taken as a rough outline.

Submerged Attacks

Submerged attacks could be launched with torpedoes or mines, although at the beginning of the war only about three-quarters of the commanders had been trained to use the latter, and only a fraction of torpedo tubes, mainly in smaller boats, had been modified to eject mines. Despite these drawbacks mines became one of the major weapons during the first winter of the war. For the majority of the crew action stations would have been the same for both weapons, although the procedures were slightly different.

Commander's Control Room
To shoot torpedoes, the commander sat on a saddle attached to the attack periscope in the commander's control room inside the conning tower. Despite this tiny compartment being exceedingly cramped, the German Navy adopted a principle of having the saddle and the eyepieces rotating around the periscope. Even with a modern wide-angled camera lenses it is almost impossible to photograph anyone sitting at this attack position in a Type VIIC boat, because one cannot get far enough away from the subject. The majority of pictures supposedly showing commanders in action were taken at the navigation periscope in the central control room. The navigation or sky periscope, which terminated one

deck lower down than the attack periscope, was used standing up and rotated by the familiar handles on both sides of the eyepieces; the saddle attached to the base of the attack periscope was moved by pressing two buttons with the feet.

There was just enough room to allow the commander to move round and for at least one other man to work the torpedo calculator. Theoretically the hatch leading down to the central control room should have been closed and orders transmitted through a voice pipe, but in practice the majority of boats kept the hatch open and had another man in the conning tower relaying orders. The settings from the torpedo calculator were transmitted automatically to the torpedo compartments at both ends of the boat.

Central Control Room
The engineering officer watched over, and gave instructions to, two hydroplane operators who were responsible for keeping the boat at periscope depth. Maintaining correct depth was an important job until automatic depth control systems were introduced in the electro-boats of Type XXI just before the end of the war. The action helmsman usually received his orders direct from the commander. The coxswain kept a record of the course on the small chart table. The chief petty officer responsible for the control room would have been standing by with a number of men to work the diving controls and vents should the order to surface be given.

Radio and Listening Rooms
These were usually manned by a warrant officer, a petty officer and two men. Underwater the use of radio was somewhat limited, but it was possible to extend a periscopic aerial and, throughout the Atlantic as far as the eastern seaboard of the United States, it was possible to receive U-Boat Command signals traffic without any part of the boat showing above the surface. The sound detection gear would have been in constant use during submerged attacks. The maintaining of radio silence meant that boats often had messages waiting for transmission, and these were often sent off once the progress of an action meant that the

Above left: U73 commander Helmut Rosenbaum with IWO Horst Deckert (who later commanded the boat) at the small chart table. Behind them is Obermaschinist Karl Keller.

Above: U73's Elektro-Obermaschinist inspecting the gyro-compass in the central control room.

Left: Like all published photos of this type, we see here the boat commander using the navigation/sky periscope in the central control room; there was no room for a photographer in the tiny conning tower compartment above, where the attack periscope was installed. The handle above the Kapitänleutnant's hands could be used for changing the magnification, and there was another for tipping the reflecting surface inside the periscope head.

Left: This U-boat man is working on the so-called "Christmas tree" or trimming controls - less than a quarter of this highly complicated set of wheels is visible here. Each wheel had a slightly different pattern so that it could be distinguished by touch, as the operators had to be able to perform the task blindfold.

Right: The hydroplane controls, forward and to starboard in the control room. The left hand man controls the forward hydroplanes, the right hand man the aft planes. The position of the hydroplanes is indicated by the two dials seen on each side of the right hand man's head.

boat's presence had already become known to the enemy.

Bow Torpedo Compartment

The torpedo mechanic (who belonged to the seaman - not the technical - division) was the only warrant officer to be accommodated with the men. He was not responsible for the day-to-day running of the bow compartment, and he did not participate in the everyday watch-keeping chores. At action stations he would have been positioned by the tubes, together with a petty officer and one or two men. Torpedo settings were automatically transmitted to an indicator situated on the deckhead close to the firing buttons by the tube doors. In later years an additional anti-convoy torpedo (FAT) adjusting device was fitted between the four bow tubes, right at the front of the pressure hull. Adjusting torpedoes already inside the tubes was an easy matter of turning some wheels until their indicators pointed to the same positions as arrows transmitted from the torpedo aimer. Although it was possible to fire torpedoes by remote control from the conning tower control room, the majority of commanders insisted that the order "release" ("*Los!*") be transmitted verbally through the boat, and that the firing buttons on the tubes be pressed as well. The stern torpedo crew usually consisted of a single seaman, who would be joined by a petty officer or the torpedo mechanic if necessary.

At the beginning of the war Types VIIA to VIIC boats carried 14 torpedoes as follows: one in each of the five tubes ready for firing; one spare between the electric motors, four on the floor of the bow torpedo compartment, two under the floor of the bow compartment, and two in external tubes situated under the upper deck. These two outside containers could only be used for storage, and torpedoes inside them had to be manhandled into the boat before they could be loaded and used. Since this was a

lengthy and awkward procedure requiring a fair amount of time on the surface, as the Allies' strength in the air and at sea increased the total number of torpedoes carried was later reduced to twelve. Stowed torpedoes were clamped down to prevent them from rolling in rough seas. Reloading time depended on the location of the spares and how much preparatory work had been done on them. In the Atlantic boats of the Second World War they had to be manhandled with a winch, and it usually took at least 30 minutes to reload one tube.

Electric Controls

The control panels for port and starboard were located over the two motors and were usually operated by an electro warrant officer, two electro petty officers and two seamen.

Diesel Controls

Although diesel engines were not used during submerged attacks, the diesel warrant officer, two petty officers and four stokers stood by to start them in case the boat was ordered to surface. (The diesel staff had the advantage of having a small workbench, and during uneventful days at sea this was often used for handicraft activities. Some most intricate hobby work was carried out, such as making unofficial boat cap badges and other modern equivalents of sailors' scrimshaw - e.g. see the boat-made U-Boat War Badge pictured on page 32.

The Cook

The cook did not undertake watch-keeping duties and his main job, even at action stations, was to prepare food. His only additional task was the reporting of leakages in the rear hatch, situated in the roof of the galley. The majority of cooks went through a short training course before going to sea, although there were a number of cases when shortages demanded that other men take over at very short notice. Placed in the position of having to go to sea without a cook, Claus Korth appointed someone and told the rest of the crew, "The first one to complain about the food will be appointed cook in his place!" Seamen usually helped with chores such as peeling potatoes and washing up. Generally the food was good, with two courses during the week and up to four or five on Sundays. Despite their unnatural life, many commanders took the opportunity to celebrate Sundays, birthdays and special holidays to add some interest to the boring routine. Although it has been claimed that alcohol was not allowed at sea, there were many boats and men capable of accommodating surprising quantities.

Emergency Controls

Steering and controlling the hydroplanes was usually achieved electrically from the central control room. Hydroplane operators held onto two handles and pressed buttons under their wrists to work the mechanism. The hydroplanes could also be moved manually by turning a large wheel mounted around the front of the control box. In addition, for dire emergencies, there was another set of manual hydroplane controls in the bow and stern torpedo compartments. The only manual steering wheel was situated in the stern compartment, aft of the electric control panel. There were also duplicate sets of essential indicator dials showing depth and position of rudder or hydroplanes.

Surface Attacks

U-boats were usually faced with three types of actions involving torpedoes, the heavy deck gun forward of the conning tower, and/or the anti-aircraft and small calibre armament. The instability of the deck as a gun platform restricted the use of the main gun, and it became less important as the war progressed. From the end of 1942 onwards many of the big guns were removed while anti-aircraft armament was greatly strengthened.

Ammunition for the deck gun - on Type VII boats usually an 88mm, and on Type IX a 105mm quick- firing gun - was stored in a magazine below the floor of the radio room. Packed individually in cardboard containers, the shells had to be manhandled through narrow circular hatches into the central control room;

up the ladder to the top of the conning tower; and then down the outside to the gun crew. Ammunition for the anti-aircraft gun was also at first stored inside the boat, but towards the end of the war pressure-resistant external containers were fitted around the guns. The idea was to supply the guns first from these containers without having to carry ammunition up from below. Around D-Day so much anti-aircraft ammunition was consumed that some boats stacked it in boxes on the outside of the bridge.

Manhandling ammunition was quite a problem. Imagine lifting up a shell weighing about 40kg (88lbs) from below the floorboards, and passing it through a 50cm (19.5in) diameter hole by your side, then through the cramped control room and through another hatch above your head, high enough for you not to be able to reach it without stepping up a ladder. Once through this opening the shell had to be carried further up the vertical ladder and through another overhead hatch. Then it was wrestled across the very confined space of a bridge already occupied by several men, and down a vertical ladder on the outside of the conning tower. Once on the deck at the back of the conning tower, the heavy weight had to be carried around the narrow side walkway, often with water washing around the feet. Having staggered forward to the gun position, the last man could well find himself uncomfortably close to the barrel of what was in effect a field artillery piece, where the blast from the muzzle not oncommonly threw unwary sailors off their feet.

At the beginning of the war the gun was the major tool for stopping merchant ships by putting shots across their bows. However, sinking a ship with the deck gun was quite a feat, and usually a torpedo was necessary. Herbert Schultze (U48) wrote in his war diary that most of the time he considered it highly irresponsible to order the gun crew on deck; it was only their guardian angel who prevented the men from being killed or seriously injured. Almost every time the gun was used he had to count upon several major injuries, and getting the artillery into action was usually simply not worthwhile. On one occasion three of his gun crew were washed overboard, and could only be retrieved because they remained attached by their safety lines. However, the quality of these lines left quite a bit to be desired: the clips became twisted and bent easily, indicating that they could only just cope with the strain.

During the early years, when there was no threat of air attack, boats travelled on the surface in a ready-to-dive condition. This meant that the ammunition containers were closed and the guns were unmanned, although they would have been checked and cleaned and were ready for use. When travelling in an air danger zone there might well be extra look-outs and the ammunition containers were kept open, the guns loaded and ready to fire, but the crews were not necessarily in position. On hearing the word "Aircraft!" the guns were manned by the men on the bridge, and the helmsman was ordered to turn the boat away from the approaching enemy - the anti-aircraft guns were mounted at the rear of the conning tower and could not be aimed forwards. At the same time, engine settings might be put onto a faster speed to enable evasive action to be taken as quickly as possible.

Later in the war, when aircraft attacks became more frequent and the armament was strengthened accordingly (e.g. from one to six 20mm cannon), it was common for the guns to be manned continuously in air danger zones - it took too long for the gun

The forward hydroplane operator. Next to him, on his left, would have been the helmsman. Usually the hydroplane operator adjusted the controls by pressing the buttons under the palms of his hands. Should the electrical power fail, then he could take manual control by turning the wheel around the control box, but this required considerable strength. The shallow depth gauge in front of his face is reading 12.5m of water over the keel; there was a separate guage for depths over 25m, and very shallow readings - when the boat was at periscope depth - were indicated on a column of mercury in front of the aft hydroplane operator.

crews to assemble on deck if some of them were below, since the only access was the single ladder and hatch to the bridge. At least eight men were usually required to work the guns, plus more to help feed ammunition.

The general rule was that a boat was only to dive to evade aircraft if it could put more than 25m (80ft) of water over the conning tower before the first depth charges exploded. Otherwise, boats were advised to remain on the surface and use the guns to put the enemy off his aim, and then perhaps try diving before the second attack. The weak link in this plan was that an aircraft running in at high speed was a considerably more stable gun platform than the top of a rocking conning tower, putting the attackers at a considerable advantage which resulted in many casualties on U-boats.

* * *

Until the end of 1939 training concentrated mainly on submerged attacks, but as the war progressed surface attacks at night became more popular. U-boat commanders found that the tiny silhouette of a surfaced submarine could hardly be seen in the dark, making it much more practical to use the more powerful diesel engines for approaching targets. The devastating blows struck against Britain's sea lanes during the winter of 1940/41 were not the result of "wolf pack" attacks, but due to the technique of U-boats attacking on the surface at night.

KL Otto Kretschmer (U99) said that the decisive factor in choosing to remain on the surface was that the boat became more or less stationary once it had submerged. For this reason his standing orders stated that the boat should only dive if aircraft came into sight; otherwise it remained on the surface and the commander was called to the bridge to assess the situation. Kretschmer, who spent much of his time reading, was known on occasion to react to the report "Mastheads in sight!" by asking casually, "Are they thick or thin?" He did not see any good reason for climbing up just because the "thin" structure of a warship came into sight; instead he suggested that they alter course to avoid the pest.

For a torpedo attack on the surface U-boats were faced either with a single ship or with a multiple target such as a convoy. In both cases action stations would have been ordered at the beginning of the attack, which meant that the first watch officer checked the torpedo gear and the second watch officer took control of the bridge to keep the boat in the best position relative to the enemy. Meanwhile, the commander kept an eye on the proceedings; and when he considered that they were close enough he took control with the words "Ich fahre weiter". His job was to break through any defences, and sometimes also to penetrate between the ranks of the convoy; to approach the target or, if there were more than one, to select the first; to estimate settings for torpedoes, and decide how many were to be launched.

In the meantime the first watch officer should have appeared on the top of the conning tower with special binoculars for attachment to the top of the torpedo aimer. By rotating these sights, essential information was automatically transmitted to the calculator in the commander's control room and on to the indicators by the torpedo tubes. In later years torpedo launching equipment was fitted with angle deflectors, but initially the whole boat had to be aimed at the target, the helmsman being directed in this by the first officer.

Both watch officers were encouraged to offer their guesses as to the target's speed, direction and range, and the commander usually had to judge which was the most correct. This sometimes led to considerable debate, and there were instances when commanders without battle experience had to be tactfully overruled by more seasoned subordinates. For example, torpedo aiming skills were introduced to "Ajax" Bleichrodt (U48) when he forbade his IWO "Teddy" Suhren from making one attack on the grounds that the target was too fast and too far away. When Suhren tactfully pointed out that "We have hit smaller and faster

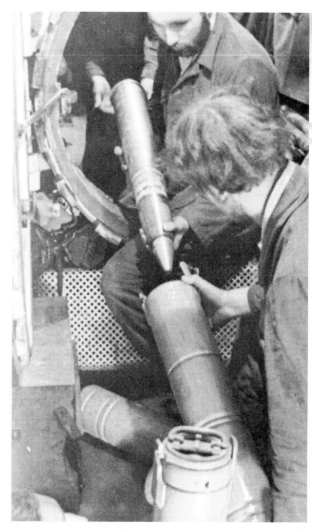

Shells for the main deck gun wre stowed in cardboard tubes under the radio room floor; during a surface action they had to be manhandled through the boat by a human chain, up the conning tower ladder, down to the aft deck, then around the side of the conning tower to the gun. Note the circular pressurised hatch leading to the control room; these divided all the main compartments, allowing them to be sealed off in an emergency.

things further away!", Bleichrodt acquiesced - mainly because he wanted to prove Suhren wrong; but at the end of an exceptionally long run the torpedo detonated on target.

It was considerably more difficult to hit a target with the deck gun than with a torpedo, and this was rarely used as a primary attack weapon. It was more common to use gunfire to accelerate sinking if the target remained afloat after a torpedo hit. Yet despite the difficulties of using deck guns a number of fairly long gun duels, lasting over an hour and consuming more than 100 shells, have been recorded. There were no hard and fast rules about who should be responsible for gunnery. Either the first or second watch officer acted as artillery officer, although it was more often the domain of the IIWO.

Chapter 5: **The U-boat Commander**

In recent years there have been a good number of attempts to define a "U-boat commander type". Virtually every analyst who has tried has made a miserable mess of the exercise, because they apparently failed to realise that these men were individuals. One American author even expressed astonishment that the three or four ex-commanders he interviewed should have different opinions of Hitler. (However, this was at least better than another so-called historian in the USA who made up his own fictitious characters, none of whom ever featured in German records.)

Was there a definable U-boat commander type? Probably not; but there were a number of individuals who had some characteristics in common. Before discussing these it is important to consider a few basic facts.

Horst Bredow of the German U-boat Archive has records of 1,171 U-boats having been commissioned between 1935 and 1945. If one combines this figure with the famous Churchill comment that the only thing which really frightened him throughout the war was the U-boat threat, then it is easy to conjure up visions of hundreds of bloodthirsty U-boat commanders prowling the waters around the British Isles and along the eastern seaboard of the United States. However, the figure of 1,171 boats is grossly misleading, and does not reflect the reality of the war at sea. The number of Allied ships which were attacked and at least damaged can be calculated from *Axis Submarine Successes* by Prof.Dr. Jürgen Rohwer. The details for the Atlantic and North Sea are as follows:

25 U-boats attacked, sunk, or at least damaged 20 or more ships
36 U-boats attacked between 11 and 19 ships
70 U-boats attacked between 6 and 10 ships
190 U-boats attacked between 1 and 5 ships

This adds up to a total of 321 U-boats. Ships sunk in the Black Sea, Mediterranean, Baltic, and Indian Ocean will make the total rather higher, and one could allow a few more for calculation errors. However, the probable total still leaves a staggering gap of about 850 U-boats which appear not to have sunk or damaged anything throughout the entire war. In fact almost all of these, representing three- quarters of the whole U-Boat Arm, never came within shooting distance of the enemy. School boats, supply boats, experimental craft, and boats commissioned towards the very end of the war which were never in a position to sink ships, could be discounted; but there still appears to be a huge discrepancy between the number of U-boats commissioned and the number which actually attacked the enemy. This makes one wonder why Germany put so much effort and so many resources into building submarines, if the majority never achieved anything other than tying down the vast enemy forces which hunted and destroyed them.

It might be worth adding that these figures were not calculated with hindsight: they were available to the U-Boat Command at the time, and the only difference between then and now is that we now know that U-boat commanders generally overestimated their tonnage sunk by about one third.

Looking at the same figures from a different angle, one might

Korvettenkapitän Wolfgang Lüth was the first naval officer to be awarded the Knight's Cross with Oakleaves, Swords and Diamonds, and second only to "Silent Otto" Kretschmer in his record of Allied tonnage sunk. Here the bald-headed Lüth was photographed trying to crawl under the table during the farewell party in November 1943 when he relinquished command of U181.

consider that these ships were sunk by men rather than by machines. Out of a total of about 2,450 Allied ships sunk in the Atlantic one finds that 30 U-boat commanders were responsible for sinking just under 800 of these. This means that 2% of the U-boat commanders were responsible for sinking almost 30% of the Allied shipping losses in this central arena of the submarine war. So who were this 2%? A considerable number of variables make calculation complicated, since it is easy to arrive at several slightly different combinations. However, the list of the 32 highest scoring commanders included in the book *60 Jahre deutsche U-boote* by Bodo Herzog will certainly yield the top 25 or so, which should be sufficient for analysing the "U-boat aces". This list is as follows, in the order rank and name; (boats commanded during the war) (boat types); Crew - i.e. year when they joined the Navy; and date of birth:

1   KK Otto Kretschmer (U23, U99) (IIB, VIIB)   30   1/5/12
2. KK Wolfgang Lüth (U13, U9, U138, U43, U181)
    (IIB, IIB, IID, IXA, IXD2)   33   15/10/13
3. KK Erich Topp (U57, U552)(IIC, VIIC)   34   2/7/14
4. KK Karl-Friedrich Merten (U68) (IXC)   26   15/8/05
5. KK Victor Schütze (U25, U103) (IA, IXB)   25   16/2/06
6. KL Herbert Schultze (U48) (VIIB)   30   24/7/09
7. KL Georg Lassen (U160) (IXC)   35   12/5/15
8   KL Heinrich Lehmann-Willenbrock (U5, U96)
    (IIA, VIIC)[1]   31   11/12/11
9. KK Günter Prien (U47) (VIIB)   33   16/1/08
10. KL Heinrich Liebe (U38) (IXA)   27   29/1/08
11. KL Joachim Schepke (U3, U9, U100)
    (IIA, IIB, VIIB)   30   8/3/12
12. KL Werner Henke (U515) (IXC)   34   13/5/08
13. KL Carl Emmermann (U172) (IXC)   34   6/3/15
14. KL Heinrich Bleichrodt (U48, U109)
    (VIIB, IXB)   31   21/10/09
15. KL Robert Gysae (U98, U177) (VIIC, IXC)   31   4/1/11
16. KK Ernst Kals (U130) (IXC)   24   2/8/05
17. KL Johann Mohr (U124) (IXB)   34   12/6/16
18. KK Klaus Scholtz (U108) (IXB)   27   22/3/08
19. KL Engelbert Endrass (U46, U567) (VIIB, VIIC)   35   2/3/11
20. KL Reinhard Hardegen (U147, U 123)
    (IID, IXB)   33   18/3/13
21. KL Adolf Piening (U155, U255) (IXC, VIIC)   30   16/9/10
22. KK Adalbert Schnee (U6, U60, U201) (IIA,
    IIC, VIIC)   34   31/12/13
23. KL Ernst Bauer (U126) (IXC)   33   3/1/14
24. KS Werner Hartmann (U37, U198)
    (IXA, IXD2)   21   11/12/02
25. KL Jürgen Oesten (U61, U106, U861)
    (IIC, IXB, IXD2)   33   24/10/13
26. KL Günter Hessler (U107) (IXB)   27   14/6/09
27. KL Helmut Witte (U159) (IXC)   34   6/4/11
28. KL Günther Krech (U558) (VIIC)   33   29/9/14
29. KL Harald Gelhaus (U143, U107) (IID, IXB)   35   24/7/15
30. KL Wilhelm Rollmann (U34, U848)
    (VIIA, IXD2)   26   5/8/07
31. KK Werner Hartenstein (U156) (IXC)   28   27/2/08
32. OL Hans Jenisch (U32) (VIIA)   33   19/10/13

(1) Lehmann-Willenbrock also commanded U256, but the boat had previously been sunk and was used only as a means of escape from Brest when the town was being cut off by advancing Allied armies after D-Day.

The classic image of a U-boat commander: KL Kurt Diggins, his cap turned backwards out of the way as he searches the horizon through the navigation periscope in the central control room of U458; the dials of the depth gauge and a hydroplane operator can be seen behind him. Diggins survived the sinking of his boat in August 1943, and later became President of the German Submariners' Association (Verband Deutscher Ubootsfahrer).

When the Aces were in command

```
          1939 1940          1941          1942          1943          1944          1945
          SONDJ FMA M J J A SONDJ FMAMJJ A SONDJ FMAM J J A SONDJFMAMJ J A SONDJ FMAMJ J A SONDJ FMAM
Kretschmer* * * * * * * + + + * * * * * * * * *
Lüth        o o o * * * * *  + + + + + * * * * * * * * * * * * * * * * * * * * * * + + + * * * * * * * * * * * * * * * * * *
Topp                          * * * *  + + + * * * * * * * * * * * * * * * * * * *  * * *
Merten                               + + + * * * * * * * * * * * * * * * * * * *
Schütze     * * * * * * * *  + + + * * * * * * * * * * *
Schultze    * * * * * * * *         * * * * * * *
Lassen                                + + + * * * * *  * * * * * * * * *
Lehmann-W   * * * * * * *  o o + + + * * * * * * * * * * * * *
Prien       * * * * * * * *  * * * * * * * * * * *
Liebe       * * * * * * * *  * * * * * * * * * * * *
Schepke     * * * * * * * *  + + + * * * * * * * * * *
Henke                                    + + + * * * * * * * * * * * * * * * * * *
Emmermann                              + + + * * * *  * * * * * * * * * * * * *
Bleichrodt          * * * *        * * * * * * * * * * *  * * * * * * * * *
Gysae               + + + * * * * * * * * * * * *  * *
Kals                       + + + * * * * * * * * * *  * * * * * * *
Mohr                          * * * * * * * * * *  * * * * * * * * * *
Scholtz             + + + * * * * * * * * * * * * * * * *  * * * * * * *
Endrass      * * * * * * * * * * * * * * * * * *
Hardegen            + + + * * * * * * * * * * * *  * *
Piening                           + + + * * * * * * * * * * * * * * * *  * * * * * * *
Schnee       * * * * * *  * * * *  + + + * * *
Bauer                     + + + * * * * * * * * * * * * * * * * * *
Hartmann    * * * * * * * * *                  + + + * * * * * * * * * * *
Oesten      + + + * * * * *  * * * * * * + + + * * * * * * * * * * * *       + + + * * * * * * * * * * * * * * * * *
Hessler             + + + * * * * * * * * *
Witte                          + + + * * * *  * * * * * * * * * *
Krech               + + + * * * * * * * * * * * * *  * * * * * * *
Gelhaus                       * * * * * * * * * * *  * * * * * * * * * * *
Rollmann    * * * * * * * *  * * * *                       + + + * * * * * * *
Hartenstein                    + + + * * * * * * *  * * * * * * * *
Jenisch              * * * *  * * * *
          SONDJ FMA M J J A SONDJ FMAMJJ A SONDJFMAM J J A SONDJFMAMJ J A SONDJ FMAMJ J A SONDJ FMAM
          1939 1940          1941          1942          1943          1944          1945
```

Key:
o = Not operational
+ = Commissioned new boat and on trials
* = Commanding a boat in service. Periods in port and other brief periods of inactivity have not been indicated.

Otto Schuhart on board U29 during the autumn of 1939; note the attachment of the forward jumping wire, and the fact that at this date the flat seaman's cap was still being worn on U-boats.

Several interesting points emerged when the present author compared this list of the top-scoring aces with another group of 20 commanders, chosen at random from among those who were themselves sunk during their first few operations. That the predominant boat type to have been lost during its first missions was the VIIC is not really significant because a greater number of these were commissioned than all the other types put together.

More interesting is that by the end of 1939 the aces had been in the Navy on average for almost ten years and their average age was almost 29. On the other hand, commanders lost during their first few missions had been in the Navy for an average of four months by the end of 1939 and their average age was under 25 years. Although this variation in age does not appear too great, the majority did not leave school until they were about 18 years old, so those few years do make a considerable difference.

Anyone with the urge to classify U-boat commanders as identifiable types should consider that although a few had participated in the Spanish Civil War, by 1939 none of them had any real battle experience comparable to what they were about to face - but neither had the great majority of their enemies. In view of this it might be reasonable to conclude that commanders fell into the following groups:
Men who were trained before 1939 and held a command during the early years of the war
Men who gained battle experience as watch officers and then became commanders later in the war

U149, with OL Adolf Freiherr von Hammerstein-Equord on the right with a white cap cover and OL Heinz Riedel behind him; interestingly, Riedel appears to wear the Crimea commemorative shield on his left shoulder. U149 was a long-range Type IID coastal boat, of which only 16 were built; note the unusual curved railing on the right. Here we can also see the special binoculars used during surface attacks clipped in position on top of the torpedo aimer; a magnetic compass can be seen to the left of this. The man in left foreground wears the narrow silver shoulder cords of a Fähnrich or midshipman.

Men who gained battle experience in surface ships and later transferred to U-boats

Men who joined the Navy and went straight into the U-Boat Arm, encountering determined enemy opposition as commanders without themselves having had any battle experience.

Young commanders and unexpected commands

The youngest commander has often been said to have been Hans-Georg Hess, who won the Knight's Cross while commanding U995 from September 1944 until the end of the war. He was born on 6 May 1923 and joined the Navy in 1940. U995, incidentally, is one of the few U-boats to have survived the war; it is now open as a museum at the Naval Memorial at Laboe near Kiel. However, there was one even younger man to have commanded a U-boat. Ludwig von Friedeburg, son of Admiral Hans-Georg von Friedeburg (Commander- in-Chief of the U-Boat Arm's Organisation Department), who was born on 21 May 1924, joined the Navy in 1941 and took up his first command in August 1944 when he was three months past his twentieth birthday. This came about when the French bases were being cut off by advancing Allied armies; having served as a watch officer in U548, von Friedeburg was instructed to take U155 to Germany. His mother said that the day she watched him arrive in Kiel was among the proudest of her life.

Some officers got their first command under even more chaotic circumstances than Ludwig von Friedeburg. There were a number of cases of commanders being injured whilst on patrol and another officer bringing the boat home. For example, OL Gerhard Kluth (U377) was very nearly killed by aircraft fire off the Canadian coast and LT "Jumbo" Gerke (IWO) brought the boat home. Bringing one's own boat home was considerably easier than having to step into a commander's position on the high seas and, at the same time, take control of a different boat with an unknown crew. This happened to Lorenz Kasch, trainee commander under KL Harald Gelhaus (U107).

In October 1942, while cruising off Freetown, Sierra Leone, U107 intercepted a distress call from U333 (KL "Ali" Cremer). Look-outs on top of the conning tower had been killed while Cremer and another trainee commander, OL Wilhelm Pohl, were seriously injured by gunfire from an aircraft. A doctor from the supply boat U459 (KK Georg von Wilamowitz-Möllendorf) administered first aid and probably saved Pohl's life; a bullet through his neck had caused him to lose his voice and rendered him unfit for further service. (Although unable to speak louder than a whisper for the rest of his life, he survived the war.) Lorenz Kasch was the most likely candidate in the area and was instructed to bring the stricken U333 home. Following this he went on to become commander of U540 and was killed in action on 17 October 1943, when the boat was sunk by British aircraft.

Bernhard Knieper became a commander in even more challenging circumstances. He had never commanded a submarine at the time when he returned to France in spring 1944 after a three-month cruise in U267 under KL Otto Tinschert. The majority of the crew went on leave to Germany while the boat was being repaired. This work had not been completed by D-Day, and soon afterwards the Allied advance threatened the French Atlantic bases. Although not seriously damaged, U267 was decommissioned and prepared for scuttling. When it became clear that the advancing armies were going to cut off rather than assault the U-boat bases, OLdR (Oberleutnant of the Reserve) Bernhard Knieper was appointed to make U267 ready for sea.

However, by this time there was not only an acute shortage of commanders along the French Atlantic coast, but also of U-boat crews. Knieper had to scrounge around for a crew, and even took on dockyard personnel. This unlikely stop-gap crew left St Nazaire on 23 September 1944, making U267 the last boat out of a French base. This in itself was quite an achievement because both the Royal Navy and the Royal Air Force were making determined efforts to prevent such escapes. Five weeks later, on 29 October, U-Knieper arrived unannounced in Stavanger, Norway, with much of the boat's machinery, including the radios, out of action. Yet despite the problems U267 continued to Germany under its own steam. Taking his first U-boat command in such unusual circumstances, going to sea with a proportion of untrained men and without a working-up period, and coping with determined opposition, must have made Knieper's achievement unique in submarine history.

Some older commanders

At the opposite end of the spectrum, there were a number of quite elderly U-boat commanders; and some dramatic instances of men losing their commands. It seems highly likely that Wilhelm Kiesewetter was the oldest when he took over the training boat UC1 (a former Norwegian submarine) in 1940 at the age of 62. It is interesting to reflect that he was born in 1878, and that when he joined the Navy in 1900 the first German submarine had not yet been built. The oldest operational commander appears to have been Georg von Wilamowitz-Möllendorf, better known as "The Wild Moritz", who commissioned the Type XIV supply boat U459 at the age of 49 on 27 July 1943.

The Wild Moritz, incidentally, also met a most extraordinary end: he was killed when an attacking aircraft crashed onto the U-boat. One airman and 41 of the crew survived the incident, but they could not prevent the boat from going down. One depth charge from the aircraft which became stuck to the casing was carelessly thrown overboard to explode, driving the final nail into the coffin. Soon after this another aircraft assured that U459 would not escape.

However, devoting space to the oldest commanders is somewhat meaningless since these two were very notable exceptions. As a rule there was an upper age limit of 40 years for commanders, and the majority were considerably younger.

Death, discipline and loss of command

All U-boat men were bad risks for life assurance companies, although the commanders did stand a slightly better chance of surviving than anyone else. Unlike surface vessels, where the commanding officer is usually the last person to abandon a sinking ship, in a U-boat he was always the first out of the conning tower hatch and the last down. This meant that the commander and the duty look-outs were in the best position to jump overboard, and usually had a chance of getting off even when things happened too quickly to evacuate the bow and stern compartments. However, this advantage did not save KL Joachim Schepke, who was crushed against the periscope support when the destroyer *Vanoc* rammed U100.

Some commanders died in quite unusual circumstances. Siegfried Lüdden had cheated death on numerous occasions as watch officer of U141 and commander of U188; but he was burnt to death in a fire aboard the accommodation ship *Daressalam*. The ace Wolfgang Lüth, holder of the Knight's Cross with Oakleaves, Swords and Diamonds, was shot by his own guard just a few days after the end of the war. It appears that he was wandering around the grounds of the naval officers' school in the dark, close to where Dönitz had set up his government, and failed to respond to a guard's challenge - probably because he had been drinking too much.

Rolf Mützelburg (U203) was killed in September 1942, some 1,200 miles west of Gibraltar, as a result of a swimming accident. He dived off the top of the conning tower, hit his head on the saddle tank, and died a few days later from concussion. The boat was then brought home by OL Hans Seidel, who was later posted to commanders' school, before he himself was killed in U361.

A number of men made it into captivity only to be killed later. Werner Henke (U515) was shot in the United States while attempting an escape from prison camp. Henke was quite a character, and worth further study for anyone seeking a "commander type". He is included in the list of the top thirty commanders and was awarded the Knight's Cross in July 1943, having seen action during a most difficult period of the war. His life is recorded in the book *Lone Wolf* by Timothy Mulligan.

Friedrich Steinhoff committed suicide by cutting his wrists with glass from his sunglasses when he could no longer bear his ill-treatment at American hands; he had been severely beaten while being dragged through the streets of Boston for the amusement of the crowd. On the whole, with very few exceptions, seamen seem to have treated each other reasonably well, but there are a good number of stories of abuse once U-boat men reached land. Looting and severe physical abuse appear to have been quite common, especially if men passed into the hands of "desk warriors". A number of U-boat men have also reported that conditions got noticeably worse after the war, when there were no longer any Allied prisoners in German hands. Some claim that the Allies then disregarded the Geneva Convention and treated prisoners pretty badly. LT Karl-Heinz Schütt made his protest against passing into captivity quite dramatically by letting off a hand grenade while inside the conning tower of U294 in Trondheim just a few days after the end of the war.

Another officer to have committed suicide shortly after capture

KL Peter Ottmar Grau, with bouquet, and KK Rolf-Heinrich Hopman. Grau survived the war, his last command being the Type XXI boat U3015; Hopman was lost with U405 in November 1943.

A shot taken by a photographer who clearly climbed part way up the periscope: the bridge of U761 under way on the surface, with OL Horst Geider wearing his white cap. The torpedo aimer, without the binoculars clipped on, can be seen in the foreground. Geider survived the loss of his boat in February 1944.

was Admiral Hans-Georg von Friedeburg, who had been chief of the U-Boat Arm's Organisation Department and was later promoted to Commander-in-Chief of the Navy. He was a member of the delegation who met Field Marshal Montgomery to negotiate the ceasefire at the end of the war. Von Friedeburg obeyed when the field marshal scratched a line in the sand of Lüneburger Heath and made the German officers stand with their toes touching it. Shortly after the arrest of the Dönitz government, higher officials and their female secretarial staff were rounded up by some British troops, taken outside into a field, made to strip naked and then forced at gunpoint to dance in front of film cameras. While this was going on their personal belongings, including wedding rings and buttons from their uniforms, were looted. Hans-Georg von Friedeburg responded by poisoning himself, something he had planned long before. When his wife Ursula heard the news on the radio that Dönitz's government had been arrested she guessed that her husband would keep his word and kill himself. She still has a letter of apology from Royal Navy authorities, who had been unaware of the incident until after the event.

A number of U-boat men ended their careers in front of courts martial which reduced them to the ranks, and some commanders were simply relieved of their duty. Helmuth Franzke (U3), for example, was sentenced to 15 months' imprisonment and reduced to the lowest rank for attempted homosexual activities with some of his men; he was killed in action on 28 May 1944 while serving with a training division. Some offences committed by U-boat men were, without doubt, real crimes; others were simply the result of too much drink at celebrations following a difficult period at sea. Some submariners suffered heavy punishment for what seem to have been incredibly trivial misdemeanours, and there were a few cases of men facing trumped-up charges in instances of personal revenge.

One could hardly quote a better example of a trivial charge

than those which dogged Siebrand Voss, radio operatior on U377. Coming home from an arduous mission, Voss found himself being detailed for guard duty before being allowed home on leave. This, in itself, seemed more like a punishment because the boat was lying in a well-protected harbour. In a moment of dejection he sat down on the capstan by the bows, from where he could get a good view of anyone attempting to board. However, this was against regulations; Voss was spotted by an administrator from the 11th U-Flotilla, and subsequently sentenced to several days' imprisonment for sitting while on duty. With the cells already full to bursting there was a considerable queue of men waiting to serve their time; and the wait cost Voss the opportunity of going home for a few days. Being locked up in cramped quarters was hardly a novelty for a U-boat man – the cells were considerably superior to his normal accommodation. But to miss precious home leave was a real punishment, and made all the more bitter in this case for being handed out by shore-bound desk warriors who never shared the hardship of action at sea.

Siebrand Voss's commander, KL Otto Köhler, fared only marginally better. He tied up a bundle of papers for the flotilla administration with tarred string which happened to have been picked up by a landing party at the deserted North Pole Hotel in Ny Alensund on Spitzbergen while U377 was establishing an unmanned weather station nearby (see Chapter 7). Incredibly, the U-boat commander was questioned about the origin of the string, and then threatened with court martial for looting. Fortunately for Köhler, not everyone on the 11th U-Flotilla staff was so short of work that they had time to think up absurdities like this, and the charge was later dropped.

(Things were not always better for U-boat men's families at home, who could not necessarily expect to be treated with decency. When the author's mother, several months pregnant, opened the door to a uniformed official holding out a telegram

U14, with Klaus Petersen on the left; note the multi-coloured Olympic rings badge painted on the front of the conning tower.

she collapsed, because she knew it could only contain the news that my father had been killed. Luckily my grandfather caught her and dragged her into a chair. Despite the occasion and her obvious distress, the official refused to hand the telegram to my grandfather because it was addressed to my mother. In a moment of rage my grandfather pulled the envelope from his outstretched hand and slammed the door. A few days later he was arrested for showing disrespect to the uniform, and only escaped the most serious consequences by giving way to my mother's pleas to make a public apology.)

There were far worse incidents, and one very nearly cost a man's life. The second radio operator of U764 (OL Hanskurt von Bremen) is reported by Günter Fismer in *Schaltung Küste* (the German submariners' journal, No. 149, November-December 1993) as having developed a strong attachment to the Nazi Party. He used threats of denouncing colleagues as a means of gaining leverage among his shipmates and covering up his own short-comings. Apparently he kept a record of any anti-government remarks he overheard, and used these notes in January 1945 to denounce a comrade, in full knowledge that the alleged offence of comments against the Party carried the death penalty. Hans Börner was brought to trial, but his defence lawyer succeeded in getting the demanded death penalty reduced to seven years' imprisonment plus a reduction in rank. Again, sadly, this happened in the 11th U-Flotilla.

One characteristic common to all successful commanders was an ability to make up their minds very quickly and then act on the decision without faltering. This "attack in ten seconds" attitude also cost a number of men their commands. When U109 returned to port in June 1941, Dönitz asked some of the old lags about the performance of their commander. On that evidence, and on the spur of the moment, the Commander-in-Chief relieved Hans-Georg Fischer of his duty and had him transferred to a

minor position aboard the cruiser *Admiral Hipper*. In his secret diary Wolfgang Hirschfeld has recorded that there had been considerable exaggeration by the old hands, making the decision most unjust. After the war Hirschfeld even mounted a one-man crusade in an attempt to clear Fischer's tarnished reputation. Such traumatic and far-reaching decisions were made very quickly, often with the victim hardly having time to offer a defence. What is more, men coming into port were usually tired and mentally worn out from prolonged concentration, making their reaction towards so-called friends somewhat unwary. Yet not all accepted a hammering at the hands of U-Boat Command meekly. In autumn 1943 U377 returned from a patrol with first watch officer "Jumbo" Gerke standing in for the wounded commander, who went straight into hospital. Gerke was accused of negligence for not spotting a destroyer which had allegedly rammed the U-boat. He shot back with such anger that the officers withdrew their indictment and looked around for alternative explanations for the damage which the boat suffered.

It will probably never be known how many men faced Admiral Dönitz "under four eyes only" and asked to be relieved of their duty. However, one commander did resign in the middle of an operational tour, and announced the fact over the radio. Dönitz was not particularly perturbed when he received the signal from "Ajax" Bleichrodt, but when he found that the commander of U109 could not be persuaded to change his mind the admiral instructed Bleichrodt to hand over command to the first watch officer and to take some specified medication from the first aid chest. Knowing full well that these were sleeping pills and that the IWO was in no position to refuse the order, the exhausted Bleichrodt dragged his wits together and made a huge effort so as not to burden anyone else with his own shortcomings. Instead of obeying, he turned the boat round and took U109 back to France. Following this incident the Commander-in-Chief refused to speak to Bleichrodt; long after the war when they met a reunion, Dönitz shrugged his shoulders and said, "What else could I have done?" Nevertheless, Bleichrodt was neither punished nor reprimanded for his behaviour; instead he was allowed some leave before being posted to a training flotilla.

After the war Bleichrodt made no effort to conceal this difficult part of his career, and stated his firm belief that many ills of the U-Boat Arm were caused by the High Command's failure to build a safety valve into the system. Once promoted to officer ranks, men were expected to give their undivided devotion to the Navy without regard to their own wellbeing. Bleichrodt said that even before the war there were ample signs that some men could not cope with the considerable pressures heaped upon them, but no notice was taken and too many were driven to destruction. It is not difficult for anyone to go through the register and find a number of names which disappeared from the list shortly after the beginning of the war. Bleichrodt thought that the Navy would have done much better to adopt a less rigid stance, allowing men who were having difficulty some time in less demanding posts before bringing them back to front line duty. Dönitz was against this approach, maintaining that a man away from operational duty lost the "feel" of the battle. Yet those men who were promoted out of operational boats towards the beginning of the war and were subsequently brought back for special commands did exceptionally well.

KS Kurt Freiwald is a prime example. In 1935 he became one of the first U-boat commanders, but during the early years of the war served as adjutant to both supreme commanders-in-chief of the Navy, first to Grand Admiral Erich Raeder and later to Karl Dönitz. In the autumn of 1943 he went back to submarine school for a refresher course, and then took U181 on a highly successful voyage to the Far East. In summer 1944 Heinrich Lehmann-Willenbrock also demonstrated that he had not forgotten very much since his glory days in U96. He took command of U256 after more than two years ashore as chief of the 9th U-Flotilla.

All volunteers accepted?

Not everybody who volunteered for U-boats was accepted, and some exceptional potential commanders never got into the U-Boat Arm although they were keen to join. One such example is Hans Bartels of Crew 31, who must rank as one of the most colourful characters in the Navy. The fact that he had a British mother did not mean that he felt any strong attachment to Germany's enemy. Incidentally, he was not the only man in the Navy with direct British connections: early in 1936 Bartels was IWO of a minesweeper whose commander, Archibald MacLean, had a similar background. The flotilla chief (KK Ernst-Felix Krüder, who later became commander of the ghost cruiser *Pinguin*) sent "Ajax" Bleichrodt over to find out why one of his boats was flying its flag at half mast. Once on board Bleichrodt was greeted by a strong smell of alcohol, and both officers sitting in the deepest of gloom. "We're mourning the death of the king", announced Bartels by way of a greeting, before pouring Bleichrodt a glass and then explaining that they had just heard the news of the passing of King George V.

The flotilla chief coped reasonably well with these two highly contrasting characters, although there were times when he wondered who put both of them into the same ship. Once he was faced by Bartels complaining that his commander was not decisive enough, and a little while later MacLean appeared to remonstrate about the recklessness of his first officer. When his adjutant asked what should be done Krüder looked up and said wearily, "They're both British, let them sort it out themselves."

In 1939 Bartels commanded minesweeper M1 with another colourful character, Albrecht Brandi, as his first officer. Despite the regulations in force at the beginning of the war M1 certainly did not follow the general rules of passive engagement, and this led ultimately to a tragic incident. The suspicion that a couple of Danish fishing boats had signalled reconnaissance information to the British resulted in everybody on M1 being ordered below decks with hatches battened down. Then, while totally alone on the bridge, Bartels used the boat's powerful cycloid propeller to destroy both fishing boats until there were no survivors. The incident did not feature in the ship's log, and the men were sent below because Bartels did not want to burden them with the guilt of his reckless action.

U81: from left to right, IWO Johann Otto Krieg, who later commanded this boat, IIWO Claus von Trotha, and LI Horst Renner.

KL Albrecht Achilles inspects the crew of U161; on the right, Maschinenmaat Reitz, Maschinenmaat Droschke and Bootmannsmaat Schöller. Achilles and his boat were lost in September 1943.

Later M1 participated in the invasion of Norway, and when the flotilla was due to return Bartels remained in port by feigning engine trouble. He could envisage a more adventurous life among the fjords than sweeping mines from a German port. Bartels was even promoted to become Commanding Officer for the Protection of the Norwegian West Coast, but he stretched his abilities a little too far. Grand Admiral Erich Raeder remarked that the man must be brought back to Germany to relearn some basic naval discipline, and appointed him as first officer of the destroyer Z34. By this time Albrecht Brandi, who had earlier succeeded Bartels as commander of M1, had gone through U-boat training and was already commanding U617. Bartels had his request to join U-boats turned down again, but later he was given his own command in the old torpedo boat T34. In 1944 KS Hellmuth Heye needed unconventional men for unorthodox projects, and he recruited Bartels to help develop midget weapons units. Bartels died in a road accident towards the end of the war, although many who knew him guessed that it was a suicide to escape possible war crimes charges.

As in other countries, there were a number of "naval families" in which son followed father or elder brother into the service. The Ites twins and "Teddy" and Gerd Suhren are examples of two brothers serving in U-boats, but some families contributed even more. Fritz Albrecht became commander of U386 in June 1943 and during the same month his brother commissioned U1062, an unusual transporter of Type VIIF. By that time the family had contributed two U-boat commanders during both world wars. This is even bettered by the von Rabenau family, which probably holds the record of having produced the largest number of naval officers - nine in all. Hellmuth von Rabenau commanded U67 in 1918 and continued as an officer of the reserve until 1945. Reinhard, who was three years younger, commanded UC77 and UB88 during the First World War. Georg served with the Luftwaffe before taking command of U528 in December 1942; he became a prisoner of war on 13 May 1943 after scuttling his

boat. Damage sustained during an attack by Halifaxes from No. 58 Squadron RAF made it impossible to dive, and once the sloop Fleetwood appeared there was no choice other than surrender or scuttle. Wolf-Rüdiger von Rabenau was not so lucky: he went down with U702 near Heligoland in April 1942. The exact cause of sinking has not yet been clarified; it appears likely that the boat was sunk by a mine, but human error cannot be ruled out.

After her capture U570 was commissioned into the Royal Navy as HMS Graph; but another U-boat had a foreign commander under even stranger circumstances. Jean-Pierre Brunet, who became the French ambassador in Bonn after the war, was the only Frenchman to have commanded a U-boat during the Second World War. The story started after the advancing armies found U766 (OLdR Hans-Joachim Wilke) in La Pallice; she had been put into dry dock and could not be got ready in time for the German evacuation. Brunet, with five years of experience in the French minelaying submarine Rubis, was told to see whether U766 could be made ready to take part in the war against the Japanese. Thinking that such a task could be only performed with a German crew, he drove to a local prisoner of war camp and asked for volunteers. Two months later U766 was fully operational.

At the time it hardly occurred to Brunet that the German sailors could easily throw him overboard before making for a neutral country. Long after the war he did indeed learn of such a plot, to ditch him overboard and then run into the Republic of Ireland. However, Brunet was such a decent chap that no one could bring themselves to carry out the grisly task. U766 must have been a strange sight, flying the French flag with a French commander and Stabsoberfunkmeister Wilhelm Kruse (earlier of U48) translating orders into German. In the end Japan surrendered before U766 left for her voyage to the Far East.

Difficult command decisions

The late Gus Britton, submariner super-extraordinary, who held the lowest rank in the Royal Navy at the beginning and end of the war, said that there was no way he ever wanted to be in a position of having to tell others what to do - although it was obvious that he had well above average ability, and had a more colourful military career than most. This burden of having to make difficult decisions under the pressure of wartime circumstances, ordering others to carry out an action and then having to justify one's judgement long after the heat of the moment has passed, is not something which civilians should judge lightly[1] .

Many U-boat men left the services with clouds on their consciences, wondering for many years afterwards whether some of their decisions were the right ones. It is interesting from the psychological point of view that many of these veterans do not hide their nightmares; instead, these difficult episodes tend to be the first things they themselves bring up during interviews. Some appalling incidents did not offer the commander any alternative choice of actions; so they just followed orders, although the consequences were sometimes hard to bear.

A few days before the beginning of the war Herbert Schultze found himself in such an unenviable predicament. Obermaschin enmaat Benno Krinitzki fell ill while U48 was attempting to reach an area off the north-west of Spain. The orders to remain undetected and to maintain radio silence were clear; but they were of no comfort when watching a close colleague suffer and perhaps die from suspected appendicitis. Yet there was nothing which could be done. The success of military missions, with their implications for the lives of many, came before the wellbeing of individuals.

A nerve-racking operational decision faced the commander of U612, KL Kurt Baberg, when attempting to break through the heavily guarded Straits of Gibraltar. The boat was first attacked by aircraft and then depth charged for 42 hours by surface ships. The damage to machinery and injuries to the men were considerable. Despite water having leaked in as deep as the floor plates, the engineering staff managed to bring U618 back to the surface, but there was no hope of going on into the Mediterranean. Both periscopes were flooded; the radio transmitter was dead, and only a limited reception was possible; the main ballast pumps were damaged; a considerable leak could not be repaired; and cracked batteries meant that electrical capacity had been drastically reduced. The damaged valves, which had allowed so much water into the boat, made it impossible to dive deeper than 20m or to withstand another depth charge attack. Baberg had no choices other than to scuttle, or to attempt to reach France by crawling through shallow coastal waters where the boat could be laid on the seabed during the hours of daylight. There was not sufficient power for maintaining diving depth for any prolonged period.

Baberg's moment of agonising decision came on 28 December 1943 when the radio brought news of German surface ships having been sunk close by. Earlier, when look-outs on U618 heard the faint thunder of gunfire, they were pleased to be well away from the action. The fact that not a single boat answered a distress call from the Supreme Naval Command to abandon operations and rescue survivors of this surface action told the men in U618 that they were the only people capable of helping; but Baberg could not communicate with the outside world. He was convinced that mounting a rescue attempt would be suicidal. The enemy was bound to be searching the area and his boat could not withstand another attack. In view of the dilemma, Baberg took the unorthodox step of asking his men to vote whether they wanted to risk helping or whether they should continue quietly on their homeward crawl. To Baberg's surprise, not a single voice objected to a rescue attempt; consequently, U618 changed course. The submariners' courage was rewarded by picking up 27 men from the destroyer Z27 (KK Günther Schultz). Despite being approached by several hostile aircraft, U618 reached home waters under the most dramatic of circumstances. Long after the war Baberg concluded a report of this incident with the words, "people who were not with us at the

time will never fully appreciate what binds our friendship together".

Rescue operations in themselves were not rare. The most famous is probably the *Laconia* incident when U156 (KL Werner Hartenstein) torpedoed a 19,695GRT troopship in the South Atlantic on 12 September 1942. The discovery that there were over 1,000 Italian prisoners of war among the survivors prompted him to mount a rescue operation. Broadcasting his intentions in plain language, he requested help and ordered his guns to be covered with red cross flags and makeshift red crosses to be painted over the upper deck. U506 (KL Erich Würdemann) took a number of the survivors of various nationalities (including British) from the mass of lifeboats surrounding U156. Everything went reasonably well until a few days later, when the United States Air Force mounted five attacks against this swimming mass of humanity. Consequently, Karl Dönitz ordered rescue operations to be avoided because U-boats were being put at obvious risk.

Despite the Allies having already adopted a similar policy, this order was cited against him at the Nuremberg Trials. It is also interesting to note that the air attack was apparently not one of opportunity, a spur of the moment reaction by aircrew who happened to pass overhead without understanding the situation, but rather that the airmen had been briefed and despatched with the attack in mind. It appears that this Allied instance of attempted murder of survivors was not explored at Dönitz's trial because the information was "secret", and it only came to light some 20 years after the war.

KL Nicolai Clausen was considerably luckier than Hartenstein. In October 1941, while commanding U129 in the South Atlantic, he picked up 119 survivors from the German supply ship *Kota Pinang*, bringing the total crew and passengers to almost 170. This must be a good contender for the maximum number of people carried in an operational U-boat under war conditions. It would have been too risky to cross the dangerous Bay of Biscay with such a load, and the U-Boat Command ordered U129 to make for El Ferrol in Spain, where a tug was organised to take off the majority of passengers on 6 October 1941. The 7,275 GRT freighter *Kota Pinang* had been taken over by the German Navy and converted into a supply ship, to be stationed in an isolated part of the southern seas as a submarine supply base. The sinking of such supply ships put a number of U-boats in dire difficulties, with some having to float around the southern oceans for days on end because they did not have enough fuel on board. In most cases operational U-boats were diverted to resupply these boats.

Claus Korth mounted a rescue operation, and was so severely reprimanded that long after the war his mind was still troubled by the incident. U93 was one of the U-boats which were due to take advantage of the *Bismarck* operation in May 1941, when several supply ships were stationed in isolated locations for the primary purpose of supplying the battleship and her consort *Prinz Eugen*. The *Bismarck* disaster is well known, and most readers will probably also be aware of the secret capture, when the Royal Navy boarded U110 (KL Fritz-Julius Lemp), of an Enigma code-writer together with a list of settings for the next few weeks. Consequently all but one of *Bismarck's* supply ships were located and sunk. When U93 arrived at its rendezvous with the tanker *Belchen* all the look-outs found was a handful of lifeboats with 50 survivors. Korth abandoned his operational orders and brought the *Belchen* crew back to France. Despite passing several Allied convoys, he was unwilling to use his radio to report them to U-Boat Command in case his presence was detected by enemy direction-finders.

After returning from this rather hair-raising Atlantic crossing, he

(1) Strange things do happen; the author had just started writing the above sentence when an envelope containing Gus's obituary dropped through the letterbox. This jolly and most generous character had friends all around the world, and knew more about naval history than the majority of officially recognised experts. He will be sadly missed.

was told by Dönitz that he should have reported the positions of the convoys. "There are U-boats all over the Atlantic," he told Korth, "which aren't finding anything - and you sit under several convoys and don't even report them." In his rage the admiral evidently failed to realise why Korth and only half a dozen or so other commanders were having similar experiences. No one seems to have asked the question why independently-operating commanders - and only such commanders - were finding so many ships. Had someone thought about the wider picture they might have made the connection that Britain was cracking the U-boat radio code. Only those commanders whose positions were not advertised over the radio were sighting enemy shipping - because their boats were the only ones of which the enemy remained ignorant.

One of the most startling of all difficult decisions was probably taken by Konteradmiral Eberhard Godt, Chief of the U-Boat Arm's Operations Department. Shortly after the D-Day landings in Normandy Dönitz told Godt that every available boat would have to go into the English Channel because the outcome of the invasion was going to be "the" decisive factor of the war. Circumstances had shown both men that boats with schnorkels stood only a tiny chance, and those without had no chance at all. Yet despite this Dönitz was adamant: the boats had to be sent into the English Channel. Günter Hessler (his son-in-law, U-boat commander, U-Boat Command staff officer, and author of the German "official" history of the war) said that Dönitz had been forced into this tragic but absurd decision, but he does not clarify how and by whom. Meanwhile in France frantic preparations were under way for getting as many boats as possible to sea.

When the fateful order came Godt did exactly what he was told: he sent the boats to sea. But he despatched the non-schnorkel boats to the Atlantic side of the Bay of Biscay, where they were relatively safe. His excuse was that they were to form a defence line in case the French bases came under attack. By disregarding Dönitz's order he almost certainly saved many lives.

It must be borne in mind that this humanitarian action was carried out at a time when special units had been sent out by the German High Command to summarily execute any German officer or serviceman who might be tempted to retreat too easily, and that these "flying courts martial" claimed many victims. So Godt took a considerable personal risk; yet when, long after the war, I confronted him with this incident, he appeared just as astonished as I was. Eagerly he read through the war diary which he had signed all those years ago; he checked my points, looked up from the papers, and said, "You know, I can't remember that." To me it appeared strange that this quiet, unassumingly modest man should have been the operations chief of Britain's most dangerous enemies. His calm patience as he elucidated history, without ever making his own role sound remotely important, was suggestive of a retired university professor. It was only his highly active mind and his ability to make quick decisions which hinted that he might have had some connection with the military.

Collisions and "friendly fire"

Peter Erich, better known as "Ali" Cremer must hold the record for having collided with the largest number of targets. He started the war aboard the destroyer *Theodor Riedel*, and it was not until the summer of 1940 that he joined U152; but he is probably most famous for having commanded U333 and for being in command of Grand Admiral Dönitz's last guards. Astonishingly, he collided with four targets on four different occasions, and every time he brought his battered boat home. In addition to making a habit of colliding with targets, Cremer was also very nearly sunk by another U-boat - though one now under British control. Captured in the Atlantic and commissioned as HM Submarine *Graph*, the former U570 now commanded by Cdr. Peter Marriot managed to get U333 into her sights, but her torpedoes failed to find their mark. A misunderstanding of signals also led Cremer to sink the German supply ship *Spreewald* on 31 January 1942. Wolfgang

Hirschfeld wrote in his secret diary that it was a real tragedy, while "Ajax" Bleichrodt shrugged his shoulders and said: "It's one of those unfortunate things which happen in war time. Cremer has British ancestors of considerable social standing, so Dönitz should let him off the hook."

There was also an incident of a merchant ship doing more than just colliding with a U-boat which was in the process of attacking it. This happened on 15 July 1942 off Cape Hatteras, United States. Hans-Dieter Heinicke of U576 instructed his IWO to concentrate on two particular steamers in a small convoy, which turned out to have been the American *Chilore* and the Nicaraguan *Bluefields*. Then, while they were choosing a third target, an aircraft attacked; and the 5873GRT steamer *Unicoi* took advantage of the confused situation by steaming at full speed towards the still-surfaced U-boat. *Unicoi's* ramming was successful; there were no survivors.

There were also a number of unfortunate collisions in waters close to home ports. For example, Peter Frahm and the entire crew of U15 were killed on 31 January 1940 after having been accidentally rammed by the German torpedo boat *Iltis*. The last boat of the Third Reich to have been lost as a result of an "own goal" was U2367 (OL Heinrich Schröder). Although this happened in the Great Belt very close to Kiel during the confusion of an air attack, the other ship involved in the collision has not yet been definitely identified. However, U2367 was raised in August 1956 and commissioned the following year as the Federal German *U-Hecht*. The boat was finally withdrawn from service in September 1968.

Although U-boats accidentally sunk a number of German ships, and several U-boats were sunk or damaged by German forces, very few were lost as a result of a definite hunt by their own anti-submarine chasers. U235 under Friedrich Huisgen was one of the unlucky few; the torpedo boat T17 depth-charged and sank U235 in the Kattegat on 14 April 1945, only a few days before the end of the war. This tragic error was partly the result of surface ships not being informed about U-boat activity and vice-versa. A ship in a small convoy spotted the wake from U235's schnorkel and immediately signalled the position to the escort T17, thinking it was a torpedo wake. Having been warned of British submarine activity in the area, T17 lost no time; the depth charges were accurate, and there were no survivors. U235 had quite an interesting history, and this final act was actually the boat's second sinking. It had already gone down on 14 May 1943 during an air raid on Kiel while under command of OL Klaus Becker. The boat was raised and re-commissioned on 29 October 1943 as a school boat shortly before Huisgen took command.

The strange thing about collisions at sea was that there were so few, despite nocturnal surface attacks on convoys demanding a number of U-boats to be milling about in fairly confined spaces. The first and probably only accidental ramming during a convoy attack took place on 8 December 1942 when U221 (KL Hans Trojer) ran into the side of U254 (KL Hans Gilardone). Although both boats survived the initial impact U254 was left unable to dive, and until recently it was thought that it was later sunk by a Catalina of No. 210 Squadron RAF. However, recent research reported by Paul Kemp in his *U-boats Destroyed* suggests that U254 went down faster than previously recorded, and the aircraft in question actually attacked U611 (KL Nikolaus von Jakobs). Only six men from U254 survived - Gilardone was among the dead; and there were no survivors from U611. Following an enquiry it was established that Trojer's look-outs could not have spotted the other U-boat, and the incident was put down to an unfortunate accident.

Chapter 6: **The Changing Face of the U-boat War**

In 1939 the misinformed youths who manned the weapon which Britain came to fear most had an incredibly narrow view of the world. The war came as an incomprehensible shock to many of them. They had not been driven into the armed forces for the opportunity of fighting or finding a glorious death for the Fatherland. They had joined up, like young men the world over, in search of adventure and the opportunity to become independent from their parents. The emotional indoctrination pumped out by a vigorous and all-pervading propaganda system had led them to the recruiting offices. Once in uniform, the lure of joining an elite made the path into U-boats easy. Although many authors have portrayed these youngsters as "bloodthirsty killers", in reality the majority of submariners of all the combatant nations seem to have displayed a tidy, passive type of character. The professional fighter type would have found the cramped space and seemingly endless stretches of confined inactivity inside a submarine quite intolerable.

The declaration of war had a subduing effect on the majority of men in U-boat crews. They knew they were being pitched into battle against a country whose empire stretched around the globe and whose Royal Navy, secure in a 200-year tradition of professional excellence, was almost more powerful than all the other combatant navies put together. Many U-boat men hoped and prayed that they might survive the expected punishment from the enemy; they did not rate their chances of success very highly. Even their Supreme Commander-in-Chief was depressed when he sent his staff into action with the words, "Britain and France have declared war on us. Gentlemen, we have no choice. Full engagement - Die with dignity." This anxiety at being at the mercy of such a powerful seagoing enemy slowly dissolved. The anticipated onslaught from Britain did not materialise, and there

were no secret anti-submarine weapons. As the men learned that their fears were ill-founded they grew bolder. Consequently the first few months of war injected a terrific confidence into the previously jittery ranks of the U-Boat Arm.

Herbert Schultze (U48) summed up his operations in 1939 by saying that the experience had been considerably better than peacetime exercises had led him to believe. He put this down to keeping strict but positive discipline, whereby every individual was encouraged to perform efficiently as a member of the team. Schultze put great emphasis on small points such as punctuality, men doing what others expected of them, tidiness, and maintaining the boat's etiquette. He said that there was no room for slovenliness, for cursing, shouting or for bawling one another out. The non-commissioned officers in U48 had been encouraged to avoid bullying tactics, even when the boat came under attack. Schultze maintained that the ringing of alarm bells was sufficient to make the crew react, and cursing them wasn't going to make them move any faster.

The majority of the better commanders seem to have banned alarming terms such as "aircraft or destroyer attacking" from their operational vocabulary; "fast ship" featured far more often than "destroyer", as being less sinister in the ears of men who could see nothing but whose imaginations were working overtime. (Incidentally, terms such as sloop, frigate, or corvette were hardly used in day-to-day language; U-boat men referred to all of these simply as "destroyers" or "fast ships".)

Comments in Schultze's diary were not limited to his thoughts about the men who served under him; he also had a polite way of telling the officers of the U-Boat Command how to run their business. For example, Schultze objected most strongly to the process of promoting and moving some of his men to other

Two crew members of U48 during her second war cruise in autumn 1939: Bootsmannsmaat Christian Duchene and IIWO Otto Ites.

U48, a Type **VIIB** boat (right), and U43 or U44, Type **IXA** (left). U48 was a single hull type with only a deck casing attached to the top of the pressure hull, while the Type **IX** had the pressure hull completely surrounded by the casing, whence the much wider deck. The device to the left of U48's bollards and directly under the jumping wire is the covered-up head of a sound detector. Note, on the front of U48's conning tower, the boat's badge of an arched and spitting black cat straddling "3x"; this would later be worn by the officers and men as an unofficial cap badge.

boats. He told Dönitz that you could not expect a crew to perform well if you kept taking out key personnel every time the boat came into harbour. His view was that it was not only the commander who suffered because he had to train someone new, but also the youngsters, because they looked up to the older hands and were unsettled by the arrival of a new face who didn't know them. Dönitz accepted this point, but he faced a quandary; the U-boat Arm also needed to withdraw good men from existing boats to help train new crews coming into service.

By the beginning of the war Dönitz had already acquired his reputation of being constantly among his men so that he could listen to their views, and it was not uncommon even for youngsters to approach him with problems. (What is more, in some 20 years of research the present author has not heard of anyone who consulted the Commander-in-Chief and did not get the matter dealt with.) Even dockyard workers and people in the street who asked casually about news of relatives in the Navy received a repy.

Although the German invasion of Norway in April 1940 was dominated by a miserable chain of catastrophic torpedo failures, morale improved well. Operating in confined areas of exceptionally clear water and coming out without only a few losses boosted confidence beyond expectations. Even the simplest of characters realised that there was very little to fear from the opposition. Everybody knew that British forces hunted with determination, but the chances of escaping were good. U-boats could outrun escorts on the surface; bombs dropped by aircraft did not have the anticipated effect, and most of the time the enemy were not even aware of the German presence until torpedo detonations alerted them.

The abandonment of Prize Ordinance Regulations in 1940, together with an escalation of the war at sea, and the harder attitudes forced upon them by war experience do not seem to have had too much of a detrimental effect upon the young men in the U-boats. The youngsters' views were swayed by reports of events such as the *Altmark* incident, when German sailors were reported to have been killed while surrendering with their hands in the air and others as being shot in the back while running away. Today we know that these alleged atrocities never happened, but in 1940 the Germans readily believed such so-called eyewitness accounts, which made them even more determined to fight.

Shortly after the Norwegian campaign came the German invasion of France, whose swift collapse gave the U-boats access to Atlantic ports. The German High Command gave the go-ahead for unrestricted sea warfare in the lucrative area to the west of

the British Isles. Consequently a completely new dimension to submarine warfare opened up, and this had a tremendous impact on operational effectiveness and thus on morale. Germany seemed to be winning; the odds were stacked high in their favour - if only someone could sort out the persistent torpedo failures.

Early in 1940 the Supreme Naval Command had ordered Dönitz to send every available boat into Norwegian waters, where the majority saw very little action. This resulted in long queues at dockyards because large numbers of boats came home for routine attention at about the same time. It was the summer of 1940 before the convoy battles resumed. When the air waves were at first dominated by news of more torpedo failures, Dönitz wrote in his diary "We can't burden the men with such miserable failures again." Even so, the combination of operating out of French bases close to the British convoy routes and the start of unrestricted sea warfare heralded in the so-called "First Happy Time", when U-boats achieved unexpected and extraordinary results. Never before, and never again afterwards, did so few achieve so much with such tiny resources. On average each boat at sea sunk almost six ships per month. Fortunately for Britain, there were only very few U-boats hunting the convoy routes.

To appreciate the difference between this period and the beginning of the war, it might be interesting to compare two actual operational cruises by summarising the surviving logbooks. U48, the most successful U-boat of the Second World War, made fast in Kiel on 17 September 1939 and a few days later left for her second war cruise. Almost exactly one year later the same boat, with an almost identical crew, left for its eighth mission, but its first from a French base.

The following passages are summaries from the logs, not verbatim copies. Although the records written by Schultze and Bleichrodt are easy to read, some logs can present considerable problems because the highly specialised technical submarine language is hardly used anymore. In the mid-1970s, while reading through a log which he had himself written during the war, KL Otto Köhler found that he could no longer understand the meaning of many technical terms and needed an interpreter. Reproducing logs exactly has another disadvantage in that at least one entry had to be made every four hours. Usually this consisted of weather details, position and course, all of which makes for rather repetitive reading.

On the bridge of U48, left, trainee commander Hans Rahmlow (who later famously surrendered U570 to the Royal Air Force), and Bootsmannsmaat Otto Petzokat, right. There seems to be an MG34 machine gun clipped ready to hand at the back of the periscope; and note the "waterwings" type lifejacket worn by the look-out second from left.

U48: SECOND OPERATIONAL CRUISE (Autumn 1939)

Commander: KL Herbert Schultze
IWO: OL Reinhard Suhren
IIWO: LT Otto Ites
LI (Engineering Officer): KL(Ing) Willi Lohner
Stabsobersteuermann Willi Kronenbitter
Stabsobermaschinist Franz Högner, Fritz Groh
Bootsmann Otto Petzokat
Maat Heinz Braune
Obermaschinenmaat Wilhelm Seifert
Maschinenmaat Erich Wunderlich, Eduard Hansen, Wilhelm Otte, Werner Bohatzsch
Bootsmaat Willi Pohle, Cristian Duchene
Funkmaat Willi Kruse
Obergefreiter Bruno Hanf, Hans Bauer
Maschinenobergefreiter Hans Haubold, Sebastian Rahbauer, August Wegmann, Heinz Prassdorf, Willi Boller, Karl Beyer, Franz Tillmanns, Helmut Werner, Johannes Klaus, Franz Franzke, Hans Müller
Matrosenobergefreiter Albert Bork, Herbert Schneider, Heinz Gralle, Horst Hoffmann, Berthold Seidel, Hans Meier
Funkgefreiter Kurt Schneegass, Waldermar Ischmer, Walter Lang

(The names are given here in the order in which Walter Lang recorded them at the time.)

Day 1: 4 October 1939
0100hrs: Left Tirpitz Quay in Kiel, through Holtenau Locks and on through the Kiel Canal into the Elbe and then North Sea. U48 negotiated the canal with the aid of three pilots, one for each of the three different stages.
Day 2: 5 October
0000: German Bight. ESE4, sea 3-4, cloudy, good visibility. On passage through North Sea.
Day 3: 6 October
0000: Central North Sea between Orkneys and Norway. ESE6, sea 6, cloudy, good visibility.
Day 4: 7 October
0000: Northern North Sea. SE1-2, sea 1, a few clouds, good visibility.
1542: Alarm dive. Aircraft sighted. At least this proves that there is air reconnaissance in this area.
Day 5: 8 October
0000: West of Shetland, south-east of Faeroe Islands, on passage to operations area. S3, sea 3, cloudy, good visibility.

Day 6: 9 October
0000: NW of Hebrides, E of Rockall, on passage to operations area. S5, sea 4-5, cloudy, moderate visibility.
Day 7: 10 October
0000: NW of Ireland, on passage to operations area. S6-7, sea 6-7, cloudy, moderate visibility.
Day 8: 11 October
0000: W of Ireland, on passage to operations area. SW4-5, sea 4, cloudy, occasional rain showers or drizzle, poor visibility.
Day 9: 12 October
0000: W of Ireland near Porcupine bank. SW3, sea 3, cloudy, moderate visibility.
0734: Sighted ship. Dived. Surfaced. Stopped the 2000GRT Norwegian freighter *Lido* with a cargo of timber for Dublin (Ireland). Master ordered over to U-boat with his papers. No war goods. Allowed ship to continue with her voyage.
1610: Ship sighted on port beam. Moved into position ahead of her. Dived. Looked like a big tanker. No signs of weapons or neutrality markings. Surfaced. Stopped her with heavy artillery. Turned out to be the French 14,115GRT *Emile Miguet*. Crew took to the lifeboats. Shot torpedo, which hit amidships. Meanwhile another ship came into sight. We have left the sinking tanker and we are making for a favourable attacking position ahead of the other target.
2024: Target with dimmed lights. Seems to have a bad conscience. We shot one torpedo, which detonated in our faces about 100m in front of us. The ship responded by sending SOS, increasing speed and then shooting at us with artillery. Shot second torpedo; no detonation. Shot third torpedo; no detonation. Shot fourth torpedo; no detonation. Turned boat and shot torpedo from the rear tube, this time a detonation - at last.
Day 10: 13 October
0000: SW of Ireland. SW3, sea 1-2, a few clouds, good visibility.
0116: The target, which is still not sinking, turned out to be the 5202GRT freighter *Heronspool*. Shot a sixth torpedo at her.
0120: Sighted smoke. Left *Heronspool*. Smoke disappeared from view and we cannot find it again, therefore we returned to *Heronspool*, which is now lying deep in the water with waves lapping around the bridge.
0145: Leaving the area to continue with our cruise.
0814: Stopped the French 6903GRT freighter *Louisiane* with shots across the bows. Then sunk her with artillery.
0917: Destroyer in sight. Shooting at us. Alarm dive. Immediately we went deep to 120m to test for any leaks. Heard a few depth charge detonations. The *Louisiane* did not use its radio, therefore

the destroyer must have been attracted by the sound of our gun-fire.

1625: Detected a ship which turned out to be a tanker. Surfaced and stopped her with flag signals. Ordered master to bring his papers over to us. Turned out to be the Norwegian *Europe* with petrol for Amsterdam. Allowed the ship to go on its way.

1900: The combination of wind WSW2 and calm sea helped in making the quick decision to bring the two torpedoes from the outside containers into the boat.

Day 11: 14 October

0000: SW of Ireland. S1, sea 1, cloudy - clear, good visibility. (Unknown to everybody aboad U48 until later in the day, this was the time when their sister boat, U47 under KL Günter Prien, was lying inside the Royal Navy anchorage at Scapa Flow, reloading torpedoes for their second attack against the battleship *Royal Oak*. The fatal shots were fired at 0116hrs.)

1000: Sighted ship on zigzag course. Moved ahead of it on the surface. Dived. Had a good look at the target. Surfaced and stopped her with artillery. Crew took to the lifeboats. This was the English 3677GRT steamer *Sneaton* with a cargo of coal. The ship transmitted an SOS with position and the news that the crew is taking to the boats.

1233: Sunk *Sneaton* with a torpedo and then went over to the lifeboats to check that everybody was in reasonable order. While doing this another ship came into sight. Dived. Identified the newcomer as a Belgian and therefore did not surface. I watched her stop and take the men from the lifeboats on board.

Day 12: 15 October

0000: SW of Ireland. NW2, sea 2, a few isolated clouds, clear, good visibility.

0840: Sighted ship and we approached cautiously. Turned out to be the 120m long bow section of the tanker *Emile Miguet* which we had attacked earlier, well afloat and no signs of sinking. Wind NE2. Ordered gun crew on deck. Shot 15 shells. The last one resulted in a brilliant flash of flame followed by a rising cloud of smoke.

Day 13: 16 October

0000: SW of Ireland. NE2-3, sea 2, cloudy - clear, good visibility.

0650: Sighted fully illuminated ship. Approached on the surface, stopped her with flag signals and ordered the master to bring his papers over. This was the Dutch freighter *Leerdam* with cotton for Rotterdam. Sent over prize crew. Everything seemed to be in order. Bought some fresh meat and fifty eggs from the master, who refused all payment, so I gave him a bottle of cognac. Allowed the ship to proceed on its way.

Day 14: 17 October

0000: North Atlantic. E3, sea 3, cloudy, moderate to good visibility.

0908: Intercepted a radio signal from KL Herbert Sohler (U46) saying he has sighted a convoy. We have changed course and are heading towards it.

2032: Sighted two ships with dimmed illumination. Shot torpedo; no detonation. Shot another torpedo at the same target; detonation. The crew abandoned ship, while we headed towards the other target. (The sinking ship was the 7256GRT *Clan Chisholm*.)

2100: Destroyer in sight on our port beam, moving at high speed towards the ship which we had just attacked. Shot the torpedo from the rear tube at it, but missed. The destroyer didn't notice our presence, so we are continuing our hunt for the other ship.

2310: Shot torpedo at range of 1500m; no detonation, but the target seems to have noticed our presence. *Sagaing* (7968GRT, belonging to Henderson and Co. of Glasgow) sending SOS with position saying she is under attack. Shot our last torpedo; again no detonation. Sank the target with artillery. (There appears to be no

record of this sinking from the Allied side and it is not recorded in *Axis Submarine Successes* by Prof.Dr.Jürgen Rohwer.)

Day 15: 18 October

0000: North Atlantic. NNE2-3, sea 2-3, cloudy, good visibility. Sent radio signal to U-Boat Command saying that have commenced our homeward bound voyage.

0655: Intercepted an SOS from a ship under attack by a U-boat. Sighted a convoy. Sighted destroyer coming towards us at high speed which started shooting at us with artillery. Alarm dive to 120m to test that there are no leaks. Counted 31 depth charge detonations. Another U-boat has got to be with the convoy. Therefore there is no need for us to shadow and we are remaining submerged for a well earned rest.

Day 16: 19 October

0000: North Atlantic. NNE2, sea 1, few clouds, good visibility.

1215: Sighted steamer and attacked with artillery. The ship returned our fire with two guns on the stern and used its radio to send an SOS. Alarm dive.

1420: Surfaced. Attacked ship a second time. Destroyer appeared at high speed, probably looking for us. We dived and let the target escape. It was the 4892GRT *Rockspool*. (Schultze seems to have got the wrong name, as there appear to be no records of a ship with this name.) Continued our homeward bound voyage.

Day 17: 20 October

0000: W of Ireland. N1-2, sea 1-2, cloud cover to clear, good visibility. Wind increasing slowly. Homeward bound voyage continuing.

U48: the coxswain on both the second and eighth war cruises, Obersteurmann Willi Kronenbitter, demonstrating the complete disregard for uniform regulations which was normal at sea. He was later commissioned, and survived the war as commander of the Type XXI boat U3527 in spring 1945.

Above left: **Maschinengefreiter Heinz Prassdorf served on U48 during her second war cruise; he later became Obermaschinist in U1203, where he was decorated with the Knight's Cross - one of only seven awarded to U-boat warrant officers throughout the war.**

Above: **Otto Ites after promotion to Oberleutnant zur See and IWO of U48. He survived to be taken prisoner when his later command U94 was lost in summer 1942.**

Day 18: 21 October
0000: NW of Ireland. NW4, sea 3-4, cloudy occasional rain showers, moderate to bad visibility. Continuing homeward voyage.
Day 19: 22 October
0000: NW of Hebrides. WSW6, sea 6, moderate visibility.
0945: Aircraft in sight. We are not diving because it probably won't spot us in this miserable weather.
1015: Two destroyers came into sight. I allowed U48 to slide between them on the surface. Distance to destroyers 800-900m. Neither of them spotted us.
Day 20: 23 October
0000: N of Shetland. W5 at times S5, sea 5, cloudy to clear, moderate visibility. Continuing homeward bound voyage.
Day 21: 24 October
0000: North Sea. W at times S3, sea 3, cloudy, reasonable visibility. Continuing homeward bound voyage.
Day 22: 25 October
0000: Approaching Little Belt. SSW3, sea 3, few clouds, good visibility. Heading southwards through Little Belt.
0945: Made fast at Tirpitz Quay in Kiel.

* * *

The commander, "Vaddi" Schultze, was later taken ill; and U48 travelled from Kiel to France under KL "Harro" Rösing, although at times one wonders who was actually in control. The boat's log, which should normally have been seen by the commander at least once every four hours, does not bear a single signature from Rösing; instead it was signed by the IWO "Teddy" Suhren throughout this voyage. Once in France, "Ajax" Bleichrodt took on U48 as

his first command. So, for both cruises the commanders were fresh with only limited experience of facing the enemy. One should not dismiss the two voyages under Rösing as uneventful; he sank 12 ships of 60,500GRT, which is considerably more than the majority of boats achieved during the whole six years of war. In fact the figures of this almost "part-time" U-boat commander make an interesting comparison with the so- called aces. OL Hans Jenisch, the 32nd on the list of most successful commanders, sank a total of 14 ships of about 100,500GRT; so the summer of 1940 was indeed a successful period for U-boats. The term "part-time" is factual, not derogatory; Rösing had been one of the first to join U-boats, and at the beginning of the war he had risen to the rank of flotilla commander. He was pushed into U48 because Schultze was taken ill unexpectedly and a man of experience was needed to control people like "Teddy" Suhren, Otto Ites and Erich Zürn, who would not have taken kindly to an inexperienced newcomer. Following his spell in U48, Rösing became liaison officer for Italian boats in Bordeaux, and later FdU West.

U48: EIGHTH OPERATIONAL CRUISE (Autumn 1940)

The number after each name below denotes the first operational cruise on which the man participated in U48; thus e.g. KL Bleichrodt was on his first patrol with this crew, and Bootsmaat Otto Petzokat on his eighth. Again, the names are listed in the same order as recorded at the time by radio operator Walter Lang.

Commander: KL Heinrich Bleichrodt (8)
IWO: OL Reinhard Suhren (1)
IIWO: LT Otto Ites (1)
LI (Engineering Officer): LT(Ing) Erich Zürn (4)
Stabsobersteuermann Willi Kronenbitter (1), Herbert Engel (6)
Stabsobermaschinist Franz Högner (1), Julius Brettschneider (7)
Bootsmaat Otto Petzokat (8)
Mechanikersmaat Heinz Braune (1)
Obermaschinistenmaat Erich Wunderlich (1), Eduard Hansen (1), Werner Zinke (5), Max Schmitz (6), Heinz Macheleidt (7)
Bootsmaat Willi Pohle (1), Cristian Duchene (1), Willi Witt (7)
Funkmaat Willi Kruse (1), Helmut Walentowitz (6)
Mechanikerobergefreiter Rudi Fischer (3), Karl Hornenbroich (5), Walter Hacker (7)
Maschinenobergefreiter Willi Boller (1), Karl Beyer (1), Johannes Klaus (1), Franz Tillmanns (1), Helmut Werner (1), Franz Franzke (2), Heinz Wittkowski (5), Werner Projahn (6), Paul Priebe (6), Erich Diefenbach (7)
Maschinenhauptgefreiter Siegfried Ilg (4)
Matrosenobergefreiter Horst Hofmann (1), Bertold Seidel (1), Hans Meier (1), Hinrich Hansen (4), Johann Dehn (5), August Androsch (6), Erich Dittkowski (7)
Funkobergefreiter Walter Lang (1), Siegfried Elser (5)

OL Reinhard "Teddy" Suhren, IWO of U48 on both the patrols summarised in this chapter. In November 1940 he became the first Watch Officer to be decorated with the Knight's Cross - just two weeks after his brother Gerd became the first Engineering Officer to be so honoured. "Teddy" went on to command U564, and seems to have taken the lucky black cat badge with him.

Day 1: 8 September 1940
This is the 10th day that the new commander had been on board.
2000: Cast off in Lorient and followed two minesweepers out to sea.
2145: Left the minesweeping escort.
Day 2: 9 September
0000: W of France. NW4, sea 3-4, clear, good visibility.
Day 3: 10 September
0000: S of Ireland. NWbyW3-4, sea 3, few clouds, good visibility.
Day 4: 11 September
0000: SW of Ireland, NW4, sea 3, cloudy, good visibility.
Day 5: 12 September
0000: W of Ireland. W4, sea 4, cloudy with rain at times, moderate visibility.
Day 6: 13 September
0000: W of Ireland. NW9, sea 8, cloudy, moderate visibility.
0809: Dived due to bad weather with a view to give the crew some rest.
Day 7: 14 September
0000: NW of Ireland. WNW5, sea 4, cloudy, good visibility.
1623: Sighted aircraft. Dived.
1711: Sighted aircraft. Dived.
2020: Sighted convoy on easterly course, speed about 6kts with warship escort. We are moving into advantageous position ahead of convoy and at best possible angle of attack in bright moonlight.
Day 8: 15 September
0000: NW of Ireland. WNW3, sea 3, cloudy to clear, very good visibility with bright moonlight.
0024: (U48 started attacking Convoy SC3.) Shot Tube I at two overlapping ships. Huge detonation after a running time of 215 seconds. A few minutes later there was another detonation, which was thought to have been caused by depth charges going off. Perhaps the target was carrying some? (It has been suggested that U48 had aimed at the British freighter *Empire Soldier*, which had been damaged earlier during a collision. It is also possible that the detonation caused the 1780GRT *Kenordoc* to sink.)
0025: Turning to shoot a G7a torpedo from stern tube, again at overlapping targets. (The G7a torpedo was propelled by an internal combustion engine with fuel injected by compressed air. This type left a wake of bubbles and a little oil which could be seen on the surface.) Detonation after running time of 230 seconds. (The target was the escort *Dundee*.)
0028: We are moving in the same direction as the convoy. Spotted three warship escorts.
0123: Shot at a ship towards the front of the convoy. Detonation after a running time of 155 seconds. We could see the target sink. (This was the 4343GRT Greek freighter *Alexandros*.) Shot Tube II. Missed. Convoy turned towards us. The ship we hit earlier was on the far side and the enemy probably thinks that we were attacking from that flank. Radio room intercepted a message on the 600m wavelength warning of a U-boat on the surface. Shot Tube III at a ship towards the front of the convoy. Torpedo seen to break the surface, but it still detonated on target, which started sinking immediately. The aft section was awash after about 1 minute. (This was the 5319GRT British freighter *Empire Volunteer*.)
We seem to have been spotted by a ship in the middle of the convoy which is shooting at us. We are turning away into the darkness, but keeping on the convoy's general course. Three destroyers appeared on our side, darting back and forth, so they probably have not seen us. Moon became covered with clouds which gave us an excellent opportunity of making for the far side

of the merchant ship columns. When we got there, the bright moon reappeared. An escort in front of the convoy was heading towards us. Either they have heard us or, more likely, seen the bright wash from our boat. Dived. Escaping on the surface seemed to be too risky.

1050: Surfaced.

1121: Sighted aircraft. Dived. Consequently lost convoy.

2047: Intercepted a radio signal which suggested one warship with the convoy seems to have been damaged. Was this ship on top of the depth charges which we heard earlier?

Day 9: 16 September

0000: NW of Ireland. SSE3, sea 3, cloudy with rain at times, variable visibility.

Day 10: 17 September

0000: NW of Ireland. SW3, sea 2, few clouds, very good visibility.

1002: Sighted convoy on westerly course, doing about 7kts. (This was OB213.) We are keeping contact because the sea is too rough for a submerged attack. WNW5, sea 5. Didn't spot any escorts.

Day 11: 18 September

0000: NW of Ireland. WNW4, sea 4, cloudy to clear, good visibility with bright moonlight.

0001: Shot Tube III and IV at a passenger ship in the middle of the convoy . Both missed because we had over calculated the settings. We are running same course as convoy.

0001: Shot Tube I. Detonation aft after running time of 119 seconds. Ship stopped and lowered lifeboats. (This was the 11,081GRT passenger ship *City of Benares*, with a large number of children on board, 77 of whom lost their lives. The liner had

not been declared as a hospital ship and was sailing in the middle of the convoy without lights, making her a legitimate target. However, after the war Bleichrodt was warned privately by his Royal Navy interrogators, as fellow warship men, that the British authorities had decided to use this sinking for another show trial and a hanging. Someone claimed - absurdly - that Bleichrodt knew there were children on board and had deliberately set out to kill them. Despite considerable intimidation, Bleichrodt was not the type to be forced into such a "confession" even under extreme pressure, and the charge was dropped for lack of evidence.)

0007: Shot Tube II at a freighter. Detonation after a running time of 43 seconds. Ship sending out SOS, saying her name is *Marina*, 5088GRT. The convoy scattered and ships are heading off in various directions. We are following a medium sized tanker. Turned and shot Tube V (stern). Still very bright moonlight, but with occasional rain. The target seemed to have spotted us and started shooting back. The passenger liner is settling in the water and sinking slowly. The *Marina* is also going down. The other target vanished from sight in a shower of rain. We dived to listen for its

January 1940: U48 in the gigantic sea-locks of the Kiel Canal at Brunsbüttel on the Elbe estuary while on the way out for her fourth war cruise. Usually the locks were crammed with ships, but following a number of collisions Dönitz insisted that U-boats be allowed through on their own. The hydroplanes, sticking out on both sides of the submarine, were rather vulnerable to being bent. There were locks at both ends of the canal because the water level was a couple of metres over "Baltic Normal".

U48 in Wilhelmshaven, having the bow protection gear removed. This metal cap was fitted while U-boats negotiated long distances in coastal ice.

sound. Heard nothing.

1325: Surfaced. Smoke in sight. Going at fast speed towards it. This turned out to be single ship heading east at about 8kts. Still good visibility, we are going on to get in front of her.

1658: Dived for submerged attack. Shot Tube V (stern). Detonation after running time of 27 seconds. Picked up radio signal with SOS from *Magdalena* (3118GRT). Surfaced.

2220: Moved the two torpedoes from the outside containers into the boat. Test dive.

Day 12: 19 September

0000: NW of Ireland. W2, sea 1, few clouds, very good visibility.

1152: Intercepted a radio call from U47 (KL Günter Prien) saying they have a convoy in sight. Changed course and gone to fast speed.

1442: Sent radio message to U-Boat Command asking U47 to send out beacon signals for us to home in on.

1720: Received a signal from U-boat Command, ordering U48, U65 (KL Hans-Gerrit von Stockhausen), U43 (KL Wilhelm Ambrosius), U99 (KL Otto Kretschmer) and U100 (KL Joachim Schepke) to take up positions in specified areas. We were allocated square 2835AL.

Day 13: 20 September

0000: NW of Ireland. NNE3, sea 2, cloudy, very good visibility.

Day 14: 21 September

0000: NW of Ireland. Bright moonlight. W2, sea 1, cloudy to clear with rain at times, generally very good visibility.

0530: Intercepted an SOS from *Elmbank*. (She had been damaged in Convoy HX72 by a torpedo from U99, which then fired 88

rounds of 88mm shells at her. Later in the day U47 used its heavy artillery against the ship, again without making too much of an impression. *Elmbank* was eventually sunk by U99 later in the day.)

0600: Shot a G7a from Tube I at range of 6-7km. Missed; the distance was too great for accurate estimation of settings. Bright moonlight, cloudy but very clear.

0620: Shot Tube V (stern), G7a, detonation after a running time of 127 seconds. Intercepted an SOS from *Blairangus* (4409GRT). Saw a high column of water rise by the side of the ship and shortly afterwards there were more explosions. Perhaps the target was carrying explosives. Lifeboats were manned, but the target then disappeared from view in a shower of rain. We are making for a tanker at the front of the convoy. Shot Tube III, G7e, but there was no detonation. (The G7e torpedo was propelled by an electric motor and did not leave a tell-tale wake on the surface.) Our last torpedo is not ready for action; it is a G7a with a bent steering fin. Keeping contact with the convoy.

2338: Shot torpedo from Tube V (stern) at a freighter; detonation. Intercepted an SOS from 5236GRT *Broompark*. U100 (KL Joachim Schepke) has taken over the role of shadowing the convoy.

Day 15: 22 September

0000: NW of Ireland. WSW3, sea 3, cloudy, good visibility.

0111: Commenced homeward bound voyage to Lorient.

1600: Sighted two ships but the wind (NW5) and excellent visibility make an attack impractical. Even if we could get within range, it would be too rough for using the deck gun. Continuing with homeward bound voyage.

Day 16: 23 September

0000: W of Ireland. NW2, sea 2, few clouds, very good visibility.

1407: Intercepted a distress call from Supreme Naval Command.

There has been a sinking just 100 miles east from our position. Both engines to full speed, making for given position.
1824: Received radio signal from U-Boat Command ordering us to continue with homeward bound voyage. Some other ship was probably closer and reached the disaster area before us.
Day 17: 24 September
0000: SW of Ireland. NW2, sea 1, a few single clouds, very good visibility.
1306: Sighted aircraft; dived.
Day 18: 25 September
W of France. W3, sea 3, a few single clouds, very good visibility.
1024: Made fast in Lorient.

* * *

The so-called "Happy Time" lasted from early autumn 1940 until the spring of 1941, when it came to a dramatically abrupt end. To appreciate the tension in this sudden change, it is necessary to remember that throughout 1940 U-boat losses due to enemy action were running at one or occasionally two per month, and not a single boat fell foul of British forces during the three months from December 1940 to February 1941, while merchant ship sinkings remained at an all time high. But then March rolled in with a bitter vengeance. First, U47 (KL Günter Prien), the heroes of Scapa Flow, failed to answer signals. U-Boat Command was still trying to raise Prien on the radio when U70 (KL Joachim Matz) also vanished from the ether. Less than a couple of weeks later the boats of the two aces KL Joachim Schepke (U100) and KL Otto Kretschmer (U99) went down, at almost the same time and place. This shock had hardly been digested when U551 (KL Karl Schrott) was depth-charged by the trawler *Visenda*; and less

than two weeks later she was followed to the bottom by U76 (OL Friedrich von Hippel). These casualties were followed by the loss of U65 (KL Jockel Hoppe) towards the end of April; and another ace, Fritz-Julius Lemp (U110) - who had fired the first torpedo of the war and sunk the passenger liner *Athenia* - was killed early in May.

This period of calamitous U-boat losses marked the first turning point of the Battle for the Atlantic. The number of ships sunk per U-boat at sea dropped to a new low, and never again were U-boats in a position to seriously threaten to strangle the Atlantic supply routes, even though the largest convoy battles were still to come. The enemy's resources would now grow steadily, and would eventually outstrip those of the BdU despite an ever increasing programme of building.

U-boats were not classified as lost just because they failed to answer their radio, although a number of them had been classified as sunk only to turn up inconveniently just in time to embarrass their memorial service. However, the uncertain period of waiting usually did not last long. Very often the B-Dienst (the German Radio Monitoring Service) intercepted messages about boats having been sunk, or the news was even broadcast by the BBC. As already mentioned, since U-boats frequently maintained radio silence many of them had a number of messages waiting, which were transmitted as soon as a battle started and their presence was obviously known to the enemy. This habit often gave the U-Boat Command an indication of what was going on

U48 at sea: a look-out uses the combination of issue sun goggles and binoculars. IWO Suhren is at the front of the bridge, wearing a "Schiffchen".

just before the bitter end. (It is worth noting, given this practice and given the British breaking of the U-boat signals code, that the unrivalled ace KL *"Stille Otto"* Kretschmer was known for his extreme reluctance to indulge in even routine radio traffic.)

After the war Britain made a determined effort to account for every U-boat, and the fates of many were confirmed. However, U47 is one of those perennial mysteries which has still not been clarified. Many sources have attributed her sinking to a number of clear-cut causes, but none of these has held water for long. It might be interesting to add that a contributing factor in her loss could well have been that the boat itself didn't seem to hold water.... U47, together with the other Type VIIBs, was no longer in prime condition and possibly not even fully seaworthy. It is known that the boat had restrictions placed on its diving depth and on rattling the engines at full speed for any length of time. The uncertainty has given rise to wild speculation that Prien survived, and it has even been claimed that he was seen in Germany after the war, but such stories are almost certainly fantasies. There is no way that a boat could have come so secretly into a port that absolutely no one knew anything about it - and who would have benefited from such a subterfuge? It would seem highly likely that U47 did indeed go to the bottom during early March 1941, although the exact circumstances will almost certainly never be known.

From spring 1941 the number of ships sunk by U-boats dwindled rapidly. American Lease-Lend gave the Royal Navy's escort assets a large boost, and bases in Iceland and Greenland increased air cover of the convoy routes. Even before entering the war the USA took over responsibility for convoy protection in the western Atlantic, thus easing the Royal Navy's burden considerably. There was what has been called a "Second Happy Time" immediately after America's declaration of war in December 1941; this opened up rich new hunting grounds for the U-boats all along the eastern seaboard of the USA, and in February 1942 nearly 70 ships were sunk there, while only six U-boats were lost off the American coast between December and July. However, the initial inexperience of the US Navy and Coast Guard did not offer dividends for long; the Atlantic war began to swing the other way, with a brief reversal in November 1942. In that month the Atlantic was swarming with shipping heading for the Allied landings in French North Africa, and 117 ships were sunk. Dönitz had about 200 U-boats by this time, and at any one time around 70 were at sea.

Despite the dramatic-seeming successes in American waters, the number of ships sunk per month per U-boat at sea actually dropped from almost six in 1940 (when there had seldom been many more than 20 boats at sea) to a maximum of two in American waters during the first months of 1942. This was largely due to the longer voyages making U-boats less effective.

The final turning point, after which the U-boats represented a dangerous but no longer a potentially war-winning weapon, came in March 1943. Put simply, the reasons for the sudden seizure of initiative by the Allies were both quantitive and qualitative. Many more escorts were available, and they were becoming more practised at their trade all the time. Both close and distant escort groups could be directed by aircraft in aggressive U-boat hunts without weakening the actual convoy escorts. Centimetric or short-wave radar was central to their new successes; unlike earlier equipment, this could detect targets as small as a U-boat on the surface, and was compact enough to fit into aircraft as well as small escort ships. The U-boats could no longer travel safely on the surface by night; and when submerged they were vulnerable to Asdic detection. The "air gap" in mid-Atlantic was closed by a combination of long range land-based aircraft being released from bomber to maritime duties, and the introduction of small escort carriers to give convoys their own eyes in the sky.

March 1943 was the last bad month for Allied shipping losses: 108 ships totalling 627,000GRT sunk by U-boats in all oceans. In May, 40 U-boats were sunk – a third of those at sea; in July, 37 more, and mostly by aircraft. In November 1943 Allied merchant shipping losses were just 80,000 tons.

To give some impression of how things had changed, we may compare the early operations of U48 with activities during the autumn of 1943. This period is of special significance because September 1943 was supposed to see Germany's great comeback in the convoy war. The Leuthen Pack, consisting of 20 boats, each with the latest weapons, was going to swing the Battle of the Atlantic back in Germany's favour. The new weapons consisted of two types of radar detectors: one for long range, warning the boat when aircraft were searching in their vicinity, and another to give warning when aircraft were close enough to attack. Earlier in the year a signal on the second set would have driven the boats "into the cellar", but now each member of the Leuthen Pack was thought to have sufficient firepower to blast even a large aircraft out of the sky. The idea was for them go in and attack convoys on the surface.

The other new weapon was an acoustic torpedo which could be shot without taking direct aim and left to home in on propeller noise. This was an ideal weapon against destroyers, which usually moved too fast for the older, conventional types of torpedoes. However, these weapons did not bring about a change in fortune for the U-boats. The radar detector did save many boats, but only to hide impotently under water - the anti-aircraft guns were too weak to make much of a difference. The acoustic torpedo had a built-in fault, its launch and erratic progress often resulting in alarm or extreme irritation aboard the target, but without fatal consequences. The figures for its performance are horrific; after the war Prof.Dr.Jürgen Rohwer calculated that of over 700 acoustic torpedoes launched less than 80 actually destroyed their target. (There were also known cases of these weapons circling to destroy the boat which fired them.)

U48 was no longer in operational service by the time the Leuthen Pack assembled on the Canadian side of the Atlantic during the autumn of 1943, having been withdrawn for training duties in July 1941. At first glance it may appear strange to compare the most successful U-boat of the war with U377, an almost unknown quantity; but they had a number of significant features in common. U377's early operations had taken the boat as far north as submarines had ever operated. Its commander, KL Otto Köhler, carried out a variety of missions around the edge of the polar ice cap, ferrying an automatic weather station and later a weather reporting detachment to Spitzbergen, where the boat was never in any position to sink ships. Köhler was then promoted to become the commanding officer of the new training detachment for acoustic torpedoes while a newcomer, OL Gerhard Kluth, took command of U377. In August 1943 he was in a very similar position to "Ajax" Bleichrodt in autumn 1940, having taken over a run-in boat with an experienced crew.

U377: TWELFTH OPERATIONAL CRUISE (Autumn 1943)

Commander: OL Gerhard Kluth
IWO: LT Ernst-August Gerke
IIWO: LT Wolfgang Herpich, or LT Kurt Menger
LI (Engineering Officer): LT(Ing) Karl-Heinz Nitschke, with trainee LT(Ing) Erich Altesellmeier
Obersteuermann Martin Weidmann
Stabsobermaschinist Jak Mallmann
Obermaschinist Willi Schulz
Maschinenobermaat Herbert Dorn, Kurt Göllnitz
Maschinenmaat Willi Hiess, Johannes Hilbert, Helmut Hofstede, Paul Jaguttis, Arthur Allenstein
Maschinenobergefreiter Helmut Bachmann, Heinz Badstüber, Karl Guth, Arthur Kobs, Norbert Pampusch, Hans Pfeiffer, Herbert Richter, Gerhard Sikorski, Alfred Schultze, Kurt Schulz, Paul Ziwiski
Maschinengefreiter Wolfgang Blümel, Peter Fehlhaber, Otto Fröhlich, Heinz Hannecke, Hermann Stehning
Funkobermaat Siebrand Voss, Paul Czinczoll, Heinz Neugebauer
Funkobergefreiter Helmut Schaar
Funkgefreiter Artur Meiser, Heinz Panning

This is probably the *Hersonspool* being sunk by U48.

The *Louisiane* sinking on 13 October 1939.

Oberbootsmaat Hermann Patzke, Albert Jungclaus
Bootsmaat Erich Köhler, Otto Schnell
Matrosenobergefreiter Otto Diening, Harry Eydam, Bruno Merkel, Horst Michel, Horst Ober, Richard Reissner, Otto Sommerer
Matrosengefreiter Kurt Dams, Stefan Istvanitz, Wilhelm Wiederhold
Obermechaniker Heinrich Böhm
Mechanikersmaat Werner Reinicke, Jakob Möhl
Mechanikersobergefreiter Karl-Heinz Schütt
Mechanikersgefreiter Erich Weinert

Sanitätsobermaat Bruno Günther
(So far we have not found a crew list for this voyage; these names have been reconstructed from the register for U377's thirteenth and final patrol.)

Day 1: 30 August 1943
0930: In Brest harbour. Followed minesweeper out to sea.
Returned to Brest.
1205: Made fast in Brest. Boat into dockyard for repairs. Periscope, port cooling water pump, various valves and other gear not work-

A life boat from *Louisiane* coming alongside **U48**.

The bow section of the *Emile Miguet* was found to be still afloat three days after the aft section had sunk; **U48** shelled it, setting it on fire.

ing properly.
1530: Boat into dry dock.
Day 2: 31 August
1600: Boat out of dry dock.
Boat being repaired.

Day 1: 6 September 1943
1710: In Brest harbour, cast off.
1730: Followed minesweepers out to sea.
1845: Man overboard. Fished out by minesweeper.
1945: End of minesweeper escort. Received back the man who had gone overboard.
Day 2: 7 September
0521: Deep diving trials. One of the engine room valves is leaking

badly.
0746: Surfaced and returned to Brest.
1920: Made fast in Brest.
2130: Into dry dock.
Day 3: 8 September
0930: Left dry dock.
2200: Into dry dock to repair damage to the port propeller by U256.
Day 4: 9 September
1000: Left dry dock.
1610: Cast off.
1624: Trimming trials.
1758: Following minesweeper escort out to sea together with U603 (OL Rudolf Baltz).

1930: End of minesweeper escort.

Day 5: 10 September

0458: Deep diving trials.

0630: Surfaced.

0920: Dismissed escorts and dived again to proceed under water.

1515: Surfaced to ventilate the boat.

1536: Dived to continue proceeding under water.

(The Bay of Biscay had become known as "The Black Pit of Biscay" because the Royal Air Force had made it far too dangerous for travelling on the surface.)

2205: Surfaced.

2235: Dived to proceed under water.

Day 6: 11 September

0505: Surfaced.

0705: Dived. Distance covered during last 24 hours; on surface 35sm, submerged 27sm, total 62sm (sm = Seemeile - nautical mile.)

2157: Surfaced. SE3, sea 2, light haze with showers at times.

2325: Alarm! Radar warning device has indicated radar being used in the near vicinity.

Day 7: 12 September

0400: Surfaced.

0657: Dived to proceed under water.

1200: Distance covered during the last 24 hours; on surface 49sm, submerged 20sm, total 69sm.

Day 8: 13 September

1200: Distance covered during the last 24 hours; on surface 52sm, submerged 20sm, total 72sm.

Day 9: 14 September

1200: Distance covered during the last 24 hours; on surface 83sm, submerged, 17sm, total 100sm.

Day 10: 15 September

(A similar pattern as on the previous days repeats itself.)

Day 11: 16 September

Day 12: 17 September

Day 13: 18 September

(1200: Being further away from land and out of the dangerous Bay of Biscay area, the boat remained longer on the surface, and the distance covered during the last 24 hours increased: on surface 135sm, submerged 24sm, total 159 sm.)

1630: Welding work necessary on the 20mm quadruple anti-aircraft gun because the armoured shield has been bent.

Day 14: 19 September

1407: Surfaced. Received signal from U-Boat Command saying boats of Group Leuthen should concentrate on surface attacks at night and during the day were only to make use of favourable conditions. "Count on a convoy on westerly course. Once it has been sighted, make towards it at fast speed." (We may recall that Dönitz stated in his diary that commanders' education had been so reduced that it was now necessary to keep sending them instructions.)

2245: Received short signal with convoy's position. We are travelling at fast speed.

Day 15: 20 September

0415: Intercepted signal from U270 (KL Paul-Friedrich Otto) with convoy's position.

0515: Received signal from U-boat Command; "Leuthen, let them have it! You are free to attack".

0850: Intercepted signal from U238 (KL Horst Hepp) with convoy's position.

1006: Received signal from U-Boat Command to all boats of Group Leuthen saying that the weather is favourable for U-boats

U48 making fast next to the *Isere*, an old hulk moored in Lorient

because it will make air attacks more difficult and we are to try attacking during the coming night.

1200: Distance covered during the last 24 hours with the boat running at fast speed for much of the time: on surface 240sm, submerged 5sm, total 245sm.

1740: Signal to attack the convoy was given by U338 (KL Manfred Kinzel) by saying "Remain on the surface and engage attacking aircraft."

1832: Signal from U-Boat Command saying all boats should remain on the surface and make for the convoy at fastest possible speed. So far two aircraft have been sighted escorting the convoy.

2322: Received signal from U-Boat Command with course corrections.

Radar detector buzzing at full volume. All our anti-aircraft guns are fully manned. (The main anti-aircraft armament consisted of twin 20mm cannon and a quadruple 20mm mount. The boat also carried lighter machine guns, but these could not be left out when diving.)

2350: Launching five radar foxers, but three of them don't work.

Day 16: 21 September

0000: North Atlantic. SW1, sea 0, cloudy, moderate visibility. Picking up spoken English on VHF. Spotted large star shells illuminating the horizon. Turned towards them and searching in that direction.

0136: Moonrise.

0825: Dived to engage the sound detection gear. Faint propeller noises detected.

0841: Surfaced, dawn is breaking.

0855: Thick fog, visibility 200m. Tried launching radar foxers but this proved pointless because the pressure in the hydrogen bottle is too low. (Foxers consisted of a balloon which trailed a number of radar reflecting foils.)

0902: The radar detector is indicating an increase in strength, which suggests the ship searching for us is drawing closer. Dived

because the risks of being surprised in this fog are too great. Faint propeller noises were detected.

1015: Surfaced. Thick fog. Brought up a new hydrogen bottle with a view to launch more radar foxers.

1020: Dived. Nothing detected with listening gear. Received signal from U-Boat Command with convoy's estimated position.

1134: Surfaced. Thick fog. Receiving impulses on our radar detector. Launched five radar foxers.

(The search pattern continued; for part of the time U377 picked up radar impulses and spoken English on the VHF receiver, but the convoy eluded them until:)

Day 17: 22 September

0445: SW2, sea 1, fog. A destroyer appeared out of the fog at range of 500m directly ahead of us. We turned away as sharply as possible. Our rudder jammed and we were directly in front of the destroyer with the danger of being rammed. Alarm dive. Convoy was clearly audible on sound detection gear and now everybody can hear the merchant ships running over the top of us. Boat gone to periscope depth. There seems to be a straggler. Taking aim on him. Shot a torpedo from Tube II with settings calculated from sound detection gear. Dived deep and continuing listening. Powerful detonation after running time of 27 seconds, but the propeller noises from the target can still be heard. Sounds of a sinking ship can be heard. (Kluth used an acoustic torpedo, which had a chronic fault of detonating some distance before reaching its target; nothing was sunk on this occasion.)

1117: Surfaced. SW2, sea 1, fog.

1348: Destroyer sighted coming out of the fog and immediately opens fire on us. Alarm dive. 26 depth charge detonations. Our lis-

KL Bleichrodt as commander of U48. Bleichrodt always made a point of wearing the oldest of clothes when out on patrol, but he nevertheless sports his Knight's Cross over his high-necked sweater.

Every inch the veteran U-boat petty officer at sea: Maschinenmaat Arthur "Assi" Allenstein of U377. His rank is shown by the braid "corners" on the collar of his old brown prewar work denims.

tening gear has picked up another destroyer and we have been located by two sets of Asdic pings. 10 more depth charge detonations.

1700: Surfaced.

1925: Received signal from U-Boat Command saying "Keep at it so that you are ready to attack when the visibility gets better."

1935: Fog is lifting and visibility is improving.

1940: Sighted Liberator flying at 300m, range 8km. Turned away from him and increased speed to maximum. Sent signal to U-boat Command, but this was not acknowledged. Aircraft is continuing its approach. Opened fire when the range had been reduced to 1500m. Aircraft flew over the boat with its guns blazing.

1955: Commander injured and taken below because he is losing a lot of blood. IWO instructed to dive at first opportunity.

1959: Alarm dive. One depth charge detonated. Commander seriously injured in both arms and will not be of further use on top of the bridge. Sent details to U-Boat Command.

At this stage it might be interesting to look at exactly the same incident from the Liberator pilot's point of view. The B24 was a Royal Canadian Air Force machine; the crew were (1st Pilot) F/L J.R. Martin, (2nd Pilot) F/O J.D.L. Campbell, (Navigator) WO2 H.C. Lindsey, (1st, 2nd, 3rd and 4th Wireless Operator/Air Gunners) WO2 N.J. Gilmour, WO2 A.C. Johns, WO2 B.J. Lielinski, and L.R. Conlin. Summary of report:

First sighting made by J.R. Martin.

Weather conditions: cloudy, sea reasonably calm, visibility to about 8 miles with fog patches.

Nature of initial contact: While carrying out instruction from senior escort commander we obtained a contact dead ahead at a range of about 18 miles. We homed in and, at a range of about 7 miles, spotted the U-boat. U-boat opened fire; the bulk of the AA was from the after portion of the conning tower; this was in salvo and "flak came up in walls" suggesting controlled fire. Bursts from a single gun were observed passing the aircraft at a range of 3 miles. (The U-boat was able to fire full salvos when only the conning tower was showing above the water).

The type of increased anti-aircraft armament fitted to boats of the Leuthen Pack in 1943, reflecting the much greater threat from the Allied air forces from winter 1942 onwards. This is an unidentified boat, but it carries the same armament as that installed on **U377** during her refit - two 20mm cannon on the original "winter garden" and a quadruple 20mm mount on the new lower platform.

Details of first attack: Four Torpex depth charges, set to shallow depth and spaced 40 feet apart, were released from a height of 50 feet while the U-boat was still on the surface. The stick appears to have been just far enough away not to have been lethal. The boat turned with the aircraft and threw up such heavy anti-aircraft fire that we were forced to retire to three miles.

Details of second attack: As the aircraft approached to make the second attack heavy anti-aircraft fire was suddenly encountered with only the conning tower visible. Aircraft attacked with depth charges from astern, 20 seconds after the U-boat had disappeared.

Day 18: 23 September
0302: Surfaced. S2, sea 1, some cloud cover. Our intention is to go southwards with a view to getting outside the range of Canadian air cover.
0410: Sent signal to U-Boat Command saying commander was out of action, but there was no acknowledgement.
1101: Received signal from U-Boat Command ordering us to with-draw to the east.
1756: Sent repeat of earlier signal to U-Boat Command and asking for new orders and a doctor.
2002: Received signal telling us to meet U386 (OL Fritz Albrecht) in square AK9777 to collect doctor and then to commence homeward bound run.

Day 19: 24 September
0400: North Atlantic. SSW2, sea 1, cloudy with moderate visibility. Received signal from U-Boat Command congratulating Leuthen Group on its success. "This battle has been won. Your rewards are the huge successes against the escorts and proving that the new weapons are effective. Had the weather not been so dreadful and in the enemy's favour, then you would have done even better. You can be proud of the fact that you are the pioneers of the re-introduction of wolf packs against convoys in the North Atlantic."

Day 20: 25 September
0628: Very strong sea luminescence, SW2, sea 1, cloudy with moderate visibility. Been on the surface since midnight. An aircraft

approached from the stern without any radar impulses having been announced by our detector. We were shot at and there were four depth charge detonations very close, but we still didn't see the aircraft. Alarm dive. Two depth charge detonations while diving. Both close. One near the conning tower and the other on the stern. Very strong vibrations throughout the boat, with odd movements which suggested we had hit the bottom, but that is too far down. The boats rolled very far to starboard and then went out of control. Blew tanks! A couple of valves had not closed. Boat clear of the water. No sign of the aircraft. The top of the conning tower and the side of the hull are badly damaged.

LI reported that the boat is now fit for diving. Dived. Sound gear picked up high pitched wine of fast moving ship. A destroyer ran over the top of us. 8 depth charge detonations were heard. Four more destroyers and a diesel corvette can be heard. They appear to be searching the surface. We presume they think that we have been sunk and they are looking for survivors. Depth charge damage: some valves not seating properly and leaking; diving tank 5 not working at all, gyrocompass not working; compressed air bottles burst and our motors have become very noisy.

(Later an analysis suggested that the aircraft, probably a small one flown off a ship, had crashed on top of the conning tower, causing the deep swing to starboard. The ships on the surface were probably looking for the airmen rather than survivors from the U-boat.)

1400: Gone up to be close to the surface where we can receive radio signals. Heard destroyer and moved away as silently as possible.

1505: 8 very close depth charge detonations, but no damage to the boat. The destroyer crossed overhead four times although

there followed no further depth charges.

2450: Surfaced.

Day 21: 26 September

0000: North Atlantic. WSW3, sea 2, fog. Received radio signal from U-Boat Command saying that U386 is indisposed due to depth charge damage.

0550: Have been submerged for the last hours. Sound gear detected a destroyer. We are running away silently.

0753: Surfaced.

0815: Radar detector indicating activity close by.

1516: Received signal saying that in case U386 has not shown up by 1800hrs, then we are to report whether we still need medical assistance and - Alarm dive! Destroyer approaching from behind. (The U- Boat Command was cut off rather dramatically.)

1600: Continuing with the meeting seems pointless because the gyrocompass is not working and we have no accurate idea of where we are. It has been too cloudy to get an accurate fix with hand-held equipment.

2328: Surfaced.

Day 22: 27 September

1000: Gyrocompass repaired.

1040: Sent short signal to U-Boat Command saying that we are at the rendezvous, have not seen or heard another U-boat and we intend to start our homeward bound voyage.

Day 23: 28 September

1200: North Atlantic. W4, sea 3, cloudy and poor visibility.

Day 24: 29 September

0910: Sighted a destroyer's mast. Dived.

1608: Surfaced.

1655: Destroyer's mast still in sight. Our intention is to avoid it by

OL Gerhard Kluth, commander of U377, after the air attack of 22 September which injured both his arms.

going southwards.
1948: Spotted smoke towards the south. Dived.
Day 25: 30 September
0515: Surfaced. SW1, sea 0, clear sky with good visibility.
(The boat is now no longer progressing on the surface, but starting the dangerous submerged passage through the Bay of Biscay, following a similar sequence as on the way out.)
Day 26: 1 October
0000: North Atlantic. SW4, sea 3, some cloud cover and slight haze.
Day 27: 2 October
2205: Sighted smoke to the west. Probably a convoy, dived.
Day 28: 3 October
0000: Bay of Biscay. NE1, sea 0, drizzle.
2235: Received signal from U-Boat Command telling us to put our clock back by one hour. It is now officially winter time.
Day 29: 4 October
0000: Bay of Biscay. NE1, sea 0, poor visibility.
Day 30: 5 October
0000: Bay of Biscay. SW4, sea 3, cloudy with variable visibility.
Day 31: 6 October
0000: Bay of Biscay. SW4, sea 3, no clouds, moderate visibility.
Day 32: 7 October
0000: NNW5, sea 4, cloudy, moderate visibility.
Day 33: 8 October
0000: NE2, sea 1, moderate visibility.
Day 34: 9 October
0000: Outside Brest. NE1, sea 0, drizzle, moderate visibility, very powerful sea luminescence.

Day 35: 10 October
0700: Met minesweeper escorts.
1100: Made fast in Brest.

Analysis of the three cruises:

U48, second cruise

Date	October 1939
Duration	22 days
Average number of U-boats at sea per day during this period	18
Number of U-boats which attacked & at least damaged a ship during period	12
Approx.total ships sunk by all U-boats in North Atlantic during period	28
Number of ships sunk per month per U-boat at sea	1.5
Approx.number of U-boats sunk during this period	5

U48, eighth cruise

Date	September 1940
Duration	18 days

U377: Jak Mallmann is at the right, next to him is Obersteuermann Martin Weidmann and then, with a cigarette in his mouth, Albert Jungclaus.

Average number of U-boats at sea
per day during this period   13

Number of U-boats which attacked &
at least damaged a ship during period 11

Approx. total ships sunk by all U-boats
in North Atlantic during period   40

Number of ships sunk per month
per U-boat at sea   3.6 (this figure would
increase to nearly 6)

Approx. number of U-boats sunk
during this period   1

U377, twelfth cruise
Date   Sept/Oct 1943
Duration   35/42 days

Average number of U-boats at sea
per day during this period   75

Number of U-boats which attacked &
at least damaged a ship during period 9

Approx. total ships sunk by all U-boats
in North Atlantic during period   17 (incl. 6 escorts)

Number of ships sunk per month
per U-boat at sea   0.2 (i.e. 4.5 U-boats
needed to sink one
enemy ship)

Approx. number of U-boats sunk
during this period   26

U377 following a minesweeper into Brest, with bow damage suffered on 25 September clearly visible. The unseen aircraft which strafed and depth-charged the boat just missed damaging the diving tanks.

Launching Torpedoes

Since commanders have always been credited with the sinking of ships, but did not always shoot torpedoes, it might be of interest to consider who actually had their finger on the trigger. Individual torpedoes were numbered and each boat had to account for every one by filling in a shooting report and attaching the pre-printed form to the boat's log. The information on this form was as follows: number of U-boat, name and rank of the torpedo marksman, date, position, time, depth of water, weather, visibility, wind, state of the sea, swell, target, success, then information about the boat's course, speed, etc., and details about the adjustment setting of the torpedo.

The following is a summary of an analysis by Bodo Herzog of the torpedoes shot by U48, the most successful U-boat of the Second World War:

Number of hits		Total number of shots
KL Herbert Schultze (Commander)	27	10*
KK Hans Rösing (Commander)	8	3
KL Heinrich Bleichrodt (Commander)	2	2
OL Reinhard Suhren (IWO)	65	30*
OL Otto Ites (II and IWO)	3	2
OL Siegfried Atzinger (IWO)	3	1
LT Hermann Becker (IIWO)	9	3
OL Johannes Liebe (Trainee Cdr.)	4	2
OL Adolf Piening (Trainee Cdr.)	5	2

(* These figures include 7 dud torpedoes for Schultze and 4 dud torpedoes for Suhren, shot during the Norwegian Campaign of 1940.)
Total torpedoes shot during surface attacks: 96, with 44 hits
Total torpedoes shot during submerged attacks: 30, with 11 hits

Bearing in mind that the commander himself generally aimed torpedoes only during submerged attacks, one quickly appreciates that there is an abnormality in these figures. This can be accounted for by 7 surface shots made by Schultze, who aimed the first six and the 16th torpedo of the war.

It is interesting to note that the most successful boat had a hit rate of 44% of the total number of torpedoes fired. So, generally throughout the whole war, one can safely assume that at least three torpedoes were fired for every ship sunk.

Opposite: **OL Gerhard Kluth is greeted by 9th U-Flotilla chief Lehmann-Willenbrock on bringing U377 back into Brest on 10 October 1943; note that Kluth still has his arms in slings.**

Chapter 7: **Some Unusual Operations**

Mediterranean Interlude

The Mediterranean held few attractions for the U-Boat Command and submarines were not moved into this inland sea until the Supreme Naval Command ordered Dönitz to do so. That is not to say that he dismissed the Gibraltar area out of hand - in fact, one of his first steps after the beginning of the war was to send a boat into the Mediterranean for reconnaissance - but the results proved to be so negative that the area was then avoided. The main reasons for this were the weather and the usually clear, smooth, relatively shallow water, which were far from ideal conditions for submarines. Traffic routes between ports were comparatively short, making it easier to escort convoys all the way; and as the choice of routes was limited the British, unable to spread shipping over a vast area, could also concentrate their defences - and these were found to be much stronger around Gibraltar than in the vicinity of the majority of British ports. On top of this, of course, Dönitz had the most valuable first hand experience of submarine warfare in the Mediterranean. Having been captured there during the First World War he knew all about the hardships of surviving in hot boats and shallow seas, and saw no reason for repeating the mistakes of 1914-18, especially as the prospects of success were so feeble.

The boat earmarked for the first reconnaissance of the Mediterranean in 1939 was U26, an oceangoing boat of Type IA. Only two of this 862/1200 ton type were ever built, because the slightly smaller Type VIIs and the marginally bigger Type IXs offered superior performance. Yet U26's commander KL Klaus Ewerth had no special gripes about his "tin can". Konteradmiral Eberhard Godt (Chief of the U-Boat Command's Operations Department, who had also commanded the sister boat, U25) said that the pair were not as bad as people have made them out to be, and that he had not experienced most of the negative characteristics of which they were accused. But then, Ewerth was not the type to be put off by trivialities either; he already had the reputation of being able to get the best out of men and machines. Having joined the Navy in 1925 he was one of the old guard who had been with U-boats ever since the creation of the new submarine flotilla in 1935; in fact he held the unique distinction of having commanded U1 at a time when the Navy officially didn't have any submarines.

U26 ran into Wilhelmshaven towards the end of September 1939 after having penetrated the western approaches of the English Channel as far as Lyme Bay on the Devon-Dorset coast of southern England. While loading stores for their next mission the men had no inkling about their destination, but thought they would probably return to the western Channel. Then, with the boat almost ready, the first suspicions that something special was afoot began to dawn. Not only was there no privacy in a U-boat, but nowhere to hide secrets. This time it was not a case of hiding anything, but the exact opposite: it was the absence of the usual Atlantic charts which made the men think. They knew they were destined for somewhere out of the ordinary, but they could not guess where.

Ewerth did not drop the bombshell until they were well under way, and even when he did the name Gibraltar didn't mean anything special to most of his crew. They knew it was a British rock at the entrance to the Mediterranean, and guessed that approaching it might be a little risky; but Ewerth did not mention that their main objective of mining the harbour would probably be impossible because of the heavy defences.

U596 in the Mediterranean, showing the typically narrow upper deck of a Type VIIC. The emblem on the side of the conning tower is "Hummel", the water carrier from Hamburg, who featured on a number of boats. U596 and her first commander, KL Günter Jahn, were both "made in Hamburg". At first glance it looks as if the boat has been fitted with a Biscay Cross for detecting radar impulses, but this photo was taken in 1942 before such devices were introduced; the cross consists of something tied to the attack periscope.

Ewerth had been given three main objectives. First and most important was to gather information about ship movements around the all-important fortress; second, to lay a mine barrage across the harbour approach; and third, to attack shipping with torpedoes. Earlier at headquarters Ewerth had already had his hand on the doorhandle of Dönitz's office when "the Lion" stopped him with the words, "Oh, Ewerth, this is going to be a tricky little number, but will you please remember that I want the boat back?" Dönitz obviously wanted information, not dead heroes.

The outward bound voyage followed a similar pattern to U26's previous cruise. Going around the north of Scotland, it headed south through the edge of the Atlantic, keeping a good distance west of Ireland. The real tension started just before daybreak on 6

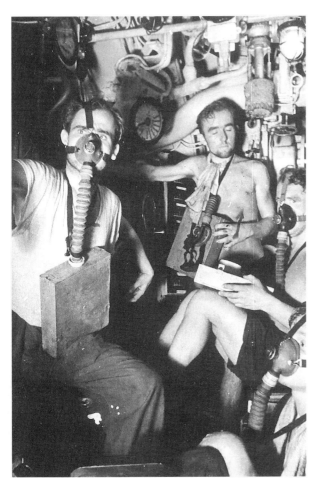

Aboard U73 (KL Helmut Rosenbaum) in the Mediterranean, showing the watch on duty in the diesel engine room breathing through Kalipatronen air purifiers which absorbed exhaled carbon dioxide. On the left is Dieselobermaschinist Erich Schmidt, who was killed on 16 December 1943.

November 1939, when U26 settled on the seabed close to the Spanish shore at Cape Trafalgar. When the vibrations of gently touching the bottom shuddered through the boat, Ewerth breathed a sigh of relief at having got so far without unusual problems. Hopefully there would be time for a good sleep before the coming night stretched everybody's abilities to the limit. Unfortunately the crew in the bow compartment had to be kept busy for some time to come with the most irksome but necessary tasks. Two torpedoes had to withdrawn from the tubes and replaced by nine mines of Type TMB (Torpedo Mine Type B). When that was done the men in this most unenviable of all accommodation were also allowed their rest.

The idea was to remain on the seabed in absolute silence until darkness fell, when Ewerth was going to attempt the first stage of the tricky part: a penetration into the Bay of Algeciras, just to the west of Gibraltar. He was planning on spending the next day in such shallow water that he could, at low tide, even observe the fortress through the periscope. On the one hand this sounded suicidal, but then he had been assured that such an attempt would be better than running the motors on silent drive. Much of the southern Spanish coast was sparsely inhabited, and the risks were worth taking. Eyes peering into the water were less

likely to spot the boat on the seabed than sensitive sound detectors in patrol boats.

The first stage went quite well. Surfacing at 1830hrs, shortly after dusk, U26 approached Tarifa with everybody on tenterhooks. Not only was there an abundance of bright lights on shore and illuminated ships at sea, but someone seemed to be practising with searchlights. Six to eight powerful beams were constantly sweeping across the water. These had just been negotiated when, a short while before midnight, a darkened boat forced U26 "into the cellar". When U26 surfaced again in the early hours there were still so many fishing boats about that Ewerth felt certain some of them must have seen the U-boat come up; but with any luck they would take no special notice, thinking it was British.

A day later the tension and caution increased even more during the last part of the approach. The navigation lights around the port were off but other lamps illuminated the harbour, making it easy to see details with the naked eye. This stage of the operation was carried out by surfacing the boat but without blowing any of the diving tanks. With the top of the conning tower just clear of the water and with the minimum of look-outs, U26 proceeded silently. The abundance of illuminated ships and the brilliant lights ashore made it easy to spot the darkened shapes of patrolling warships, but that did not improve the look-outs' jittery nerves. There was hardly a breath of wind, the surface of the water was smooth, above them stars were shining extra bright and visibility was exceptional. Only a few patches of haze made the far distance occasionally slightly blurred. Being able to observe Gibraltar harbour, Ewerth dictated copious notes about the movements of the numerous British patrol boats until the coming of daylight forced him to seek out another quiet spot on the seabed.

The silence in the boat - never speaking above a whisper, and having to take perpetual care not to clank anything, especially cooking pots - was starting to fray nerves, but there was no way of expressing frustration safely. Worse was still to come. By now all auxiliary machinery had been shut down, not to save power, but to prevent the noise being detected by the patrol boats which had the irritating habit of stopping too frequently, suggesting that they definitely carried sensitive listening gear.

When U26 surfaced on 8 November, just before 2200 hours at night, auxiliary machinery remained switched off. Everything which moved had been silenced, including the almost noiseless gyrocompass. This meant that the boat had become so hot and stuffy that men were forced to wear breathing apparatus. Having found what looked like a dark part of the bay, Ewerth allowed a few limited machines a brief running period, not for the comfort of the crew but because he was obliged to clear the bilges - though once the pumps were running he saw no reason for not blasting fresh air through the interior.

The prospect of laying mines in the approaches of Gibraltar harbour appeared suicidal. Never before had any man aboard seen so many lights at sea; there was such an abundance that look-outs stopped reporting them and only focussed on those which might come too close - and of course, on the dreaded blacked-out silhouettes of warships. The ultra smooth surface of the water reflected the lights from shore as if the boat were floating on an illuminated mirror, making it possible to see the slightest of disturbances. Raising the periscope from a submerged position would have been suicidal because there would have been no one watching the commander's back while he was concentrating on laying mines. When Erwerth announced the cancellation of the mine-laying he had the impression that the sigh of relief throughout the boat could have been heard on shore.

While he was making these calculations something inexplicable happened. A large, light-coloured oval object was seen approaching the boat. At first it was put down to some type of sea luminescence, but the shape was too distinct and the outline too sharp. The men watched it for a short while before it vanished, seeming to dissolve or fade into nothing. Ewerth was puzzled, and ordered extra cautious silence in case there was a submarine underneath them ventilating its tanks and sending a large bubble of air to the surface. Yet he knew full well that one usually saw lots of little bubbles rather than a single large one. The yellowish object was quickly forgotten as the men concentrated on the enemy, but one wonders what caused this entry in the log. In a moment of boredom men might be forgiven for imagining strange shapes, but during this night of high tension they were concentrating hard and their senses were fine-tuned; they hardly had time for allowing their imaginations free rein.

Following this incident U26 passed through the Straits of Gibraltar and proceeded eastwards as far as the approaches of Almeria. Nobody in the boat was particularly keen on the Mediterranean; there was nothing about it to offer the slightest appeal to submariners. The inside of the boat was exceedingly hot although it was almost mid-winter, and limited ventilation made it exceptionally stuffy. On top of this, the sea was too clear, the surface too calm and visibility too good. Even when the wind whipped up to a westerly of Force 6, with moderate waves and good cloud cover, the visibility remained crystal clear. Ewerth took advantage of the storm to attack a ship, but the usual miserable torpedo failures ensured that the target escaped.

Everybody was pleased when the rougher Atlantic weather started tossing them about again. The real laugh came some way out of the danger area when the radio room intercepted instructions for every boat to converge on a convoy sighted by U53 (KL Heinz-Günther Heinicke). The navigator grinned, remarking, "Yeah, that's somewhere around here where we are, but we haven't got any grid charts for the Atlantic, so we can't work out exactly where." The crew of U26 had to satisfy themselves with a lone freighter, the 4576GRT *Elena*, which they sunk a couple of miles south of the Shambles lightship while on their way home.

U26's experiences had proved beyond doubt that these southern waters, and even the area to the west of Gibraltar, were no place for U-boats. So when the Naval War Staff ordered boats to be made ready for voyages into the Mediterranean they sparked off immediate protests from Dönitz. However, despite his pointing out that the decision would reduce the numbers astride the Atlantic convoy routes by 25%, the first wave left their French bases towards the end of September 1941. Group Goeben, consisting of six boats and named after the First World War battleship which had been handed over to Turkey, made a successful breakthrough without serious incident. There was a Mediterranean submarine squadron in position by the middle of October.

The next wave were not so lucky. Urgent orders from the Naval War Staff required that instructions be radioed to boats destined for the Atlantic. They were told to abandon their planned missions and to change course; even boats which had reached the waters off Newfoundland were diverted to the Mediterranean, although they carried only very general charts for the vital area and were without important reconnaissance details.

Such highly secret messages arrived in a quite dramatic manner. After passing the radio signal addressed to the individual boat through the Enigma code-writer the radio operator still ended up with a mass of jumbled letters; to decode the signal once more an officer would have to readjust the wheel settings of the machine to a combination contained in a sealed envelope and not available to anyone else in the boat. Despite all the secrecy, most officers used the gadget so rarely that they needed one of the radio operators to help them set the mechanism. At first glance the result appeared to come out as a miserable mistake, but this second set of jumbled letters included a code saying the message had to be handed to the commander, who then passed it once more through the machine using another combination of settings kept locked in his safe.

Since no one in any of the boats had been briefed on how to make such difficult passages, it was a case of the men having to work things out on their own as best they could. The area covered by British patrols necessitated boats having to remain submerged for at least 40 nautical miles, which was quite beyond the

endurance of a Type VII. Larger, long range boats of Type IX were thought to be unsuitable for the inland sea because they were less manoeuvrable and more susceptible to depth charge attack, so they remained on station in the Atlantic. Type VIIs could cover about 80 nautical miles at 4 knots or slower under water; but that meant charging the batteries on the surface for several hours beforehand, and then surfacing to recharge them afterwards. Timing was another crucial factor because at 4 knots it would take 20 hours to cover the distance. If battle conditions drove the boat to faster underwater speeds, as could well be the case around Gibraltar, then the submerged range could easily be cut to much less than 40 miles. In other words, there was a good possibility of exhausted boats being forced to surface during daylight and in full view of land, and such risks were not worth contemplating. Part of the hazards had to be negotiated at night, on the surface.

Travelling submerged had another disadvantage in that too little was known about a deep, 2 to 4 knot current running into the Mediterranean, beneath the westerly surface current. U26 had already reported some of the problems; expecting one night to advance around a dangerous headland close to Gibraltar, the crew discovered that they had already been carried through this danger zone during the previous day without having been aware of it. By 1941 it was general knowledge that boats could probably get into the Mediterranean with the help of the deep easterly current, but repeating the feat in a westerly direction would be another matter. There was no way that their limited electric power could muster the force to fight against the deep current. Once past Gibraltar they would remain effectively trapped in the Mediterranean. In October 1939 U26 was lucky because guarding the narrow straits was still regarded as a somewhat academic task. Once Britain was involved in a serious fight for her national life vigilance became considerably more concentrated; and after September 1941 about one third of all attempts to get through the straits failed due to British opposition. The project of bringing boats back to the Atlantic ports of western France for overhaul, initially conceived because repair facilities in the Mediterranean were inadequate, had to be abandoned.

The horrors experienced by men attempting to crawl past Gibraltar have been dramatised in the film *Das Boot,* and men who were there at the time seem to agree that this portrayal is fairly accurate (although they point out feelingly that the aircraft used to attack U-boats were much larger than the single-engine fighters faked up for the film). It is also true that a number of boats short of oil were refuelled from German ships in Vigo or Cadiz, although the shifty characters in the film appear to have been a little over-dramatised.

By the end of 1941 boats were operating in the eastern Mediterranean and on both sides of Gibraltar, and this is where the U-Boat Command received another unexpected shock. A group of U-boats approaching the western side of Gibraltar ran into convoy HG76, which was escorted by a novelty - an auxiliary aircraft carrier, HMS *Audacity*. Two merchantmen and the carrier were sunk, but not without heavy German loss: five U-boats went down during the attack. This largest single loss to date threw the U-Boat Command into considerable turmoil, wondering whether some new weapon had been introduced. Finally, after a calm assessment and debriefing of survivors, it became apparent that it had been a case of specially skilful anti-submarine forces. The small aircraft flown off the carrier were certainly an unexpected threat, being too persistent and too manoeuvrable for the U-boats' clumsy anti-aircraft armament. These losses were especially painful because Dönitz had anticipated determined opposition and he had therefore thrown experienced "old lags" into battle.

All of this is not to say that the Mediterranean did not see some dramatic successes for U-boats. The aircraft carrier HMS *Ark Royal* was torpedoed near Gibraltar by U81 (KL Friedrich Guggenberger). The attack was rather confusing because U205 (KL Franz-Georg Reschke) also fired torpedoes against the carrier, and U81 was in fact aiming at the battleship HMS *Malaya*;

however, after a careful reconstruction it would appear that a single hit from U81 caused the carrier to go down while on tow to Gibraltar.

Perhaps some of the most dramatic pictures of a sinking were those taken after a submerged attack on the battleship HMS *Barham* by U331 (KL Hans-Dietrich Freiherr von Tiesenhausen). It would appear that the torpedo salvo caused the boat to break the surface momentarily until the trim was readjusted. At the same time the 31,100 tons of *Barham* started heeling over, settling slowly in the water until the tops of her funnels were touching the sea. Then, seconds later, with the boilers probably still running, water ran down the funnels where it instantly vaporised, causing massive expansion and a huge explosion which was captured by numerous cameras. Many books claim that *Barham's* magazine exploded, but study of motion picture footage suggests that a boiler explosion was the more likely cause.

Landings on Hostile Shores

Throughout the war a variety of missions forced U-boats uncomfortably close to hostile shores. Perhaps some of the most remarkable landings were instrumented by Heinrich Garbers, a yachtsman whose exploits were so stunning that Allied intelligence did not believe his story and, after the war, branded him as a secret U-boat commander. Apparently he was placed in solitary confinement, beaten up and fed only on potato peel and water for several weeks. Yet the stories told by this quiet, somewhat clumsy character, who couldn't even salute properly, were true. He had indeed landed a number of agents in Ireland, South America and South Africa. What is even more incredible is that his last journey took him through the Atlantic during the turmoil of 1944 - and that all of his voyages were made in small sailing boats, *Passim* and *Kyloe*, both of less than 40 tons.

The landing of agents was thoroughly disliked by the U-Boat Command, but Dönitz could not prevent such ventures because the orders came direct from the Supreme Naval Command. His main objections were that the men appeared to be adventurers and lacked patriotic motives for their hair-raising ventures. Although Dönitz was forced into these operations, he did not lose control; he ensured that the boats were specially prepared for their passengers so that they could not learn too many U-boat secrets. Code-writers, handbooks and other sensitive material usually freely available were locked away. On some boats these preparations went as far as removing the numbers from the dials of the deep depth gauges: the argument was that U-boat men did not need them, and it would be best if outsiders did not know the usual diving depths. Dönitz argued that these men would probably be captured very quickly, and might well disclose U-boat secrets while bargaining for their lives with their captors.

U81, with OL Friedrich Guggenberger and Hans Harald Speidel. The emblem on the side of the conning tower with the inscription "Jaffa" underneath appeared early in 1942 after U81 had been ordered to bombard that port. Note that this boat has a large dazzle pattern painted over the basic shipyard pale grey; and note too the very narrow walkway beside the tower - this was the route for carrying deck gun shells forward during surface actions.

Left & opposite: **Photographs taken during U377's mission to establish a secret weather station on the northern shore of Spitzbergen in autumn 1942. The crew later had the remarkable experience of exploring the abandoned mining settlement of Ny Alesund, where they found the hotel bar still well stocked.**

Agents appear to have been landed in a number of locations, and the majority of these missions went relatively smoothly. Unfortunately the image of secret agents landing from U-boats seems to have a considerable attraction for the postwar tourist industry; a large number of seaside towns have invented their own histories which now feature in local guidebooks, and it is necessary to take some stories with a very large pinch of salt. What is more, a number of yarns have been concocted by people who should have known better; a Chief of Research and Planning in the United States Navy's Special Warfare Branch has muddied this water in his memoirs.

Two landings which did take place in the United States and which were recorded by the U-Boat Command occurred on 13 June and 17 July 1942. First, U202 (KL Hans-Heinz Linder) landed a four-man sabotage team (E.P.Burger, G.J.Dasch, H.H.Heinck and R.Quirin) on Long Island near New York City. Subsequently U584 (KL Joachim Deecke) landed four agents (H.H.Haupt, E.J.Kerling, W.Thiel and N.Neubauer) on Jacksonville Beach. The procedure on both occasions was roughly the same. The boats were trimmed bow heavy and then, under cover of darkness, they ran slowly onto the beach using the silent drive of their electric motors. Once they touched ground dinghies were used to row the agents ashore for the last stretch. Although this sounds rather simple, it was an exceptionally frightening experience for the majority of the crews, who could not see what was going on.

U202 made some miscalculation over the tides, and after making the landing the boat failed to respond to propellers turning in reverse; she remained stuck for several hours until the water rose again. To make matters worse, Mechanikersobergefreiter Zimmermann was in considerable agony with what looked like an acute appendicitis. When the boat eventually pulled itself free and was back in mid-Atlantic her look-outs made a chilling discovery. At a range of over 1000km (620 miles) from land, inside the so-called "air gap", they spotted a large four-engined bomber, indicating that the aircraft-free zone in mid-Atlantic had finally been slammed shut. (Linder, incidentally, was one of the few U-boat commanders who died in bed from illness rather than as a result of an injury; after his death, on 10 September 1944, he was promoted to Korvettenkapitän.)

Not all secret agents were successfully landed. U65 (KL Hans-Gerrit von Stockhausen) found that one of their agents had died

on them inside the U-boat. They were due to land Sean Russell and Frank Ryan near Ballyferriter, County Kerry in the Republic of Ireland. Although the surviving Ryan abandoned his mission and was returned to France, he also died shortly afterwards in Germany; and von Stockhausen himself also met an unusual end. He was killed as a result of a road accident in Berlin on 14 January 1943.

Performing the procedure in reverse, that is picking men up from hostile shores, was considerably more difficult, especially as the tremendous organisation involved was vulnerable to leaks in numerous quarters. Yet the risks were sometimes considered to be worth taking, and Dönitz himself seems to have been quite keen on some of these ventures. The idea of rescuing prisoners of war had floated through the minds of the more adventurous for some time, but it seems that "Ali" Cremer was the first person to seriously plan the intricate details of such an escape attempt, early in 1943.

The big problem at the time was that Cremer had no idea which commander was going to be selected for the undertaking, because no one on the German side could determine the exact time of the planned breakout. All Cremer knew was that radio contact with Camp 70 near Fredericton, New Brunswick, suggested that such an escape could become reality. The planning was made more difficult because the matter could not be thrown open for general discussion even in tight naval circles; the U-Boat Command had already been shaken by the suspicion that there were spies within its ranks. This mania for security went so far that the usual secretaries were excluded from typing sensitive notes.

Today it is well known that security had been compromised by Britain's ability to intercept the U-boats' secret radio traffic and decrypt the signals at Bletchley Park. However, at the time nothing sensitive was discussed with anybody who was not directly involved. In view of this, the U-Boat Staff considered the briefing of all likely commanders to be too much of a risk; so they would simply have to send out an unprepared officer when the time came. All candidates likely to be in a suitable position for the mission were handed a plain, thick, securely sealed envelope with a code word printed boldly on the front.

Thus when U262 left her French base on 6 April 1943 no one aboard had an inkling of the unusual adventure ahead of them.

after more than a week at sea, when another U-boat with instructions for "mission impossible" in its safe had been lost, Heinz Franke received a special signal ordering him to open the sealed package. The instructions sounded simple - a little matter of going over to Prince Edward Island in Canada, and picking up escapees from a prisoner of war camp. The envelope contained a reasonable amount of supportive documentation, the all-important recognition signals and other essential details. But Franke knew that all seemingly simple missions usually guaranteed an unpredictable sting in the tail.

His first big problem came towards the end of April, when U292 got stuck in the still quite thick ice of the narrow Cabot Strait, leaving Franke with the choice of either walking the 100km (60 miles or so) to the shore or abandoning the operation. The third possibility, although exceedingly dangerous, was the one he chose. After the machinery had been checked and double-checked to make sure that batteries and compressed air bottles were charged to capacity, U292 plunged down for an almost 18-hour-long voyage under the ice, to reappear near the designated spot close to the beach. The first attempt to surface was frustrated by the thickness of the ice. It was not until the engineering officer pointed out in the coarsest terms that they no longer had sufficient power to go all the way back that Franke used the full lifting power at his disposal to break the stubborn ceiling holding his boat down. Luckily there was no military opposition, because both the top of the conning tower and the guns were somewhat bent in the process, and two torpedo tubes were also twisted out of alignment. Although the escape at Camp 70 had been well planned, the U-boat prisoners suffered from an earlier failed attempt by a different group which had alerted the guards. Consequently U262 waited in vain, and had to return empty-handed; yet the performance of commander and crew was so exemplary that Germany started planning more rescue attempts.

The big carrot of the next venture was the prospect of getting the ace KL Otto Kretschmer (U99, and the most successful commander of the Second World War) out of the Bowmanville camp. Prisoners in this Canadian camp had succeeded in making a radio transmitter with which they reached receivers in Germany. On 9 August 1943, U536 (KL Rolf Schauenburg) left Lorient to attempt a rescue. The planned breakout was compromised, how-

ever, and the men of U536 found themselves in a trap with nine Canadian warships surrounding them. Schauenburg demonstrated his remarkable skills by extracting U536 from this predicament, but his luck did not hold. On his way home and on the German side of the Atlantic, U536 became the first victim of a Canadian Support Group. Ships of EG5 were protecting the combined convoys SL139 and MKS30, both from African ports. The first attack by the corvette HMCS *Snowberry* damaged U536's trimming system, making it impossible for the hydroplanes to correct the downward plunge. Tanks had to be blown, and while on its way to the surface HMCS *Nene* launched another and fatal pattern of depth charges. Rolf Schauenburg and some of his men succeeded in getting off the stricken boat before it plunged uncontrollably into the depths.

The name Prince George's Island sounds as if it should be Canadian; yet on consulting the log book of U387 (KL Rudolf Büchler) one finds that this small collection of uninhabited Arctic rocks lie deep inside Russian territory. U387 called there with a view to establishing a secret unmanned weather station; Germany desperately needed access to Arctic climate data for forecasting weather on the European latitudes. Since the beginning of the war the numerous Allied stations had either been evacuated or they had taken to transmitting in code. This left Germany with only one practical alternative: installing their own weather recording stations on far distant shores. The first ones were fully automatic devices which only needed to be erected in the appropriate spot. This in itself sounds quite simple, but in reality it involved considerable hardships and little chance of the type of success which U-boat men longed for.

Long after the war some of these top secret activities were themselves uncovered in quite dramatic fashion. Early in 1970 Otto Köhler, the first commander of U377, happened to bump into a Dr. Sommermeyer in the street in Freiburg. U377 had been instrumental in setting up one of the doctor's projects on Spitzbergen. Unfortunately Sommermeyer died shortly after this meeting, but his son was kind enough to lend me a number of photos taken during the erection of a weather station, thinking there might be pictures of my father among them. One of his photos showed a close-up of some radio gear with the name Canadian Weather Service printed on the side. We knew that Canadian troops had remained on Spitzbergen after the Allies had forcibly evacuated the settlements there; so it appeared quite likely that this was part of their portable transmitter.

Some time later, when the Austrian historian Franz Selinger saw the picture, he immediately noticed that the rounded rocks in the background did not look like any of the typically jagged Spitzbergen features. Instantly the hunt for a new location was on. Of course officials assured him that the Canadian coast was too well protected for U-boats to have landed there, and Germans never set foot on Canadian soil, not even in the desolate Arctic wastes. However, after considerable diligence Selinger discovered the number of the U-boat which had erected the weather station and from its log found the location at Martins Bay on the northern tip of Labrador. When a Canadian Coast Guard cutter took Selinger up there, the captain considered it too dangerous to approach the land in the way U537 (KL Peter Schrewe) had done way back in October 1943. Instead the ice breaker remained well clear of the coastal ice and sent a helicopter over to remove the rusting remains.

Unfortunately Schrewe had not known enough about the local inhabitants and his location, at the end of a long and narrow peninsula, was not ideal for a secret weather station; it was a perfect spot for hunting caribou, and the peninsula was frequently visited by nomadic locals. (The trick was to drive part of a massive herd onto the headland, where it could remain confined until animals were singled out for shooting. This was done by aiming at one of the legs; killing the animal outright meant the carcass could not be transported. It had to be made to limp to a settlement where it was finally killed. This rather cruel method of

With the boat frozen in by ice in a fjord near Cape Mitra, the crew of U377 used sledges for unloading the heavy equipment.

hunting was necessary because an uninjured animal would have been too agile for hunters.) So, when Selinger's expedition arrived long after the war, he found the remains of the weather station thoroughly vandalised; but it was still of sufficient interest to be removed to a museum in Montreal.

While setting up a similar venture on the shores of an isolated fjord in North Spitzbergen in autumn 1942 the men of U377 found themselves in a somewhat compromising situation. Look-outs spotted lights in the supposedly deserted settlement of Ny Alesund. Knowing its occupants had been evacuated, they thought that a British radio detachment might have been left behind, giving KL Otto Köhler no alternative other than to capture or kill them before they could betray this secret mission. Edging its way south, U377 landed at Ny Alesund in an dramatic attempt to storm the small, isolated collection of houses. Only when the U-boat men were standing among the remains of the mining settlement did they realise what they had seen. The buildings surrounded a coalmine, and the reason for its evacuation had been to prevent the Germans from gaining access to the coal. The mine had been destroyed by British forces and even the stockpiles waiting to be loaded onto ships were set on fire. Now, about a year later, these coalheaps were still smouldering under a thick blanket of ash and snow. Now and again, when the wind disturbed the delicate covering, gasses would escape and burst into flames, which looked very similar to the light of a hurricane lamp.

Finding the place deserted was a great relief, and exploring the North Pole Hotel brought even greater amazement. The Allied evacuation came as a surprise and was carried out so quickly that

there had not even been time to clear up; there was still food on the tables, and the low temperatures had prevented it from going rotten. Even more startling was the discovery that the bar remained well stocked. Finding an old rail wagon from the mine, the men filled it with crates of alcohol and then pushed their find down to the boat - where they were confronted by the commander. Picking up a couple of bottles in great anger, Köhler smashed them at his men's feet. He told the keen young lads that they were looting, and ordered the booty to be tipped into the sea. Although feeling rather hard done by, the men had no choice but to obey.

Later, when the crates washed up on the beach, torpedo mechanic Heinrich Böhm and radio operator Siebrand Voss came to the logical conclusion that their booty had become jetsam, and thus perfectly legitimate salvage; accordingly they stuffed some of the bottles into the barrel of their 88mm, which had watertight tampons at both ends. Köhler had actually been aware of this little enterprise, and long after the war he said that there were times when it was best for commanders not to inquire too deeply about what the men were doing. The last twist to the story came in the mid-1970s. After having related this tale at a reunion, Köhler was told that the other crates had also been brought back to Norway, but the men did obey his order and not a single bottle was brought into the boat. Instead they had lashed the boxes to the outside of the pressure hull, under the deck planking where they could not easily be seen.

Appendix 1: **Operational Boat Types**

The following is a brief summary of the important operational U-boat types of the Second World War. Further technical data can be found in the author's *U-Boats under the Swastika* and even more detailed information in Gröner's *Die deutschen Kriegsschiffe* (see Bibliography).

Different U-boat types were identified by a number which was usually written as a Roman numeral, differences or modifications within each type being distinguished by a letter after the number - e.g. Types IIA, VIIB, etc. There has been considerable discussion as to whether it is appropriate to use the letter A after the type number; it is held to be more correct to start each sequence with a plain number and to progress straight to "B". For clarity, the type numbers and letters adopted in this book are those used by the U-Boat Command.

Individual boat identification numbers prefixed with the letter "U" were usually allocated during the planning stages, often before the actual construction contract was issued. Therefore boats were not built or commissioned in numerical order, and some numbers were not even laid down.

Boats had two further identification numbers: they were often allocated a building number, and they also had a five-digit postal number, always prefixed with the letter "M" for Marine, meaning Navy. The tabulated technical data are as follows:
Number commissioned: (Total number built) Identification numbers of boats commissioned
Complement: Officers / men
Displacement: Surface / submerged in metric tons
Length, Beam, Depth: in metres
Maximum speed: Surface / submerged in knots
Radius of action:
at high speed: Speed / range, in sea miles
at cruising speed: Speed / range
submerged: Speed / range
Torpedo tubes: bows; stern
Number of torpedoes carried: Some of these were accommodated in external containers and had to be moved into the boat before they could be fired. This became impractical after 1942 and the number each boat carried was thus reduced.

Germany had two different types of mines for ejection through torpedo tubes; one was half the size of a torpedo and the other a third the size, so submarines could carry approximately twice or three times as many mines as torpedoes. However, such calculation is academic, because for the majority of operations boats carried both mines and torpedoes. The mines carried in the bow shafts of the minelayer Type XB and in the mine shafts aft of the conning tower in Type VIID had a larger diameter than torpedo mines and these could not have been ejected through torpedo tubes.
Guns: Number of guns x calibre (approximate number of rounds carried)

Large deck guns were usually removed during 1942/43 and replaced by strengthened anti-aircraft armament. The figures given here are for the pre-1942 combination.
Diving depth: The goal was generally a maximum diving depth of 200m (650ft), but Type II should not have gone deeper than 150m (490ft) and Type VIIC could reach 250m (820 feet). Some VIIC boats have been recorded as having dived deeper than 300m (985ft) and returned to the surface. The electro-boats of Type XXI and probably also Type XXIII could go down to 250 metres, and perhaps deeper.

Type I
Number commissioned: (2) U25 & U26

Complement: 4 / 39
Displacement: 862/1200t
Length: 72.4m
Beam: 6.2m
Depth: 4.3m
Maximum speed: 18 / 8kts
Radius of action:
  at high speed: 17kt/3300sm
  at cruising speed: 12kt/6700sm
  submerged: 4kt/90sm
Torpedo tubes:
  bows: 4
  stern: 2
Number of torpedoes carried: 14
Guns: 1 x 105mm (150 rounds); 1 x AA 20mm (2000 rounds)

The design for this oceangoing submarine was based on a successful boat of the First World War and the Turkish Gür, which had been built as an experimental boat by German engineers. Today it would seem that many of the negative attributes of this class were overemphasised for political ends, and the two boats were not as bad as they have been made out. One of the major problems was a difficulty in venting the tanks. Apparently some air usually remained lodged inside and changed in volume as the boat dived and this, together with bubbles rolling from one end to another, made depth control somewhat difficult. On top of this, both Type I boats had a mobile centre of gravity which tended to slide forwards when travelling at fast speeds. This presented no problems for experienced operators, but easily caught out the unwary when diving. In any case, both boats were sunk relatively early in the war, making a detailed analysis of their characteristics somewhat speculative. It might be of interest to add that Germany built a similar type for Russia and this boat, S56, not only survived the war but is now on display in Vladivostok.

Type II
Number commissioned:
IIA: (6) U1 - U6
IIB: (20) U7 - U24, U120, U121
IIC: (8) U56 - U63
IID: (16) U137 - U152

Complement: 3 / 22
Displacement: 254 / 380t
Length: 42m
Beam: 4.1m
Depth: 3.9m
Maximum speed: 12 / 7kts
Radius of action:
  at high speed: 12kt / 1800sm (IID: 3450sm)
  at cruising speed: 8kt / 3500sm (IID: 5650sm)
  submerged: 4kt / 43sm (IID: 56sm)
Torpedo tubes: bows: 3; stern: 0
Number of torpedoes carried: 5
Guns: 1 - 4 x AA 20mm (850 rounds)

These small coastal submarines, originally conceived at a time when the Versailles diktat prevented Germany from constructing or owning submarines, were the first to be built by the National Socialists. After the outbreak of the war the majority were used for training, but quite a number saw successful operational service during the first winter of war, when they were engaged mainly as minelayers close to British harbours. Conditions inside were exceptionally cramped and it was this human factor, rather than the boats' performance, which limited their operational employment. The other problem was that they could carry only five torpedoes.

Type VII
Number commissioned:
VIIA: (10) U27 - U36
VIIB: (24) U45 - U55, U73 - U76, U83 - U87, U99 - U102
VIIC: (Over 600) U69 - U72, U77 - U82, U88 - U98, U132 - U136, U201 - U212, U221 - U232, U235 - U 329, U331 - U458, U465 - U486, U551 - U683, U701 - U722, U731 - 779, U821 - U822, U825 - U828, U901 - U908, U921 - U930, U951 - U1032, U1051 - U1058, U1063 - U1065, U1101 - U 1110, U1131 - U1132, U1161 - U1172, U1191 - U1210, U1271 - U1279, U1301 - 1308.
VIIC/41: Included with VIIC
VIID: (6) U213 - U218
VIIF: (4) U1059 - 1062

Complement: 4 / 40 - 56
Displacement: 770 / 1040t
Length: 66.5m
Beam: 6.2m
Depth: 4.7m
Maximum speed: 17 / 7.5kts
Radius of action:
  at high speed: 17kt/3300sm
  at cruising speed: 10kt/8500sm (could be extended to 9500sm if running on diesel/electric drive.)
  submerged: 4kt/80sm
Torpedo tubes: bows: 4; stern: 1 (some boats had the stern tubes welded shut)
Number of torpedoes carried: 14, later 12
Guns: 1 x 88mm (250 rounds) 1 x 20mm AA (4400 rounds); AA armament strengthened from 1942 onwards.

Type VIIC is the largest submarine class ever to have been built by any country, and a number of different shipyards participated in their construction; there were thus a large number of variations on the basic design. In addition to this many boats were ret-rospectively modified, producing still further divergences from the basic appearance. Type VIID had an additional section with mine shafts just aft of the conning tower; and VIIF was intended as a transporter for carrying torpedoes or mines.

Type IX
 Number commissioned:
IXA: (8) U37 - U44
IXB: (14) U64, U65, U103 - U124
IXC and IXC/41: (143) U66 - U68, U125 - U131, U153 - U176, U183 - U194, U501 - U550, U801 - U806, U841 - U846, U853 - U858, U865 - U870, U877 - U881, U889 - U891, U1221 - U1235
IXD1: (2) U180, U195
IXD2: (30) U177 - U179, U181, U182, U196 - U200, U847 - U852, U859 - U864, U871 - U876, U883, U884

Complement: 4 / 44 - 51
Displacement: 1120 / 1430t
Length: 76.5m
Beam: 6.8m
Depth: 4.7m
Maximum speed: 18 / 7kts
Radius of action:
  at high speed: 18kt/5000sm
  at cruising speed: 110kt/13500sm
  submerged: 4kt/65sm
Torpedo tubes: bows: 4; stern: 2
Number of torpedoes carried: 22
Guns: 1 x 105mm (200 rounds); 1 x 37mm AA (575 rounds); 1 x AA 20mm (8000 rounds)

A large oceangoing long-range patrol submarine which was modified as IXD1 and IXD2 to become very long range boats capable of covering 32,000sm at 10kt.

Type XB
Number commissioned: (8) U116 - U119, U219, U220, U233, U234

Complement: 5 / 47
Displacement: 1763 / 2710t
Length: 89.8m
Beam: 9.2m
Depth: 4.7m
Maximum speed: 17 / 7kts
Radius of action:
  at high speed: 17 / 6500sm
  at cruising speed: 10kt / 18500sm
  submerged: 4kt/80sm
Torpedo tubes: bows: 0; stern: 2
Guns: 1 x 105mm (200 rounds); 1 x AA 37mm (2500 rounds); 1 x AA 20mm (2000 rounds)

A special minelayer with free-flooding mine shafts in the bow compartment and smaller shafts along both sides of the hull. The shafts along the sides accommodated torpedo mines while the free-flooding shafts in the bow held an especially large submarine type. By the time this cumbersome type became operational the mission of approaching harbours to lay mines was thought too risky, and many of these boats were used instead as supply craft.

Type XIV

Number commissioned: (10) U459 - U464, U487 - U490

Complement: 6 / 47
Displacement: 1688 / 2300t
Length: 67.1m
Beam: 9.4m
Depth: 6.5m
Maximum speed: 15 / 7kts
Radius of action:
  at high speed: 14kt/5500sm
  at cruising speed: 10kt/12000sm
  submerged: 4kt/80sm
Torpedo tubes: none
Guns: 1-2 x AA 37mm (2500 rounds); 2-4 x AA 20mm (4000
  rounds)

A purpose built supply boat capable of carrying about 650 tons
of fuel. This gave it a range similar to a Type IXC plus enough
spare fuel to fill four Type VIIs. By the time Type XIVs became
operational Britain had broken a fair proportion of the U-boat
radio code and a great effort was made to eliminate these vulnerable submarine tankers; attractive targets, the majority were
sunk very quickly.

Type XXI

Numbers commissioned: U2501 - U2552, U3001 - U3035, U3037 -
U3041, U3044, U3501 - U3530
Only two boats set sail for operational missions.

Complement: 5 / 52
Displacement: 1621 / 2100t
Length: 76.7m
Beam: 8m
Depth: 6.3m
Maximum speed: 15.6 / 16.8kt
Radius of action:
  at high speed: 15kt/5100sm
  at cruising speed: 10kt / 15500sm
  submerged: 10kt/110sm
Torpedo tubes: bows: 6; stern: 0
Guns: 1 x AA 20mm twin (16000 rounds) with provisions to
  accommodate bigger guns

The hull was made up of two roughly circular sections as in a figure 8, with the lower part containing mainly batteries to give it
revolutionary underwater speeds. Type XXI should have replaced
Types VII and IX in the Atlantic convoy war, but only two saw
operational service before the end of the war.

Type XXIII

Number commissioned: U2321 - U2371, U4701 - U4707, U4709 -
U4712
The following sailed on operational missions: U2321, U2322,
U2324, U2326, U2329, U2336

Complement: 2 / 12
Displacement: 243 / 275t
Length: 34.5m
Beam: 3m
Depth: 3.7m
Maximum speed: 10 / 12.5kts
Radius of action:
  at high speed: 8kt / 2600sm
  at cruising speed: 6kt / 4450sm
  submerged: 10kt / 35sm or 4kt / 194sm
Torpedo tubes: bows: 2; stern: 0
Number of torpedoes carried: 2
Guns: none

These small electro-boats also had a large number of batteries for
very fast underwater speeds, but only a few saw operational service before the end of the war. The insides were so cramped that
even torpedoes had be loaded from the outside and spares could
not be carried. In 1945 it was quite widely believed that this type
had been fitted with underwater jet engines, but this is untrue;
the high speeds were achieved with batteries powering conventional propellers.

Appendix 2: **Register of U-boat Commanders**

This register of U-boat commanders was compiled over a period of several years and finally assembled and sorted with an English version of Microsoft Excel, which could not recognise Umlauts; it was also necessary to write titles such as "von" in the Christian names column. The spreadsheet was then converted and Umlauts inserted using the word processor Microsoft Word. As a result of this the order of names does not always follow exactly the conventional German sorting procedures.

Although great care was taken to avoid mistakes, the register should not be taken as being absolutely definitive.
The information is arranged as follows:
Column 1 - Fate:
a = died as a result of an accident
d = died of natural causes, i.e. illness
e = executed; note that Heinz-Wilhelm Eck was executed by order of the Allies; others were executed by order of the German authorities
i = interned in a neutral country
k = killed in action
p = prisoner of war. This means that the boat was sunk by enemy action but the commander survived and became a prisoner. Men who passed into captivity after the national capitulation at the end of the war have not been included in this category.
s = committed suicide
v = vanished; disappeared, exact cause of death unknown

Column 2 - Family name
Column 3 - Forenames
Column 4 - Crew (i.e. the year he joined the navy)
Column 5 - Date of birth
Column 6 - Boats in which he served, but did NOT command
Column 7 - Boats commanded

Notes:
The following could not be fitted into the tabulated register:
Christophersen, Erwin: was killed aboard U2503 when the boat was attacked by an RAF Beaufighter in Little Belt on 3/5/1945 and then beached.
Damerau, Wolf-Dietrich: died from illness on 21/5/44.
Franzke, Helmut: Stripped of his rank, and killed in action on 28/5/44 as Gefreiter with a naval anti-aircraft unit.
Eck, Heinz: found guilty by a court martial following a confession that he had shot survivors, and executed by Allied forces on 30/11/45.
Grasse, Martin: died from illness 28/1/45.
Greger, Eberhard: killed by depth charges on 14/4/42 after U85 had been sunk. It appears that this was a deliberate attempt to murder swimming survivors.
Hewicker, August Wilhelm: discharged from the officer corps on 4/5/43.
Hirsacker, Heinz: shot by order of German authorities on 24/4/43.

Kluth, Gerhard: killed by an acoustic torpedo which he himself had launched.
Koch, Leopold: joined the Midget Weapons Unit in December 1944 and was killed by a landmine on 20/4/45.
Kusch, Oskar-Heinrich: shot by order of German authorities on 12/4/44.
Lüdden, Siegfried: died in a fire aboard an accommodation ship in Kiel on 13/1/45.
Lüth, Wolfgang: shot accidentally by his own guard on 15/5/45.
Michahelles, Hermann: died as a result of an accident.
Michalowski, Hans: died due to illness 20/5/41.
Rademacher, Rudolf: killed 30/6/44 when depth charged while in a life-raft after U478 had been sunk - apparently a deliberate attack to murder the survivors.
Sauerbier, Joachim: killed 19/4/45 while in U251.
Singule, Rudolf: discharged 31/8/43 and murdered 2/5/45.
Steinhoff, Friedrich: committed suicide 20/5/45 in USA, apparently after being exposed to mob violence and fearing further abuse.
Zedelius, Günther: relieved of his duties on 21/7/44.
Zschech, Peter: committed suicide through depression on 24/10/43 while on operations.

KL Herbert "Vaddi" Schultze" on the bridge of U48 in autumn 1939.

	Surname	Forename		Date		
k	Abel	Ulrich Dr.	39	03/03/12	154	193
k	Achilles	Albrecht	34	25/01/14	66	161
	Ackermann	Paul	39	16/09/20	177	1221
	Ackermann	Wolf	39	08/03/21	509	994
	Ady	Gerhard	40	05/09/23	672, 704	677
	von Ahlefeld	Hunold	40	02/04/23	455, 95, 967	150, 4714
	Ahlers	Kurt	39	31/07/22	301, 566	10, 1201, 3512, 3041
p	Albrecht	Fritz	37	10/05/20	43	386
k	Albrecht	Karl	23	21/04/04	62, 9, 214	1062
k	Aldegarmann	Wolfgang	39	24/04/16		297
	Altmeier	Friedrich	38	16/07/20	80, 508	1227, 155
	Ambrosius	Wilhelm	15	17/05/86		21, 28, 43
	Andersen	Klaus	37	19/10/18	81	708, 481
	Angermann	Walter	40	22/01/23	272, 618	2323, 2324
	Anschutz	Hans-Helmut	41	27/06/23	427, 586	150
	von Arco	Ferdinant Graf	39	06/06/21	346, 617	151
	von und zu Arco-Zinneberg	Ulrich-Phillip Graf	40	12/12/17	117	922, 29
	Arendt	Rudolf	39	25/01/23	18	18, 23
	Argens	Kuno	39	03/05/20	8, 873	?MidgetWeaps
	Atzinger	Siegfried	36	22/10/16	61, 72, 48	48
k	Auffermann	Hans-Jürgen	34	01/10/14	69	514
k	Auffhammer	Leonhard	36	09/06/17	86	265
	Augustin	Hans Eckart	41	07/01/24	255	62
k	Aust	Eduart	39	11/08/20	613	29, 34, 922, 679
	Baberg	Kurt	36	23/02/17	UA	30, 618, 827
	Bach	Helmut	39	05/12/06		681
	Bach	Joachim-Werner	37	07/08/18		1110
k	Bade	Hans-Botho	39	15/11/09	69	626
k	Baden	Hans-Heinrich	38	30/04/15	558	955
	Bahn	Rolf	36	06/03/18	128	1235, 876
k	Bahr	Rudolf	35	01/04/16	69	305
	Balduhn	Ernst-Ludwig	38	27/10/19	211	1163
	Baldus	Hugo	39	12/04/21	618	773
	Balke	Diethelm Dr.	37	22/09/19	134	991
	Ballert	Rene	39	03/03/20	518	1196
k	Ballert	Sarto	37	21/04/17	198, 758	1166, 3520
	Baltz	Rudolf	38	02/07/20	603	603
k	Barber	Bruno	22	06/03/04	57, 93	58, 220
p	Bargsten	Klaus	36	31/10/11	99	563, 521
k	Barleben	Kurt	35	28/03/09	553	271
k	Barsch	Franz	30	30/11/11		1235
	Barschkis	Hans-Heinrich	39	28/03/09	46, 72, 421	2321
	Bart	Fritz	?	30/11/11	96, 107, 3501	UD4
k	Bartels	Robert	35	08/04/20	21	139, 561, 197
k	Barten	Wolfgang	31	18/08/09	29	52, 40
k	Bartke	Erwin	40	28/04/09	403	488, 1106
	Bartsch	Hans-Jürgen	39	31/03/21	957, 1023	18, 17
k	Basse	Georg-Wilhelm	36	27/08/17	751, 575	339, 314
	Bauer	Ernst-Ludwig	33	03/01/14	10, 37	120, 126
k	Bauer	Hermann	36	14/08/17	67	30, 169
k	Bauer	Max Hermann	30	24/07/12		18, 50
	Baum	Heinz	40	05/11/12		1197, 1303, 290
p	Baumann	Arend	22	30/03/03		131
	Baumann	Heinz	40	06/03/22	672	2333
k	La Baume	Günter	29	29/04/11		355
	Baumgärtel	Friedrich	40	24/03/23	969, 592	17, 142
p	Baur	Götz	35	01/08/17	552	660
	Beck	Dieter	34	07/05/15		3051
	Becker	Klaus	36	17/03/18	586	235, 360
i	Becker	Klaus	39	29/04/20	260	367, 260
	Becker	Philipp	40	21/10/21	269	794
	Becker	Richard	34	21/02/11	43	218, 2503
	Beckmann	Hans	39	06/01/18	214	2330
k	Beckmann	Heinz	39	29/06/13	504	159
k	Beduhn	Heinz	26	11/08/07		10, 16, 23, 25
	Behnisch	Günter	39	12/06/22	952	2337
	Behrens	Udo	30	09/04/11	30	16, 24, 17, 845
k	Bender	Werner	36	28/10/16	161	841
k	Benker	Hans	36	21/02/17	75	152, 80, 625
	Bensel	Rolf-Rüdiger	40	12/06/23	129, 101, 34, 667	120
	Benthin	Karl-Dietrich	40	25/09/21	518	2335
k	Bentzien	Heinz	37	28/01/17	73	425
k	Berends	Fritz	33	23/09/06		321
	Bergemann	Wilhelm	39	06/04/20	375	152
k	Berger	Joachim	34	23/06/13		87
	Berkemann	Paul	33	20/01/13	530	4709
	Bernardelli	Richard	32	22/11/08		805
	Bernbeck	Hinrich-Oskar	34	05/07/14	43	4, 461, UD4, 638
	Bertelsmann	Hans-Joachim	36	29/04/16	71	142, 603
	Besold	Heinrich	39	18/10/20	981, 518	1308
	Beucke	Heinz-Ehler	22	12/01/04		173
k	Bielfeld	Heinz	34	30/08/16	151	703, 1222
k	Bigalk	Gerhard	33	26/11/08		14, 751
k	Bischoff	Gustav	39	11/05/16	710, 953	2359
a	von Bitter	Georg	39	23/03/21	38, 160	750
	Bitter	Otto	37	12/10/18		1010, 2535
	Blaich	Ferdinand	40	08/02/12		3024
k	Blaudau	Ernst-Ulrich	35	09/11/14		1001
k	Blauert	Hans-Jörg	39	21/03/18	553	734
	Bleichrodt	Heinrich	31	21/10/09	8, 6	48, 67, 109
k	Blischke	Heinz	38	01/09/19	755	744
k	Block	Helmut		04/02/17		771
	Blum	Otto-Ulrich	36	04/02/17	373	760
	Boddenberg	Karl	33	23/05/14	201	963
	Bode	Thilo	36	19/02/18	505	858
	Böhm	Hermann	37	24/12/10	1061, 758	2341
p	Böhme	Kurt	37	21/01/17	575, 751	450
p	Boehmer	Wolfgang	39	09/08/20	431, 263, 575	575
k	Börner	Hans-Joachim	37	24/07/18	507	735
	Böttcher	Richard	25	02/10/06		139

Robert Bartels aboard his first command, U139, a Type IID boat; he would be killed when his U197, a Type IXD2, was sunk in August 1943.

Korvettenkapitän Wolfgang Lüth; he made his name commanding U43 with the 6th U-Flotilla in 1940-42, and U181 with the 12th in 1942-43. Ironically, he died in a tragic accident only days after the end of the war.

k	Bohmann	Heino	34	11/03/14	94	88
	Bokelberg	Max Hermann	37	15/04/19		323, 2530
	Boldt	Walter	39	05/12/21	415	720
	Boos	Hans-Heinz	37	14/02/13		1002, 1015
k	Bopst	Eberhard	33	25/12/13		6, 597
k	Borchardt	Gustav	37	25/12/16	460, 135	563
k	Borcherdt	Ulrich	31	13/09/09		8, 555, 587
	Borchers	Rolf	33	01/11/13	206	149,226,276,2515?
	Borchert	Günther	36	17/05/14		24, 566
k	Borger	Wolfgang	36	04/04/13	94, 34, 251	394
	Bork	Helmut	39	29/05/10	134	275
	Borm	Karl	34	10/08/11		592
k	Bornhaupt	Konrad	37	06/06/20	88	285
	Bornkessel	Dieter	39	07/08/20	124,178,616,29,354	2332, 2370
	Bortfeldt	Karl-Hermann	39	12/04/21	71	14, 1167
	Bosüner	Harald	34	17/10/12	161	1223, Midgets
k	Bothe	Friedrich	36	01/07/17	30	5, 101, 447
	Brachmann	Hans-Günther	22	11/02/04		518
	Braeucker	Friedrich	37	13/07/19		889
k	Brammer	Herbert	37	24/04/14	118	1060
	Brand	Wilhelm	39	18/11/15		1196
k	Brandenburg	Karl	24	25/07/06		457
	Brandi	Albrecht	35	20/06/14	552	617, 380, 967
k	Brans	Hans-Joachim	35	21/08/15	84, 169	801
	Brasack	Paul	37	09/05/16	590	737
	Brauel	Wilhelm	37	17/09/14	103	256,92,3530,975
	Braun	Kurt		27/08/23	763	763
	Breckwoldt	Friedrich	39	16/06/12		679, Midgets
	Breinlinger	Siegfried	39	24/04/20	152, 267, 152, 108	320, 3018
k	Breithaupt	Wolfgang	33	19/09/13		599
	von Bremen	Hanskurt	38	11/08/18	598	764
	Breun	Gerhard	40	07/04/20	266, 410	2358
	Brischke	Ernst				255
k	Brockmann	Karl	39	17/10/14	UD1, 588	UC1,
k	Brodda	Heinrich	21	09/05/03		209
k	Brosin	Hans-Günther	36	15/11/16	572	634, 134
	Bruder	Hermann	39	05/03/21	471	1058
	Brückner	Werner	34	13/10/15		2351
	Brüllau	Heinz	39	12/12/17		905
	Brüller	Ernst-Ulrich	36	23/09/17	4, 28	7, 23, 407,
	Brümmer-Patzig	Helmut	10	26/10/96		UD4
	Brünig	Matthias	38		195	108,884, 3038
	Brüninghaus	Herbert	31	11/10/10		6, 148, 1059
k	Brünner	Joachim	37	12/04/19	703	703
	Brünning	Herbert	35	13/09/15	98	137, 642, 3518
k	Bruns	Heinrich	31	03/04/12	75	175
k	Buchholz	Heinz	29	03/08/09	8, 22	15, 195, 177
	Budzyn	Sigmund		01/01/16	18, 155	2352
p	Büchel	Paul	25	03/08/07		32, 860
k	Büchler	Rudolf	36	14/10/15	161	387
	Bühring	Klaus-Jürgen	37	02/07/20	657, 148	360
	von Bülow	Otto	30	16/10/11		3, 404
p	Bürgel	Friedrich	36	24/10/16	565	97, 205
k	Bugs	Hans-Helmuth	37	11/03/17	435	629
k	de Buhr	Johann		23/03/12	86	347
k	Buhse	Heinz	39	03/01/17		399
d	Bungards	Hans	36	01/07/17		1103, 2513
	Burghagen	Walter	11	21/09/91		219
k	Burmeister	Walter	37	09/02/19	267	1018
	Buscher	Hans	38	02/08/18		1307
	Buttjer	Johann	31	26/05/12		768, 774
	Cabolet	Servais		24/04/08		907
	Callsen	Peter	39	28/10/11	1060	3033
k	von Carlowitz	Dietrich	36	11/07/16	98	710
p	Carlsen	Klaus-Peter	37	07/10/19	251	732
	Christiansen	Helmut		24/09/18		1305
	Christiansen	Uwe	38	25/01/20	572	28,71,2508,2365
k*1	Christophersen	Erwin	36	13/04/15	753	228, 3028
	Clausen	Heinz-Ehlert	32	12/07/09	101, 18	403
	Clausen	Nicolai	29	02/06/11	37	142, 37, 129, 182
k	Claussen	August-Wilhelm	37	13/03/19		1226
k	Claussen	Emil	37	06/10/17	576, 578	469
k	Clemens	Johannes	35	25/05/11		319
k	Coester	Christian-Brandt	37	13/11/19	124	10, 542
	Cohausz	Hans	26	30/11/07		30, UA
	Collmann	Herwig	35	01/09/15	56	17, 562
k	Conrad	Gerhard	39	18/08/22	260	214
k	Cordes	Ernst	34	26/06/13		560, 763, 1195
k	Cranz	Wilhelm	39	19/04/15	653	398
	Cremer	Peter Erich	32	25/03/11		152, 333, 2519
	Creutz	Horst	35	19/05/15		400
	Curio	Oskar	37	28/02/18	373	80, 952, 2528
	Czekowski	Martin	40	18/01/22	608	2362
k	Czygan	Werner	25	25/11/04		118
	Dähne	Wolfgang	39	06/08/21	257, 29, 960	349
k	Dahlhaus	Eberhard	38	24/07/20	753	634
k	Dahms	Hermann	36	31/03/16		980
d	Damerau	Wolfdietrich	37	28/05/19	521	106
k	Dangschat	Günther	35	08/07/15	38	184
k	Dankleff	Walter	35	13/11/06		767
p	Dau	Rolf	26	01/04/06		5, 31, 42
	Daublebsky von Eichhain	Karl	29	09/07/09		13
p	Dauter	Helmut	37	09/08/19	454	448
	Davidson	Heinz von	37	29/12/18	135	281
p	Deckert	Horst	37	11/10/18	73	8, 73
k	Deecke	Joachim	33	29/06/12	37	9, 584
k	Deecke	Jürgen	31	28/04/11		1
k	Deetz	Friedrich	35	11/09/16	205	757
p	Degen	Horst		19/07/13	552	701
	Deiring	Hugo	38	25/07/20	151, 255	56, 3503

	Name	First name		Date		
	Denkleff ?	Walter	35	12/11/06		767
	Dick	Hans-Peter	39	13/11/20	713	612
	Dierks	Hans-Joachim	40	16/07/23	739, 978,23,572	14, 137
k	Dierksen	Reiner	33	24/03/08		176
k	Dieterich	Max	34	06/09/14	572	78, 637
k	Dieterichs	Horst	34	01/03/12	46	406
k	Dietrich	Willi	28	20/12/09	35, 28, 125	286
p	Diggins	Kurt	34	17/10/13		458
	Dingler	Gottfried	39	16/02/22	92	748
k	Dobberstein	Erich	38	15/12/19	155	988
	Dobbert	Max		13/04/10	593	969, 2537
	Dobenecker	Günter	40	09/02/22	203, 650	11, 2524
	Dobinsky	Hans-Jürgen	39	24/07/22	758, 932 or 952, 333	323
	Dobratz	Kurt	22	09/04/04		1232
k	Döhler	Hans	37	05/12/17	751	21, 606
k	Dohrn	Erwin	38	18/03/20		325
	Dommes	Wilhelm	31	16/04/07	4, 96	431, 178
	Drescher	Günther	38	13/10/19	196	3026
k	von Dresky	Hans-Wilhelm	29	27/01/08	20	4, 33
k	Drewitz	Hans-Joachim	33	14/11/07		525
	Drews	Ulrich	36	24/05/16		321, 2534
	Driver	Heinrich	33	10/07/12	13	23, 145, 371, 20?
	Dübler	Rudolf	39	12/10/21	203, 83, 464, 81	1101
k	Dültgen	Gert	37		508	391
	Düppe	Joachim	40	23/01/16	432	4, 2505
	Duis	Hans-Diederich	39	06/02/22	48, 462, 351, 365	792
k	Dumrese	Adolf	29	13/11/09		78, 655
	Dunkelberg	Hans	37	07/08/18	406	716
	Duppel	Martin	38	09/02/20	201	959
p	Eberbach	Heinz-Eugen	39	02/07/21	407	967, 230
v	Eberlein	Otto	38	15/11/13		1020
	Ebersbach	Hans-Joachim	39	17/10/18	618	975
	Ebert	Eberhard		27/06/07		1201, 3010
k	Ebert	Jürgen	37	25/09/16		927
e*	Eck	Heinz-Wilhelm	34	27/03/16		852
	Eckel	Kurt	39	16/05/21	979	2325
k	Eckelmann	Heinz	37	24/07/16	75	635
	Eckermann	Hans	25	30/05/05		29, UA
k	Eckhardt	Hermann	36	15/06/16	94, 28	28, 432
	Edelhoff	Ernst	36	13/10/17		324
	Ehrhardt	Walther	38	23/12/19		1016
k	Ehrich	Heinz	37	15/09/19	175	334
k	Eichmann	Kurt	37	11/10/17	553	151, 98
	Eick	Alfred	37	09/03/16	176	510
	von Eickstedt	Wolfgang	35	01/12/15	553	668
	Eilers	Horst				3013(?)
	Eisele	Wilhelm	27	16/03/07	4, 10, 59	57, 78, 1103
p	Elfe	Horst	36	23/04/17	99	139, 93
	Ellerlage	Hermann	40	03/02/13		2344
k	Ellmenreich	Helmut	35	16/07/13		535
	Elsinghorst	Josef	39	26/08/16		822
	Emde	Bernhard	37	06/12/17		248, 299
	Emmermann	Carl	34	06/03/15	UA	172, 3037
k	Emmrich	Heinz	41	19/01/13		320
	Endler	Siegrfried	34	14/04/15	748	4711
	Endrass	Engelbert	35	02/03/11	47	46, 567
	Engel	Hans	36	16/08/15	83	273
	Engel	Herbert	39	29/06/12	559	666, 228
k	Engelmann	Kurt-Eduard	23	08/04/03		163
k	Epp	Dietrich	37	09/08/17	572	62, 341
k	Eppen	Günter	33	27/08/12	38	519
	Erdmann	Dieter	38	11/04/20	406	555, 904
	Ernst	Hans-Joachim	37	17/08/18		1022
k	von der Esch	Dietrich	34	31/01/15	98	586, 863
	Euler	Klaus	37	21/01/19		1162
k	Ewerth	Klaus	25	28/03/07		1,35,36,26,850
p	Ey	Hans		19/06/16	94	433
	Faber	Ulrich	37	10/10/18	1018	1271
	Fabricius	Friedrich	37	18/05/19		637, 234, 1028
	Fabricius	Ludwig	39	12/04/21	95, 210, 666	821, 30, 721
	Fahr	Theodor	30	30/11/09	123	567
k	Falke	Hans	37	07/01/20		1279
	Falke	Hans	39	16/06/20	118	992
k	Faust	Erich	39	22/04/21	412	618
k	Fechner	Otto	24	15/11/05		164
	Fehler	Hans	36	20/09/10		234
	Feiler	Gerhard	34	06/09/09		653
	Feindt	Hans-Arend	39	29/10/21	34, 641	758
	Fenn	Heinz-Konrad	37	20/07/18	108	139, 445
p	Fenski	Horst-Arno	37	03/11/18	752	34, 410, 371
k	Ferro	Otto	40	24/01/11		645
	Feufel	Karl	38	09/09/18		1301, 2529
	Fiebig	Günter	38	06/03/20		1131
k	Fiedler	Hans	36	14/10/14	562, 120	120,564,998,333
k	Fiehn	Helmut	35	19/02/16	67	191
p	Findeisen	Eberhard	36	25/05/16		877
k	Finke	Otto	36	24/09/15		279
k	von Fischel	Unno	34	05/11/15	97	374
	Fischer	Erich / Georg	40	27/01/22	363	137
	Fischer	Ernst	39	20/02/21	596	30, 821, 749, 3006
	Fischer	Hans-Georg	26	03/02/08	38	109
k	Fischer	Klaus	38	07/10/19	148, 659	961
k	Fischer	Ruprecht	37	17/11/16		244
k	Fischler Graf von Treuberg	Ruprecht	39	20/02/20	214	749, 445
k	Fitting	Hans-Hermann	39	27/05/20	1056	1274
	Flachsenberg	Walter	28	26/10/08		71
	Fleige	Karl	24	05/09/05	20, 123	18
k	Förster	Hans-Joachim	38	20/02/20	380	479, 480
k	Förster	Heinz	40	25/06/09		359

U566, with Günther Borchert and his IWO Hans-Joachim Klaus, who later became commander of U340. Both officers are sporting the boat's polar bear emblem on the side of their caps.

ps	Förster	Hugo	23	21/01/05		501
k	Folkers	Ulrich	34	06/03/15		38, 125
k	Forster	Ludwig	36	09/10/15	29	62, 654
pk	von Forstner	Siegfried Freiherr	30	19/09/10		59, 402
	von Forstner	Wolfgang-Friedrich Freiherr	37	03/10/16	572	472
k	Fraatz	Georg-Werner	35	30/03/17	3, 101	652, 529
	Fränzel	Otto	39	29/04/21	510	903
	Frahm	Karl	31	03/08/13	6, 190	2363
k	Frahm	Peter	32	14/06/12	15	15
	Franckschi	Gerhard	41	01/10/21	156, 764	4704
	Franke	Hans-Heino	40	27/05/21	373	2355
	Franke	Heinz	36	30/11/15	84	262, 148,3509,2502
ka	Franken	Wilhelm	35	0/9/14	331	565
p	Franz	Johannes	26	18/05/07		27
k	Franz	Ludwig	37	30/01/18	463	362
	Franze	Joachim	37	09/01/18		278
	Franzius	Rudolf	32	05/06/11		145, 438
k*	Franzke	Helmut	27	02/12/07	26	3
	Frauenheim	Fritz	30	09/03/12		21, 101
	Freiwald	Kurt	25	29/10/06		7, 33, 181
	Frerks	Paul		25/06/08		975
	Fresdorf					17
k	von Freyberg-Eisenberg- Allmendingen	Walter Freiherr	35	05/11/15	552	52, 610
s	von Friedeburg	Hans-Georg	14	15/07/95		25
	von Friedeburg	Ludwig	41	21/05/24	548	155, 4710
k	Friederich	Karl	37	12/06/14	74	5, 74
	Friedland	Klaus	38	28/06/20		310
k	Friedrich	Rudolf	35	15/06/14	558	759
k	Friedrichs	Adolf	35	04/03/14	98	253
k	Frischke	Karl-Heinz Dr. jur.	36	25/11/12	970	881
	Fritz	Detlef	39	01/06/21	73	905, 555
k	Fritz	Karl-Heinz	41	20/02/21	103	107
	Fritze	Günther	39	12/06/22	1206	1206, 3514
k	Fröhlich	Wilhelm	29	10/03/10		36
k	Frömmer	Heinz	39	21/04/21	228	923
k	Frömsdorf	Helmut von	39	26/03/21	853	855
	Frohberg	Günther	39	06/02/21	980, 952	1275
	Fuchs	Karl-Heinz	35	18/01/15	154	528
	Fuhlendorf	Harald	39	11/05/19		2343
	Gabert	Paul	33	13/04/13		1210
k	Gänge	Albrecht	37	01/06/19	378	226
k	Ganzer	Erwin	35	08/12/12		871
	Gaude	Hans-Ludwig	36	23/01/16	83, 558	19, 3525, 2343
	von Gaza	Jürgen	39	07/09/20	863, 739	312
p	Gebauer	Werner	39	10/09/22	212	681
	Gehrken	Heinrich	37	12/07/11		UF2, 298
p	Geider	Horst	37	07/09/18	73	61, 761
	Geisler	Hans-Ferdinand	38	26/03/21		152, 21, 3006
	Geissler	Hans		01/10/16		561, 440
k	Geissler	Heinz	38	29/08/17	376	390
k	Gelhaar	Alexander	27	24/11/08		45
	Gelhaus	Harald	35	24/07/15	103	143, 107
k	Gemeiner	Gert	37	02/10/18	38, 160	146, 137, 154
k	Gengelbach	Dietrich	34	07/10/14	52	574
k	Gericke	Otto	33	29/12/08	17	503
	Gerke	Ernst-August	39	09/05/21	377	382, 673, 3035
k	Gerlach	Peter	39	25/02/22	453, 37	223
p	Gerlach	Wilhelm	39	15/08/05	124	490
	Gessner	Hans	38	06/05/19	1105	1008
p	Giersberg	Dietrich	37	26/11/17	155	419
	Giesewetter	Herbert	39	09/09/22		60, 368
	Giessler	Hans-Henrich	31	12/01/11		455
k	Gilardone	Hans	32	09/07/12	203	254
k	Glaser	Wolfgang	37	24/02/19		1014
p	Glattes	Gerhard	27	06/02/09		39
	Gode	Heinrich	39	24/01/22	549	3536
	Godt	Eberhard	18	05/08/00		25
k	Göing	Walter	34	02/08/14	38	755
k	Göllnitz	Heinrich	35	30/08/09		657
	Görner	Friedrich-Karl	39	24/11/21	958	145
	Götze	Hans	39	12/01/16	586	586, 2527
k	Goldbeck	Heinz	36	10/02/14	288	1169
	Goschzik	Georg	31	06/01/12	367, 642, 586	2348
k	Gosejakob	Henri	36	14/12/15		713
	von Gossler	Curt	30	21/09/05		49
k	Gossler	Johann-Egbert	35	16/11/14	125	538
p	Graef	Adolf	36	22/04/16	652	664
k	Gräf	Ulrich	35	15/12/15	74	23, 69
i	Grafen	Karl	35	09/05/15		20
p	Gramitzki	Franz	36	18/05/16	17, UA, 19, 138	138
k	Grandefeld	Wolfgang	36	11/02/17	108	174
d	Grasse	Martin		10/11/12		1168, 3511
k	Grau	Peter	39	08/03/20	601	1191
	Grau	Peter-Ottmar	34	03/05/14	201	46, 601, 872, 3015
	Grave	Günther	37	13/07/17	71	56, 470
	Grawert	Justus	40	13/01/23	80, 333	750
k	Greger	Eberhard	35	15/09/15	30, 110	85
k	Gretschel	Günter	36	26/10/14	6, 93	59, 707
	Greus	Friedrich-August	39	27/04/21	217, 214	737
k	Grimme	Wilhelm	25	12/05/07	146	146, 116
	Groschowiak	Edmund	37	24/10/17		982
k	Grosse	Harald	25	17/11/06		8, 22, 34, 53
	Grote	Henrich	38	09/11/20		3516
	Groth	Gerhard	37	20/08/17	96	143, 958, 397
	von Gudenus	Karl-Gabriel Graf	38	10/10/20	71	427
	Günther	Horst	39	29/01/22	275	1287, 2504, 2533
p	Guggenberger	Friedrich	34	06/03/15	28	28, 81, 847, 513
	Guse	Joachim	39	08/06/21	77	1193

	Surname	First name		Date		Boats
k	Gutteck	Hans-Joachim	35	10/04/14		1024
	Gysae	Robert	31	04/01/11		98, 177
k	Habekost	Johannes	33	13/02/07		31
p	Hackländer	Burkhard	33	17/12/14		454
k	Hackländer	Klaus	37	26/07/16	172	423
	Hälbich	Gerhard		12/11/16	404	673
p	Hänert	Klaus	36	01/02/18	68	550
	Hagenau	Karl-Heinz	37	31/08/19		704
k	Hagene	Georg	27	24/07/08		1208
k	Hahndorff	Jobst	37	30/03/18		864
k	Hamm	Horst	35	17/03/16	26, 96	58, 562
	Hammer	Ulrich	39	26/03/18	621	367, 430, 733
	von Hammerstein-Equord	Addolf Wilhelm Freiherr	37	11/03/18		149
	Hanitsch	Hans-Ulrich	39	12/08/22	441	428
	Hansen	Hans-Johann	37	15/06/18		1026
	Hansen	Hermann	39	06/05/18	129, 462	999, 2517
k	Hansen	Otto	37	23/04/18	435, 269	269, 601
k	Hansmann	Bruno	33	01/12/07	95	127
k	Happe	Werner	36	23/09/15	68	192
k	Hardegen	Reinhard	33	18/03/13	124	147, 123
k	Harflinger	Karl-Heinrich	35	02/08/15	84	269
	Harms	Erich	39	20/01/10	255	255, 3023
p	Harms	Otto	34	22/04/09		6, 56, 464
k	Harney	Klaus	35	26/03/17	84	756
k	von Harpe	Richard	37	19/08/17	108	129, 3519
	Hartel	Friedrich	40	10/01/23	989	2356
k	Hartenstein	Werner	28	27/02/08		156
	Hartmann	Curt	39	14/10/20	171, 170	236, 554, 236, 982
	Hartmann	Ernst	39	08/04/21	704	3
	von Hartmann	Götz	34	30/10/13	93	555, 563, 441
k	Hartmann	Klaus	33	07/02/12		38, 441
k	Hartmann	Otto	36	18/04/17		77
k	Hartmann	Werner	21	11/12/02		26, 37, 198
p	Hartwig	Paul	35	14/09/15	125	517
k	Hasenschar	Heinrich	36	27/09/16	59, 751	29, 628
k	Hashagen	Berthold	37	26/08/09	515	846
	Hass	Hans-Heinrich	40	12/10/22	96, 543	2324
	Hauber	Hans Gerold		08/07/13	170	170
k	Haupt	Hans-Jürgen	35	19/02/11	203	665
k	Hause	Karl	35	15/07/16		351, 211
	Hechler	Ernst	29	21/11/07		870
	Heckel	Fridtjof	39	25/10/20	541	2322
k	Hegewald	Wolfgang	37	05/07/17	332	671
k	Heibges	Wolfgang	40	01/07/22	278	999
k	Heidel	Werner	33	24/6/9		7, 55
p	Heidtmann	Hans	34	08/08/14	33, 14	2, 14, 559, 21
k	Heilmann	Siegfried	36	08/06/17		659, 389
	Heilmann	Udo	33	04/03/13	18	24, 97
k	Hein	Fritz	38	25/12/19	333	300
k	Heine	Karl-Franz	34	13/10/15		303, 403
p	Heinecke	Hans-Jochen	26	26/09/07		111
	Heinicke	Ernst-Günter	27	24/09/08		3, 51, 53, 2561
k	Heinicke	Hans-Dieter	33	18/05/13	73	576
	Heinrich	Erwin	40	27/03/23	752, 963	2357
p	Heinrich	Günther	38	20/01/20	596	960
	Heinrich	Helmuth		04/10/13		255
k	Heinsohn	Heinrich	33	12/02/10		8, 573, 438
	Heintze	Werner	35	16/03/16		708
	Heitz	Horst		09/04/22	664	6, 792, 1407
k	Heller	Wolfgang	30	16/06/10	155	842
ka	Hellmann	Hans	39	08/03/21	262	903, 733,
k	Hellriegel	Hans-Jürgen	36	16/06/17	46	140, 96, 543
k	Hellwig	Alexander	35	05/03/16	405	239
	Hengen	Dieter	40	19/10/22	255	2364
pk*	Henke	Werner	34	13/05/08		515
k	Henne	Wolf	24	07/08/05		157
	von Hennig	Heinz	40	17/03/22	421	2361
k	Hennig	Helmut	-36	30/04/14	52	24, 533
	Henning	Fritz	37	10/04/17	561	561, 565, 668
k	Hepp	Horst	36	10/10/17	162	727, 238
	Herbschleb	Karl-Heinz	35	19/10/10		21, 354
	Herglotz	Helmut	38	15/03/18	143, 408	2, 290
	Hermann	Wolfgang	28	31/12/08		662
k	Herrle	Friedrich-Georg	39	13/08/10		307, 393
	Herrmann	Werner	38	14/01/20		2510
k	Hertin	Willi	35	11/09/14	552	647
k	Herwartz	Oskar	35	01/01/15	67	843
	Herwartz	Wolfgang	37	25/6/17		1302
k	Hesemann	Siegfried	35	07/07/12	95	186
	Hess	Hans-Georg	40	06/05/23	466	995
k	Hesse	Hans-Joachim	25	18/01/06		654, 444
k	Hesse	Hermann	35	10/03/09		133, 194
	Hessler	Günter	27	14/06/09		107
k	Hetschko	Gert	33	06/08/13	89	453, 121,
k	Heusinger von Waldegg	Burkhard	38	10/03/09	177	198
	Hewicker	August-Wilhelm	37	30/07/18		671
p	Heyda	Wolfgang	32	14/11/13		120, 434
k	Heydemann	Ernst	36	20/06/16	142, 141	17, 268
k	Heydemann	Günther	33	11/01/14	69	575
	Heyse	Ulrich	33	20/09/06		128
	Hilbig	Hans	36	05/07/17		1230
	Hilbig	Kurt	38	18/05/19	601	993, 3526
	Hildebrandt	Hans	36	24/12/11		636
	Hilgendorf	Klaus	39	29/02/12		1009
	Hille	Wolfgang	36	12/03/18	202	762
	Hillmann	Jürgen	40	21/09/20	371	2353
k	Hilsenitz	Erich	36	28/09/16	108	108, 146
	Hinrichs	Johannes	33	29/05/13	2518	3005
	Hinrichs	Otto	36	30/11/13		1061, 2504

Karl Heinz Herbschleb of U354, wearing clean, badged-up overalls for a homecoming.

	Surname	First name				
	Hinsch	Hans-Peter	34	30/07/14	30	4, 140, 569
	Hinz	Rudolf	39	22/02/20	30, 618	1004
p	von Hippel	Friedrich	34	02/01/15	65	144, 76
e	Hirsacker	Heinz	34	14/08/14		572
	Hoeckner	Fritz	33	22/12/12		215
	von der Hoeh	Hermann	40	23/04/20	445	2346
k	Höltring	Horst	33	30/06/13		149, 604
	Hoffmann	Dietrich	32	17/06/12		594
k	Hoffmann	Eberhard	25	16/05/07		165
k	Hoffmann	Eberhard	33	24/10/12	51	146, 451
k	Hoffmann	Erich-Michael	38	14/06/19	437	738
	Hoffmann	Günther	26	04/10/08	206	?
	Hoffmann	Heinrich-Dietrich	40	19/08/21	238, 957	141
p	Hoffmann	Hermann	39	27/04/21	172	172
	Hoffmann	Rudolf	36	28/04/17	123	8, 845
	Hofmann	Horst	37	18/01/19	48, 134, 672	
	Hohmann	Otto	37	01/04/10		298, 2526
k	von Holleben	Heinrich	38	13/03/19		1051
k	Holpert	William	34	11/06/14		1021
k	Holtorf	Gottfried	36	21/05/12		598
	Homann	Hans	38	04/03/18		1165
k	Hopman	Rolf-Heinrich	26	26/03/06		405
k	Hoppe	Joachim	33	20/03/15		65
	Hoppe	Konrad	35	20/04/17	168	
k	Horn	Karl-Horst	35	16/12/16	201	705
	Hornbostel	Klaus	34	04/06/16		806
	Hornkohl	Hans	36	07/04/17	753	566, 1007,3512,3041
k	Horrer	Hans-Joachim	33	06/02/08		555, 589
	Horst	Frierich	39	12/04/17	11, 565	121
	Hoschatt	Alfred	27	10/02/09		378
k	Hossenfelder	Albert	35	05/03/08	37	342
	Hübsch	Horst	39	31/12/21	262	145, 78
	Hübschen	Otto	38	06/12/19	7, 60, 121	121, 145,2501,2542
k	Hülsenbeck	Ewald	38	21/12/19	704	121, 146, 1209
k	Hüttemann	Eberhard	37	25/06/19	590	332
k	Huisgen	Friedrich	36	01/03/15	1162	235, 749
k	Hummerjohann	Emmo	37	15/04/16	205	964
	Hunck	Wilhelm	37	15/12/14		829
k	Hunger	Hans	35	16/03/15	75	336
p	Hungerhausen	Heinz	36	05/12/16	128	91
k	Hungerhausen	Walter	38	22/03/19	218	280
k	Huth	Walther	37	14/04/18	562	414
k	von Hymmen	Reinhard	33	05/11/14	97, 564	408
k	Hyronimus	Guido	37	17/11/18	351, 461	670, 678
	Ibbeken	Hans	18	20/09/99		178, 27
	Issermeyer	Hans-Adolf	38	01/02/20	752	80, 2562
p	Ites	Otto	36	05/02/18	51, 48	146, 94
k	Ites	Rudolf	36	05/02/18	709	709
	Iversen	Jürgen	39	24/04/21		8, 1103
k	von Jacobs	Nikolaus	33	05/01/13	751	611
	Jacobs	Paul	34	23/03/15	332, 738	560
	Jaeckel	Kurt	39	06/12/19	529, 714	2366
	Jaeger	Walter	43	27/05/97		1061
	Jaek	Bernhard	37	14/10/18	218	3044
	Jaenicke	Karl	39	14/07/15	801	3533
	Jahn	Günter	31	27/09/10		596
k	Jahrmärker	Walther	35	23/09/17		412
	Janssen	Gustav-Adolf	36	09/04/15	65	151, 37,103,3037
k	Jaschke	Heinz or Hans	39	16/07/20	592	592
k	Jebsen	Johann	35	21/04/16		565, 859
p	Jenisch	Hans	33	19/10/13		32
kv	Jenisch	Karl-Heinrich	29	20/04/10		22
k	Jensen	Kurt	37	23/02/18	376	644
k	Jenssen	Karl-Joachim	38	31/07/20	141, 705, 563	477
	Jeppener-Haltenhoff	Harald	-33	20/09/07	17	17, 24
	Jeschke	Hubert	39	24/04/21		975
p	Jeschonnek	Wolf	38	13/07/19	607	607
k	von Jessen	Ralf	35	25/02/17		222, 266
	Jestel	Erwin	40	31/03/23	642	6, 1204
k	Jewinski	Erich	38	10/03/20		46, 1192, 2539
	Jobst	Karl	36	24/04/13	744	2326
	Johann	Johann	27	04/09/09	2539	2539
p	Johannsen	Hans	35	03/06/10	506	569
	John	Alfred	38	05/05/20	415	828
k	Jordan	Günther	37	12/02/19	132	274
	Juers	Ralf	37	07/05/19		778
k	Jürst	Harald	32	18/03/13		59, 104
	Juli	Herbert	35	08/06/16	83	382
	Junker	Hanns-Joachim	40	19/08/23	121, 5, 72, 716	5, 72,716,2370,2332
	Junker	Ottoheinrich	24	12/07/05		33, 532
p	Just	Paul	36	24/12/15	156	546
	Justi	Friedrich	37	10/04/19		1170
	Käding	Walter	35	14/09/15	123	4713
	Käselau	Erich	-41	25/03/22	237, 990	922
k	Kaiser	Hans Dietrich	40	06/10/21		2338
	Kaiser	Hermann	25	09/03/07		3002
k	Kaiser	Karl-Ernst	38	21/04/20	555, 608	986
	Kallipke	Fritz	37	28/11/09		397, 2526, 2529
	Kals	Ernst	24	02/08/05		130
k	von Kameke	Horst-Tessen	35	21/02/16	116, 84	UD5, 119
k	Kandler	Hans-Albrecht	37	31/10/17	565	386, 653
k	Kandzior	Helmut	38	25/09/19	333	743
k	Kapitzki	Ralph	35	28/06/16	93	615
k	Karpf	Hans	35	14/05/16	566	10, 632
k	Kasch	Lorenz	33	20/08/14	107	333, 540
	Kaschke	Walter		09/09/11		746
	Kasperek	Walter	39	13/12/21	466	143
p	Kaufmann	Wolfgang	33	23/06/12	7	9, 19, 79
k	Keerl	Hans	39	05/01/21	598	291, 80

p	Kelbling	Gerd	34	12/06/15	557	593
k	Kell	Walter	33	04/12/13		204
k	von Keller	Alexander Graf		12/03/19	564	731
k	Keller	Günter	37	18/02/17		68
	Keller	Günther	39	25/08/21	321, 366, 372	981, 3521
	Keller	Siegfried	37	30/10/17	109	38, 130
	Kellerstrass	Gerhard	25	08/07/06		2043
	Kelling	Heinrich	25	20/12/04	28	150, 37, 423
k	Kellner	Adolf	36	28/04/10		357
	Kentrat	Eitel-Friedrich	28	11/09/06		8, 74, 196
	Kessler	Horst	34	15/8/14		704, 985
	von Ketelhodt	Eberhard Freiherr	40	30/01/20	307	712
	Ketels	Hans-Heinrich	37	11/03/18	571	970, 2523,3511,1168
	Ketelsen	Wolfgang	35	14/08/11	130	UD1
k	Kettner	Paul-Hugo	33	20/07/12		142, 379
	Kiesewetter	Wilhelm	0	28/10/78		UC1
	Kiessling	Ulrich	39	17/12/18		1306
k	Kietz	Siegfried	37	04/01/17	130	126
	Kimmelmann	Walter	40	23/08/22		139
k	Kindelbacher	Robert	35	18/05/15	96	627
k	Kinzel	Manfred	35	27/03/15	404	338
	Klapdor	Heinrich	36	06/07/14	9	9, 2538
	Klatt	Johannes	35	02/06/16	557	606
p	Klaus	Hans-Joachim	37	17/05/18	560, 566	340
k	Kleinschmidt	Wilhelm-Peter	33	27/01/07		111
	Klingspor	Leonhard	37	17/06/17	129	293
	Kloevekorn	Friedrich	37	19/02/18		471, 3012
kv	von Kloth-Heydenfeldt	Harro	31	25/04/11		20, 102
k	Klug	Werner	39	15/01/20	69, 552	794, 1406
	Klusmeier	Emil	30	27/07/12		2340, 2336
k*	Kluth	Gerhard	37	31/08/18	91	377
k	Knackfuss	Ulrich	38	18/06/20	257	345, 821
	Knecht	Joachim	37	13/08/18	653	46, 748,3036,3059
	Kneip	Albert	39	09/07/21	174, 171, 170	1223
	Knieper	Bernhard	41	01/03/11		925
	Knipping	Erwin	34+	22/11/10		1273
kv	Knoke	Helmuth	41	11/08/06	462	925
k	Knollmann	Helmut	37	09/08/18		1273
k	Knorr	Dietrich	31	13/02/12		53, 51
k	Koch	Heinz	39	10/07/14	331	304
k*	Koch	Leopold	37	15/09/18		258, 382
	Koch	Walter	38	05/06/19	309, 601	1132
	Koch	Walter-Ernst	38	30/09/19	563, 737	712, 975
	Kock	Uwe	36	25/11/11		249
k	Köhl	Kurt	39	04/02/12	562	669
	Köhler	Otto	31	17/11/09		377
	Köhlzer	Karl	31	13/03/12		2, 1221
	Köhntopp	Walter	37	19/04/11	77	14, 995
	Kölle	Walther	26	03/08/07		
	Kölzer	Kurt	29	14/03/10		603
k	Könenkamp	Jürgen	32	14/08/13		14, 375
k	König	Alois	39	05/07/20	410	6
	König	Gottfried	39	24/10/21	43, 181	316
kv	König	Klaus-Dietrich	37	14/11/15	UB, UD5	972
	König	Lothar	39	14/03/21	440	237
k	Köpke	Klaus	35	05/01/15	569	259
k	Köppe	Helmut	33	01/04/09	751	613
k	Körner	Willy-Roderich	35	26/12/14		120, 301
k	Köster	Helmut	34	25/04/14		72
p	Koitschka	Siegfried	37	06/08/17	552	7, 616
p	Kolbus	Hans	38	05/10/19		421, 596, 407
	Koopmann	Hermann	40	04/02/10		1171
	Korfmann	Freitz-Otto	40	24/04/23	375, 340, 362	2365
	Korndörfer	Hubertus	39	20/11/19	593	139, 407
	Korth	Claus	32	07/10/11		57, 93
k	Kosbadt	Hans-Karl	37	15/12/17	94	224
	Kosnick	Fritz	36	04/03/11		739
p	Kottmann	Hermann	36	04/12/15		203
	Kranich	Franz	33	29/08/13	3525	3525
k	Krankenhagen	Detlef	36	03/07/17		549
p	Kraus	Hans-Werner	34	01/07/15	47	83, 199
p	Krech	Günther	33	29/09/14	100	558
	Kreglin	Ludo	38	20/10/19	432	60, 38, 236, 3003
k	Krempl	Erich	39	15/05/21	108	71, 28, 548, 1162
k	Kremser	Horst	36	05/09/17		383
p	Kretschmer	Otto	30	01/05/12		23, 8, 99
	Krieg	Ernst	35	19/11/15		
	Krieg	Johann Otto	37	14/03/19	81	142, 81
	Kriegshammer	Jürgen	40	04/08/22	286	8, 150
k	Krönig	Ernst	25	13/01/05		656
	Kronenbitter	Willy	28	28/03/05	48	3527
	Krüger	Erich	39	21/04/18	382	307
k	Krüger	Jürgen	37	18/07/18	141	141, 631
k	Krüer	Werner		23/11/14	591	590
	Kruschka	Max	37	05/07/19	554, 217	621
	Kühl	Peter	41	19/10/22	565	57
	Kühn	Herbert	39	24/04/19	331, 73, 81	38, 708
	Kühne	Johannes	40	01/01/22		2371
	Kugelberg	Rudolf	39	15/11/17	565	21
k	Kuhlmann	Hans-Günther	37	12/11/13	37	580, 166
k	Kuhlmann	Jürgen	38	03/03/20		1172
	Kuhn	Hans-Joachim	31	04/07/10		1233
	Kuhnke	Günter	31	07/09/12		28, 125
k	Kummer	Heinz	36	25/05/15	754	467
k	Kummetat	Heinz	37	19/11/18	455	572
	Kummetz	Hans-Erich	39	19/08/22	79, 642	235
k	Kuntze	Jürgen	36	12/09/17	40	227
k	Kuppisch	Herbert	33	10/12/09		58, 94, 516, 847
k	Kurrer	Hellmut	35	16/02/16	128	189

OL Friedrich Kloevekorn, commander of U471: a clear image of the officer's reefer jacket, with the Minesweeper War Badge below the submariner's equivalent, marking earlier active service in small surface warships. He later commanded U3012, and survived the war.

KL Lehmann - Willenbrock of U96, wearing here the officer's greatcoat with shoulder straps of rank.

k*	Kusch	Oskar	37	06/04/18	103	154
	Kuscher	Fedor	39	19/01/19		1274, 3515
k	Kutschmann	Günther	29	21/01/11		5, 54
	Kuttkat	Martin	40	18/01/22	468, 740	429
	Lamby	Hermann	36	30/12/13	754, 202, 584	437, 3029
	Landt-Hayen	Martin	39	03/11/20		24, 4705
	Lange	Georg	11	12/10/82		UC1, UF2
k	Lange	Gerhard	37	22/05/20	436	418
k	Lange	Hans	35	29/05/15		61, 261
	Lange	Hans-Günther	37	28/09/16	431	711
p	Lange	Harald		23/12/03	180	180, 505
k	Lange	Helmut	37	31/08/16		72, 1053
k	Lange	Karl-Heinz	37	10/02/18		667
	Lange	Kurt	22	12/08/03		530
	Lange	Richard	40	14/11/12	73	773
k	Langenberg	Bruno	38	10/11/20		366
k	Langfeld	Albert	37	28/01/18	571	444
	Lassen	Georg	35	12/05/15	29	29, 160
	Lau	Kurt	39	04/03/22	953	1197
p	Laubert	Helmut	37	05/04/19	125	38
	Laudahn	Karl-Heinz	39	05/09/15	138, 652	142, 1194, 262
	Lauterbach-Emden	Hans-Jürgen	37	20/05/19	511	539
	Lauth	Hermann	39	10/11/20	959	1005
k	Lauzemis	Albert	37	12/03/18	68	139, 37, 68
p	Lawaetz	Ulf	37	05/11/16	564	672
	Lawrence	Peter	38	04/08/20		328, 2328
	Leder	Joachim	40	26/06/18		4707
	Lehmann	Hans	38	24/09/15	454	997
	Lehmann-Willenbrock	Heinrich	31	11/12/11		8, 5, 96, 256
	von Lehsten	Detlef	37	14/08/17	548	373, 3508
	Leilich	Hans	37	12/02/18		977
k	Leimkuehler	Wolfgang	37	10/08/18	60, 201	4, 225
	Leinenmann	Hannes	28	15/12/08	98	266
k	Leisten	Arno	38	24/12/19	336	346
	Lemcke	Hans	37	09/12/18		327
k	Lemcke	Rudolf	33	08/05/14		210
k	Lemp	Fritz-Julius	31	09/12/13	28	30, 110
	Lenkeit	Paul-Ehrenfried	35	22/06/15		1301
	Lenzmann	Dieter	39	14/09/18	24	24, 3522
k	Lerchen	Kai	33	27/04/11	85	525
	Lessing	Hermann	21	20/10/00		1232
k	Leu	Wolfgang	37	06/07/17	456	921
p	Leupold	Günter	38	11/02/21	355	1059
	Ley	Wolfgang	38	21/06/20	591	61, 310
	Lichtenberg	Philip	28	09/09/08	16, 18, 96, 37, 516*	652
	Liebe	Heinrich	27	29/01/08		38, 2
	Liebe	Johannes	33	08/07/13	48	6, 332
k	Liesberg	Ernst	37	15/06/18	454	962
k	von Lilienfeld	Erich	35	22/11/15	553	661
k	Linck	Gerhard	37	30/05/19		1013
	Lindemann	Kurt	40	31/07/12		1207
	Linder	Gerhard	38	21/03/20		579, 2515,3006,3516
k	Linder	Hans-Heinz	33	11/02/13		18, 202
	Lindke	Siegfried	20	12/12/00	62	142, ?
	Lindschau	Rudolf	36	02/11/14		249, 3017
k	Link	Günther	37	04/03/18	86	240
	Litterscheid	Gerhard	35	10/06/14	554	19, 411
k	Loeder	Herbert	38	03/04/19	380	967, 437, 309
k	Loeschke	Günther	39	30/08/21	264	7
	Loeser	Paul-Karl	35	26/04/15	43, 108	30, 373
	Loewe	Axel-Olaf	28	03/01/09	74	505
k	Loewe	Odo	34	12/09/14		256, 254, 954
k	Lohmann	Dietrich	30	12/10/09		554, 579, 89
p	Lohmeyer	Peter	32	02/01/11	19	19, 138, 651
k	Lohse	Bernhard	32	06/04/13		585
kv	Looff	Hans Günther	25	10/2/06		122
p	Looks	Hartwig	36	27/06/17	375	264
k	Loos	Johann	39	20/04/21	636	248
p	Lorentz	Günther	32	23/10/13		10, 62
p	Lott	Werner	26	03/12/07		25, 32, 35
	Lottner	Ernst	39	15/08/20	92	349, 746
	Lube	Günther	39	19/10/20	254	139, 552
	Lübke	Olaf	37	27/08/19		826
k	Lübsen	Robert	37	30/09/16	98	277
ka	Lüdden	Siegfried	36	20/05/16	141, 129	188
k	Lüders	Günter	38	18/07/20	653	424
	Lüders	Konrad	34	05/01/15	2511	2511, 884
p	Lührs	Dierk	38	18/11/19	596	453
k	Lüssow	Gustav	37	30/12/17	566	571
	Lüth	Günter	37	23/03/17		1057
k*	Lüth	Wolfgang	33	15/10/13	27, 38	9, 138, 43, 181
k	Luis	Wilhelm	35	13/12/15	505	505
p	Luther	Otto	37	18/09/18		135
	Luttmann	Bernhard	39	07/04/21	758	141, 3030
	Lutz	Friedrich	30	09/08/11		485
	Mackeprang	Hans-Peter	35	03/12/11	244	244
p	Mäder	Erich	36	03/10/15	80, 508	378
k	Märtens	Hans	37	30/01/18		243
k	von Mässenhausen	Wilhelm	35	16/01/15	79	258
	Mäueler	Heinrich	40	10/04/20	1204	3020
	Mahn	Bruno	11	03/12/87		UB, UD5
	Mahrholz	Hans-Gert	38	10/10/18	89	309
k	Makowski	Kurt	36	01/09/15	61, 66	78, 619
k	Manchen	Erwin	36	18/06/18		879
k	Mangels	Hinrich	38	24/08/19	636	1200
k	Manhardt von Mannstein	Alfred	25	09/03/08		753
k	Manke	Rolf	35	21/12/15	576	358
k	Mannesmann	Gert		14/10/10	563, 156	545, 2502
	Manseck	Helmut	34	22/12/14	553	143, 758,3002,3007,3...

	Surname	First name		Date			Boats
	Marbach	Karl-Heinz	37	05/07/17	101		29, 28, 953, 3014
	March	Jürgen	33	08/03/19			452
	Marienfeld	Friedrich-Wilhelm	38	01/03/20	205		4, 1228
	Markert	Albrecht	38	10/09/19	107		140
k	Marks	Friedrich-Karl	34	05/06/14	75		376
	Markworth	Friedrich	34	14/02/15	103		66
	Martin	Lothar	37	19/06/16			776
p	Massmann	Hanns Ferdinand	36	25/06/17	17, 137		137, 409
k	Mathes	Ludwig	28	23/11/08			9, 44
k	Matschulat	Gerhard	38	25/05/20	458		247
k	Matthes	Peter	37	09/01/18			326
k	Mattke	Willy	28	25/01/09	62		61, 544
k	Matuschka	Helmut Freiherr von Toppolczan und Spaetgen	3	29/1		482	
			4	2/14			
p	Matz	Joachim	32	01/10/13			6, 59, 70
	Maus	August	34	07/02/15	68		185
	Mayer	Karl-Theodor	39	15/08/21	382		72?
	Meckel	Hans	28	15/02/10			3, 19
	Meenen	Karlheinz	39	12/03/21	30, 188		1192
	Meentzen	Bernhard	38	25/04/15			1272, 3016
	Meermeier	Johannes	37	14/11/16			979
	van Meeteren	Kurt	39	13/03/08			3021
	Mehl	Waldemar	33	07/09/14			62, 72, 371
	Mehne	Karl	37	14/07/14			3027
	Meier	Alfred	39	31/12/07	183		UIT25
	Meinlschmidt	Rudolf	39	01/02/21	223		235, 2544
	Melzer	Volker	39	09/01/18	714		994
	Menard	Karl-Heinz	37	18/10/17			237
	Mengersen	Ernst	33	30/06/12			18, 101, 607
	Merkle	Reinhold	39	10/12/21	516		1201
	Merten	Karl-Friedrich	26	15/08/05			68
k	Methner	Joachim	37	17/05/18	592		423, 1005, 2521
k	Metz	Helmut	35	26/09/06	UA, 129, 373		487
	Metzler	Jost	32	26/02/09			69, 847
k	Meyer	Fritz	34	12/02/16	34		34, 207
	Meyer	Gerhard	35	15/04/15			486
	Meyer	Heinrich	39	08/04/22	154		287
k	Meyer	Herbert	37	30/11/10			804
p	Meyer	Paul	36	27/08/17	505		505
k	Meyer	Rudolf	38	01/02/20			1055
k	Meyer	Willy	36	02/10/12			288
a	Michahelles	Hermann	17?	18/05/99			2, 36, 35
d	Michalowski	Hand-Bernhard	33	13/04/12			62
	Michel	Georg-Heinz	-33	19/09/09			54, 8
k	Miede	Heinrich	35	04/03/15	1274		56
k	von Mittelstaedt	Gert	32	14/01/12			144
	Möglich	Hans	35	29/01/16	130		526
	Möhle	Karl-Heinz	30	31/07/10			20, 123
	Möhlmann	Helmut	33	25/06/13			143, 571
	Möllendorff	Goske von	37	12/03/18	196		235, 148, 38
k	Möller	Günther	37	30/06/18	989		141, 844
k	Mohr	Eberhard	35	12/10/15	111		148, 133
k	Mohr	Johann	34	12/06/16			124
	Mohr	Kurt	40	12/01/22			930
	Mohs	Hans-Dieter	37	22/09/19	203		5, 60, 956
	Mokowski	Kurt	36	01/09/15			619
	von Morstein	Hans-Joachim	28	01/08/09			483
	von Müffling	Hans-Bruno Freiherr	38	24/09/19	263, 952		76, 2545
	von Mühlendahl	Arved	23	01/11/04			867
k	von Mühlenpfordt	Karl	40	27/06/09	86		308
k	Müller	Bernhard	37	10/10/16	584		633
	Müller	Hans-Georg	36	14/03/16	69		662
p	Müller	Heinz-Eberhard	40	15/10/22	276, 596		2349
k	Müller	Rudolf	37	17/06/17	509, 91		282
	Müller	Werner	39	04/08/20	239, 953, 1167		953, 2327
	Müller	Willi	39	25/04/12			1000, 3523
	Müller-Arnecke	Wilhelm	-33	30/10/10			19 ?
k	Müller-Bethke	Erich	37	23/07/17			1278
	Müller-Edzards	Heinrich	-33	18/03/10			590
	Müller-Feldhammer	Name adopted after the war:See Müller,Werner					
	Müller-Koebl	Harro	38	17/10/19			3051
k	Müller-Stöckheim	Günther	34	17/12/13			64
k	Münnich	Ralph	35	11/02/16	106		187
	Münster	Helmut	37	14/09/16			101, 428, 3201, 3517
	Münster	Rolf	32	23/06/13			10, 203
	Mürl	Heinrich	32	11/02/12			2327
ka	Mützelburg	Rolf	32	23/06/13			10, 100 planned, 203
k	Mugler	Gustav-Adolf	31	10/10/12			41
k	Muhs	Harald	38	01/10/19			674
k	Mumm	Friedrich	36	15/01/15	564		52, 594
	Mumm	Herbert	39	03/09/20	354		4, 236
	Musenberg	Werner	25	24/09/04			180
	Muths	Werner	30	26/02/12	37, 32, 124		32, 124, ?
	Nachtigall	Richard	37	24/09/14			1171, 3513
k	Nagel	Karl-Heinz	37	17/01/17	586		640
	Neckel	Herbert	35	14/08/16	30, 108		531
	Nees	Werner	28	20/07/11			363
	Neide	Kurt	36	08/07/16	134		415
	Neitzel	Karl	23	30/01/01			510
	Neitzsch	Wilhelm	39	14/05/20	518, 3509		3509
	Neubert	Kurt	36	24/03/10	126		167
k	Neuerburg	Helmut	36	25/08/17			869
k	Neumann	Hans-Werner	25	03/09/06			72, 117
k	Neumann	Heinz-Joachim	30	29/04/09			372, 371
p	Neumann	Hermann	38	07/09/19			3057
	Neumeister	Hermann	40	04/01/23	306, 281		3, 291
k	Ney	Günter	39	27/03/22	431		283
	Ney	Johannes	40	16/06/22	739		739

	Surname	First name		Date		
	Nicolay	Kurt-Heinz	37	06/10/17	163	312
	Nielsen	Karl	35	30/09/11		370
	Niemeyer	Heinrich	39	15/06/10	515	547
	Niester	Erich	39	19/09/21	617	350
	Niethmann	Otto	38	12/08/19		6, 476, 3507
	Niss	Hellmut	23	08/03/06		1275, 2531
k	Nissen	Jürgen	36	28/05/16		146, 105
k	Nölke	Kurt	35	05/09/14	82	20, 263
	Nollau	Herbert	36	23/03/16	505	534
k	Nollmann	Rolf	36	29/12/14		1199
d	Nolte	Gerhard	39	23/01/22	648	1194, 704
	Nonn	Victor-Wilhelm	37	02/04/17	97	152, 596
	Nordheimer	Hubert	36	03/02/17	206	237, 990, 2512
	Oehrn	Victor	27	21/10/07		14, 37
	Oelrich	Adolf	35	15/03/16	568	92
	Oesten	Jürgen	33	24/10/13		61, 106, 861
k	Oestermann	Johannes	33	19/05/13		151, 754
k	Offermann	Hans	39	02/07/21	129	518
i	Ohlenburg	Willy	34	12/03/15	19	19
	Ohling	Klaus	37	04/02/18	51 or 511	965
k	Ohlsen	Prosper	36	16/01/18	218	855
k	Oldörp	Hans-Jürgen	35	23/06/11	558	90
	Opitz	Herbert	34	07/03/15	25, 7, 22	206
k	Otto	Hermann	34	30/05/14	408	449
	Otto	Paul-Friedrich	37	03/04/17	136	270, 2525
	Otto	Walter	37	11/03/17	436	285
k	Paepenmöller	Klaus	37	25/02/18	134	973
	Pahl	Hans-Walter	38	16/08/19		2331, 2327
	Pahls	Heinrich	39 ?	13/12/19	511	UIT24
k	Palmgren	Gerhard	38	11/11/19	441	741
k	Panitz	Johannes	37	14/08/13		1065
k	Parduhn	Paul	37	27/11/18		1107
	Paucke	Karl-Wilhelm	38	04/10/15	402	242
	Pauckstadt	Hans	26	27/09/06		193
k	Paulschen	Ottokar	34	11/10/15	26, 18	20, 557
k	Pelkner	Hans-Hermann	35	16/04/09		335
	Perleberg	Rüdiger	33	09/03/13		1104
	Peschel	Otto	34	28/08/15		3004
	Peters	Georg	4	03/03/88		38
	Peters	Gerhard	39	14/12/21	410	1198
	Peters	Wilhelm	37	20/06/16		96, 999,3045,3001
	Petersen	Klaus	36	13/01/17	563	14, 24, 9, 3042
	Petersen	Kurt	36	20/09/16	146, UB, 371	541
	Petersen	Theodor	34	14/01/14	43, 181	612, 874
	Petran	Friedrich	38	06/12/19	178	516
	Pfeffer	Günther	34	23/10/14		67, 171, 170, 548
p	Pfeiffer	Werner	33	02/05/12	138	56, 58
p	Pich	Helmut	34	26/06/14	103 ?	168
	Pick	Ewald	34	27/05/12		481, 1025
	Piening	Adolf	30	16/09/10	48	155
k	Pietsch	Ulrich	36	05/12/15	373	344
k	Pietschmann	Walter	37	31/07/19	377	712, 762
p	Pietzsch	Werner	35	30/04/17	123	523
	Piwowarsky	Wolfgang	32	07/07/07	2534	?
	Plohr	Helmut	33	02/12/13	145, 371	149
	Poel	Gustav	36	02/08/17		413
k	Poeschel	Wolfgang	38	25/03/20	28, 604	737, 422
k	von Pommer-Esche	Gerd	37	22/01/18	159	160
	Pommerehne	Walter	31	04/04/08		866
	Popp	Klaus	35	30/05/17		140, 552
p	Poser	Günter	36	23/09/16	432	59, 202
	Poske	Fritz	23	23/10/04		504
	Praetorius	Friedrich-Hermann	34	28/02/04		135
	Pregel	Siegfried	42	02/02/15		323
	Prehn	Wilhelm	34	23/12/14	97	3034
p	Prellberg	Wilfried	33	18/10/13	34	19, 31
k	Premauer	Rudolf	37	08/05/11	510	857
k	Pressel	Kurt	30	01/04/11	56, 5	5, 951
	Preuss	Georg	36	30/12/16	433	1224, 875
p	Preuss	Joachim	33	30/05/14	UA	10, 568
k	Prien	Günter	-33	16/01/08		47
	Prützmann	Robert	24	04/05/03		30
	Przikling	Huertus - Adopted the name Purkhold during the war.				
k	von Pückler und Limburg	Wilhelm or Walter-Heinrich Graf	34	09/03/13	101	381
	Pulst	Günther	37	26/03/18		978
	Purkhold	Hubertus	35	06/06/15		14
	Puschmann	Hans-Friedrich	39	07/06/22	410, 385	748
k	von Puttkammer	Konstantin	36	31/07/17	146, 46	443
p	Quaet-Faslem	Jürgen	34	25/05/13	98	595
	Queck	Horst-Thilo	35	09/01/15	372	622, 92, 2522
k	Raabe	Ernst	26	05/02/07		246
	Raabe	Karl-Heinz	38	23/05/20		1161, 1007
p	von Rabenau	Georg	36	03/07/08	504	528
k	von Rabenau	Wolf-Rüdiger	33	07/01/08		10, 52, 702
	Racky	Ernst-August	38	01/09/19		52, 429, 3019
k	Rademacher	Erwald	37	01/12/17		772
k	Rademacher	Rudolf	37	19/02/19		478
	Radermacher	Alfred	33	13/09/13		120, 393
ka	Radke	Hans-Jürgen	28	10/01/16		148, 657
k	Rahe	Heinz	36	15/03/16	73	257
k	Rahlf	Peter	39	07/03/09		317
p	Rahmlow	Hans-Joachim	28	18/10/09	48	58, 570
k	Rahn	Hermann	38	14/10/18	83	5
k	Rahn	Wolfgang	38	31/10/20	458	343
	Ranzau	Emil	39	04/06/08		71
	von Rappard	Konstantin	36	13/06/17	103	560, 2324
	Rasch	Hermann	34	26/08/14	106	106
k	Rasch	Karl-Heinz	34	06/04/14		296

	Surname	First name		Date		
p	Rathke	Hellmut	30	03/12/10		352
k	Ratsch	Heinrich	34	18/10/14	38	28, 583
	Rauch	Dietrich	36	18/12/16	107	141, 868
	Rave	Ernst-Wolfgang	37	09/09/17	105	554, 3002 ?
	Reche	Reinhardt	34	13/12/15	751	255
	Reckhoff	Johann	28	15/01/11		398
	Reeder	Günther	35	02/11/15	58	7, 214
k	Reese	Hans-Jürgen	37	27/04/18	561	420
p	Reff	Reinhard	37	07/09/13	453	736
	Rehren	Hellmuth	39	04/03/22	529, 564, 998	926
	Rehwinkel	Ernst-August		30/10/01		578
k	Reich	Christian	36	21/11/15	202	416, 426
	von Reiche	Heinz	29	18/03/08		17
k	Reichenbach-Klinke	Kurt	35	21/02/17	57	23, 217
k	Reichmann	Wilfried	34	10/09/05		153
	Reimann	Ernst	39	09/09/20	953	3050
k	Reimers	Hans	-40	19/10/16	454	983, 722
p	Reisener	Wolfgang	38	13/10/18	223	608
	Reith	Hans-Edwin	39	17/01/20	105, 190	190
	Remus	Gerhard	36	10/05/16	652	2364
	Remus	Werner	39	26/09/19	406	339, 554
k	Rendtel	Horst	36	27/11/16	202	555, 641
	Reschke	Franz-Georg	29	26/05/08	94	205
	Rex	Herbert	37	27/08/18		
	Rex	Wilhelm	35	26/10/10	680	1405
k	Richard	Hellmut	36	02/03/17	453	446
	Richter	Freimut	39	29/11/29	517, 639, 302, 564	2547
k	Riecken	Werner	34	08/06/12		1017
k	Riedel	Heinrich or Heinz	39	30/12/21	612, 230	242
k	Rieger	Eberhard	40	?/?/23	201, 564	4, 416
	Rieger	Hubert	39	26/05/20		4
k	Riekeberg	Wolfgang	37	14/10/18		1054, 637
	van Riesen	Friedrich	38	09/07/11		1109
k	Riesen	Rolf	38	18/12/19		180
	Rigele	Hermann	9	16/09/91		UD1, UD3
	Rinck	Hans	41	02/06/12		1019
k	Ringelmann	Helmuth	31	21/04/12		75
	Rix	Robert	39	20/03/07		58, 96
	Robbert	Heinz	39	20/08/16	107	3040
k	Rodig	Johannes	36	24/03/17		878
k	Rodler von Roithberg	Hardo	37	14/02/18	96	24, 71, 989
	Roeder-Pesch	Hans	37	25/04/14	86	1167
p	Römer	Wolfgang	36	22/10/16	52, 103	56, 353
	Rösing	Hans Rudolf	24	22/09/05		48
	Röther	Josef	27	07/10/07		380
k	Röttger	Helmut	37	15/12/18	203	715
k	Rogowsky	Peter	38	10/06/19	595, 185, UF2, 552	866
	Rohlfing	Karl-Heinz	35	22/11/10	1193	4712
k	Rollmann	Siegfried	34	13/09/14	52	82
k	Rollmann	Wilhelm	26	05/08/07		34, 848
	Roost	Werner				926
k	von der Ropp	Dietrich	29	27/07/09		12
ka	Rosenbaum	Helmut	32	11/05/13		2, 73
k	Rosenberg	Günther	36	19/01/17	372	351, 201
k	von Rosenberg-Gruszczynski	Hans-Achim	37	04/06/17	37	18, 384
k	von Rosenstiel	Jürgen	33	23/11/12	38	143, 502
k	Rossmann	Hermann	37	23/07/18	582	52, 273
k	Rostin	Erwin	33	08/10/07		158
	Roth	Goetz	38	19/12/19		351, 748, 1232
	von Rothkirch und Panthen	Siegfried	38	23/10/19	407, 604	717
k	Rudloff	Klaus	35	24/01/16	559	609
	Rudolph	Johannes	37	24/04/16		155, 2552
	Rüggeberg	Rolf	26	04/03/07	107	513
	Ruperti	Günter	39	07/07/14		777, 3039
k	Ruppelt	Günther	37	13/09/19		579, 356
k	Ruwiedel	Kurt	36	18/09/17		337
ka	Saar	Franz	38	12/12/19	202	46, 555, 30, 957
	Sach	Heinrich	38	28/04/13	374	3031
k	Sachse	Dietrich or Dieter	39	22/08/17	413	1162, 28, 413
	Säck	Franz	28	31/12/09	120, 552	251
	Salman	Otto	32	05/07/08		7, 52
k	Sammler	Karl-Heinz	37	15/01/19	66	59, 675
	Sander	Paul	38	05/10/08	25, 103	4, 38, 72
k	Sass	Paul-Heinrich	39	03/10/19	757	364
k	Sass	Werner	37	16/01/16	171, 554, 525	676
	Sauer	Heinz	39	07/04/15	592	673
k	Sauerberg	Ernst	34	11/01/14	515	1225
k*	Sauerbier	Joachim	39	25/09/19		120, 56, 251
k	Sausmikat	Werner	37	07/10/17	371	56, 1103, 774
	Schaafhausen	Ludwig	37	30/11/13	565	369
	Schaar	Gerd	37	05/03/19	704	957, 2551
k	Schacht	Harro	26	15/12/07		507
k	Schad von Mittelbiberach	Berchtold	36	01/09/16		2342
	Schäfer	Friedrich	14	28/02/93		UD4
kd	Schäfer	Heinrich	25	30/01/07		183, UIT23
	Schäfer	Heinz	39	28/04/21	445	148, 977
k	Schaefer	Wolf-Axel	30	03/03/11		484
	Schäfer	Wolfgang	39	04/04/22		368, 3018?
	Schaiper	Wolfgang known as Wolfgang Schäfer				
p	Schamong	Klemens	37	15/04/17	333	468
	Schattenburg	Johannes	39	16/05/22	968	1272
	Schauenburg	Günther	39	26/04/20	621	793
k	Schauenburg	Herbert	31	29/05/12		20, 577
p	Schauenburg	Rolf	34	30/05/13		536
	Schauer	Werner	40	10/09/22	616, 369	2350
	Schauroth	Karl	40	11/07/21	228	142, 146
	Scheer	Werner	12	06/06/93		25?
k	Scheibe	Hans-Martin	36	17/04/18	431	72, 455

KL Werner Schulte of U582, and his Engineering Officer LT(Ing) Karl Cords.

	Scheltz	Hans-Ulrich	34	15/11/09		UD5
k	Schendel	Eberhard	39	06/06/20	758	636
	Schendel	Rudolf	32	10/01/14		19, 134, 2509
k	Schepke	Joachim	30	08/03/12	13	3, 19, 100
	Scherfling	Wolfgang	40	29/06/23	518, 548	140
p	Scheringer	Heinz	27	29/08/07		13, 26
	Scherraus	Ekkehard	38	01/10/19	507, 107, 68	1225
k	Schetelig	Robert	37	06/10/18	87	229
	Schewe	Georg	-30	24/11/09		60, 105
	Schewe	Peter	34	03/12/13	48, 378	537
	Schiebusch	Günter	33	26/10/09		252
	Schild	Hans-Juerg	38	13/05/20		924
	Schimmel	Günther	39	13/08/20	711	137, 30, 382
k	Schimmelpfennig	Hertmuth	37	04/10/19	586	1004
	Schimpf	Karl		23/03/14	514	803, 3009
	Schley	Hans-Jürgen	39	20/10/20	563	59, 351, 3507
k	Schlieper	Alfred	34	15/01/15	96	208
	von Schlippenbach	Egon Reiner Freiherr	34	10/04/14	18, 101	121, 453
	Schlitt	Karl-Adolf	37	16/04/18		1206
	Schlömer	Fokko	28	25/08/09		1164, 3008
	Schlott	Heinrich	40	10/07/22		2329
p	Schmandt	Adalbert	40	26/12/09		489
k	Schmid	Heinrich or Hermann	34	22/05/15	555	7, 663
	Schmidt	Friedrich	39	01/06/21	732, 129, 190	793
	Schmidt	Karl-Heinz	36	20/01/11	351, 211	17, 37, 3526
k	Schmidt	Werner	26	17/04/06		12, 15, 25, 40, 116
p	Schmidt	Werner-Karl		15/04/15		250
	von Schmidt	Werner	39	11/07/20	84	292
	Schmidt-Rösemann	See Schmidt, Karl-Heinz (Name changed after the war.)				
	Schmidt-Weichert	Hans-Joachim	36	07/05/15	95	9
	Schmoeckel	Helmut	36	18/12/17	504	802
	Schnee	Adalbert	34	31/12/13	23	6, 60, 201, 2511
k	Schneewind	Fritz	36	10/04/17	506	511, 183
k	Schneider	Herbert	34	25/06/12	123	552
	Schneider	Manfred	39	11/12/20		4706
	Schneidewind	Hermann	36	07/03/07		1064
k	Schnoor	Ebe	15	22/06/95	153, 108	UA, 460
	Schöler	Clemens	36	30/05/15	564	20, 24, 20
k	Schönberg	Adolf	37	07/08/18		62, 404
k	Schöneboom	Dietrich	37	04/12/17	205	58, 431
k	Schötzau	Gerhard	36	16/04/17		880
	Scholle	Hans-Ulrich	38	30/09/09	388, 985	2328, 328
	Scholtz	Klaus	27	22/03/08		108
	Scholz	Günther	38	27/02/19	371	284, UD2, 1052
	Scholz	Hans-Ulrich	40	07/05/11	101	4703
d	Scholz	Heinz-Günther	37	12/01/18	172	283
	Schomburg	Heinz	35	28/09/14	78, 561	145, 561
	Schomburg	Oskar		19/08/97		26
k	Schonder	Heinrich	35	23/07/10	51	58, 77, 200
k	Schramm	Joachim	36	03/06/16	109	109
p	Schreiber	Gerd	31	02/04/12		3, 95
p	Schreiber	Heinrich	37	30/04/17		270
	Schrein	Herbert	37	30/05/17	UIT25, 183, 219	UIT25
k	Schreiner	Wolfgang	37	20/04/17	593	417
	Schrenk	Hans	37	18/09/17	593	7, 901
	Schrenk	Hermann	37	19/06/18	178	3511
k	Schrewe	Peter	34	05/12/13	48, 378	537
k	Schreyer	Hilmar	33	28/08/14	558	987
	Schrobach	Kurt	35	11/09/14	596	2360
	Schröder	Gustav	39	06/07/21	184, 311	1056
	Schröder	Heinrich	36	25/01/16	385, 155	2367
k	Schröder	Hermann	37	07/04/12	751	623
	Schroeteler	Heinrich	36	10/12/15		667, 1023
	von Schroeter	Horst	37	10/06/19	123	123, 2506
k	Schroeter	Karl-Ernst	34	03/12/12	9, 78	121, 752
	Schröter	Karl-Heinz	39	13/03/21	603	1195, 763, 3062
k	Schrott	Karl	32	25/03/11		7, 551
	Schubert or Schubart	Albrecht	36	19/07/14		1002, 2520
	Schuch	Heinrich	25	28/08/06		37, 38, 105, 154
k	Schüler	Philipp	35	17/01/11	100	141, 602
	Schüler	Wolf-Harald	39	22/08/21	123	720, 2325
k	Schümann	Henning	36	24/11/15	402	392
	Schünemann	Horst	34	02/01/14	71	62, 621
	Schütt	Heinz	36	24/11/15		294
k	Schütze	Herbert-Viktor	35	24/02/17	77	605
	Schütze	Viktor	25	16/02/06		11, 25, 103
k	Schug	Walter	34	22/10/10	74	86
p	Schuhart	Otto	29	01/04/09		29
p	Schulte	Max	33	24/09/15	9	9, 13
k	Schulte	Werner	37	07/11/12		98, 582
	Schultz	Dietrich	40	05/11/19	284	4708
	Schultz	Hermann	38	07/02/20	209	150, 3502
k	Schultz	Karl-Otto	34	09/11/14	22	34, 216
k	Schultze	Heinz-Otto	34	13/09/15	31	4, 141, 432, 849
	Schultze	Herbert	30	24/07/09		48, 48
	Schultze	Rudolf	39	19/05/22	608	61, 2540
k	Schultze	Wolfgang	30	03/10/10		17, 512
	Schulz	Hermann	34	22/04/13	255	2389, 2367
	Schulz	Richard	39	20/09/17	636	58
	Schulz	Werner	30	28/09/19		929
	Schulz	Werner-Karl	28	25/10/10		437
	Schulz	Wilhelm	-32	10/03/06		10, 64, 124
	Schulze	Wilhelm	28	27/07/09	71	177, 98
	Schumann-Hindenberg	Friedrich	32	28/03/13		245
	Schunck	Hans-Norbert	38	31/03/20	554, 660, 377	348, 103, 369
k	Schwaff	Werner	36	03/03/15	654	2, 333, 440

	Surname	First name		Date		
	Schwager	Erwin	37	09/01/17	573, 404	143
	Schwalbach	Bruno	37	11/09/17	3508	1161
k	Schwantke	Hans-Joachim	36	30/08/18		43
k	Schwarting	Bernhard	36	30/01/13		1102, 905
k	Schwartzkopff	Volkmar	34	25/04/14		520
	Schwarz	Hans-Joachim	38	28/09/19		1105
	Schwarz	Rudolf	36	19/07/14	471	1056
k	Schwarzenberg	Hans-Dietrich	40	23/05/23	711	579
	Schwarzkopf	Wolfgang	39	10/01/21	605	2, 21, 704
k	Schwassmann	Heinz	35	03/02/16	753	742
k	Schwebcke	Hans-Joachim	37	22/03/18		714
k	Schweichel	Hand-Adolf	36	26/05/15		173
	Schweiger	Friedhelm	37	07/03/17	125	313
	Schwirley	Ernst-Werner	39	07/06/19	413	982, 3510
	Seeger	Joachim	39	11/02/12		393
	Seeger	Sigurd	39	06/07/20	560, 382	348, 1203
k	Seehausen	Gerhard	37	29/07/17	518	68, 66
	Seeliger	Edgar	40	27/07/20	956	4702
k	Seibicke	Günther	32	30/08/11		436
k	Seidel	Hans	37	15/05/18	203	203, 361
	Seiler	Wolfgang	39	04/08/18		37
	Sell	Erwin	40	03/05/15	4	1102
	Selle	Horst	39	14/02/21	255	795
k	Senkel	Hans	33	04/01/10		658
k	Sickel	Herbert	35	30/06/14	73	302
	Siebold	Karl-Hartwig	36	19/03/17	66, 557?	554, 3504
k	Sieder	Heinz	38	28/06/20	440	984
	Siegman	Paul	35	24/05/13		230, 2507
k	Siemon	Hilmar	34	29/03/15	97	334, 396
	Simmermacher	Volker	37	01/02/19		107, 3013
k*	Singule	Rudolf	1	08/04/83		UD4
k	Sitek	Walter	39	05/01/13	581	17, 981
	Slevogt	Horst	39	04/07/22		62, 3032
k	Sobe	Ernst	24	02/09/04		179
k	von Soden-Fraunhofen	Ulrich Graf	36	02/08/13	552	624
	Sohler	Herbert	28	25/07/08		10, UB, 46
	Sommer	Helmuth	35	24/08/14		139, 78, 853
k	Sons	Friedrich	40	14/08/10		479
	Spahr	Wilhelm	21	04/04/04	47, 178	178
p	Speidel	Hans Harald	36	20/05/17	81	634
k	Spindlegger	Johann	35	31/07/15	561	616, 411
	Sporn	Wolfgang	34	12/09/12		439
k	Staats	Georg	35	13/03/16	5, UA	80, 508
	Stahler	Hellmut	37	08/09/16		928
k	Stahl	Peter	38	01/08/13	575	648
k	Stark	Günther	36	01/02/17	653	740
k	Staudinger	Oskar	36	13/05/17		638
k	Steen	Hans	25	29/09/07	117	233
	Steffen	Karl	40	16/10/09	1132	2345
k	Steffens	Klaus-Dietrich	37	17/06/18	373	719
	Stege	Friedrich	39	12/11/20	212	291, 397, 958
k	Stegemann	Hasso	39	30/07/20	1227	367
	Stegmann	Hans	35	05/03/12		779
k	Stein	Heinz	37	21/08/13	24, 8, 139, 98	554, 620
k	von Steinaecker	Walter Freiherr	35	25/03/17	130	524
	Steinbrinck	Erich	38	13/03/19		1203, 296?,293,953
p	Steinert	Hermann	36	10/12/16	155	128
	Steinfeld					UIT25
	Steinfeldt	Friedrich	40	15/12/14	371	195
	Steinhaus	Rolf		01/04/16	101	8, 802
s*	Steinhoff	Friedrich	35	14/07/09	96?	511, 873
k	Steinmetz	Karl-Heinz	39	19/02/21		993, 714
k	Stellmacher	Dietrich	39	27/03/15		865
	Stellmann	Ernst-August	35	19/04/15	956	2541
	Stephan	Karl-Heinz	36	18/09/15		1063
k	Sternberg	Heinz	36	16/02/17	659	473
	Stever	Ehrenreich	37	04/10/18		1277
k	Sthamer	Hans-Jürgen	37	26/07/19	593, 604, 91	354
p	Stiebler	Wolf	32	04/08/07		8, 17, 21,61, 461
	van Stipriaan	Johannes	40	09/12/13	539	237, 3046
k	Stock	Hans	35	02/08/15	96	659
	Stock	Rupprecht	37	16/02/16	214	214, 218
ka	von Stockhausen	Hans-Gerrit	26	11/08/07		13, 65
	Stoeffler	Otto	39	12/03/10		475
	Stoelker	Gerhard	39	26/05/10		825
	Stolzenburg	Gottfried	38	08/12/12		11, 2543
k	Sträter	Wolfgang	35	21/05/16		20, 83, 614
k	Straub	Siegfried	39	22/06/18	652	625
	Strauch	Günter	34	05/12/08		1010
	Strehl	Hugo	39	05/10/21	3507	351
k	Strehlow	Siegfried	31	15/04/11		435
	Strenger	Hartmut	36	12/01/17		290
	Strenger	Wolfgang	37	09/02/19	553	10, 1023
kv	Striegler	Werner	37	30/06/18	511	UIT25, UIT23,196
	Struckmeier	Rolf			205	608
k	Strübing	Werner	42	25/05/07		UD4?, 1003
k	Stuckmann	Hermann	39	02/01/21	571	316, 621
k	Studt	Bruno	39	06/04/18	108, 459	488
	Stührmann	Günter	40	11/03/22	453	904
	Sturm	Kurt	25	30/01/06		410, 167, 547
	Suerenhagen	Albert	36	25/03/16	593	855
k	Sues	Peter	38	26/09/19	204, 558	388
	Süss	Walter	40	27/10/08	1210	1210?, 1304
	Suhren	Reinhard	35	16/04/16	48	564
	Sureth	Kurt	39	08/07/22	625	625, 2549
	Tammen	Renko	41	21/12/22	380, 967	148
	Taschenmacher	Erich	38	01/11/19		775
	Techand	Werner	37	21/01/19	135	731
k	Teichert	Max-Martin	34	31/01/15	94	456

	Surname	First name		Date		
	Thäter	Gerhard	36	18/11/16		466, 3506
	Thiel	Gernot	40	13/05/22	305, 763	152
	Thienemann	Sven	39	04/12/12		682, 1271
	Thilo	Ulrich	22	04/01/03		174
	Thimme	Jürgen	37	26/09/17	214, 294	276, 714
	Thomsen	Rolf	36	06/05/15		1202
	Thurmann	Helmut	35	05/01/15		1234, 3004
k	Thurmann	Karl	28	04/09/09		29, 553
p	von Tiesenhausen	Hans-Diedrich Freiherr	34	22/02/13	23, 93	331
	Tiesler	Raimund	37	07/03/19	578	649, 976, 2503
	Tillessen	Hans-Rutger	34	16/04/13	506	516
	Timm	Heinrich	33	30/04/10		251, 862
	Tinschert	Otto	35	02/03/15	97	267, 650, 3010?,3011,903
k	von Tippelskirch	Helmut	37	07/12/17	160	439
k	Todenhagen	Diether	37	22/07/20	703	48, 1008, 365
	Topp	Erich	34	02/07/14	46,	57, 552,2513,3010
k	Trojer	Hans	36	22/01/16	34, 67	3, 221
k	von Trotha	Claus	36	25/03/14	81	554, 306
kv	von Trotha	Wilhelm	36	07/08/16	582	733, 745
k	Trox	Hans-Georg	36	21/01/16	83	97
	Turre	Eduard	39	31/01/20	530	868
	Uebel	Johannes		15/04/01		883
	Ufermann	Friedrich	38	06/10/12		2368
k	Uhl	Georg	39	04/01/15	512, 592	269
p	Uhlig	Herbert	35	27/02/16	105	527
	Ulber	Max	35	12/10/16	358	680
	Ulbing	Willibald	39	19/08/20	129	2347
	Umlauf	Hans	37	29/01/18	270	1168
	Unterhorst	Ernst-Günther	37	05/04/19	403, 359	394, 396
k	Unverzagt	Günter	39	03/05/21	307	965
k	Uphoff	Horst	35		46	84
	Utischill	Karl-Erich	39	25/02/21	37, 565	151, 2548
p	Valentiner	Hans-Guido	37	12/01/19	584	385
k	von Varendorff	Amelung	35	20/12/13	47	213
	Vernier	Franz	12	15/6/93	UD3	UD1, UD2
i	Verpoorten	Hubert	40	07/09/22	23	19
	Vieth	Joachim	36	10/01/16		3041
k	Vockel	Jürgen	41	19/09/22	198, 969	2336
	Vöge	Ulrich	38	05/11/19		239, 2536
	Vogel	Hans	37	22/05/18	453	143, 3001, 3025
k	Wolfbauer	Leo	13	21/07/95		463
	Wolff	Günter	39	31/01/20	441	2550
	Wolff	Heinz	37	13/03/18	437	974, 985, 3534
	Wolff	Karl-Heinz	28	16/10/09		509
k	Wolfram	Ralf-Reimar	30	31/03/12		108, 864
	Wollschläger	Otto	22	31/03/02		17, UC1, UC2, 721
	Wrede	Hans-Christian	39	09/08/20	448	1234
	Würdemann	Erich	33	15/01/14		506
	Wüst	Helmuth	39	31/07/20	307	146
k	Wulff	Heinrich	40	11/02/08	584	646
k	Wunderlich	Karl	41	28/05/11	106, 29, 628	UIT22
k	Wysk	Gerhard	38	02/05/20		322
	Zahn	Wilhelm	30	29/07/10		56, 69
	Zahnow	Günter	39	05/06/20	167, 547	747
	Zander	Hermann	29	28/07/10		1205
k	Zander	Joachim	36	20/04/17	201	3, 311
k	Zapf	Werner	36	23/07/15		61
	Zapp	Richard	26	03/04/04		66
	Zaubitzer	Joachim	37	28/04/18		974, ?
	Zech	Alois	25	14/09/07		119
	Zedelius	Günther	35	19/05/15	130	639
	Zehle	Dietrich	39	19/09/21	360	?
	Zeissler	Herbert	38	17/09/20	373, 30, 338	1192, 140, 1194
	Zenker	Walter	31	02/01/14	17, 553	57, 393, 3535
p	Zeplien	Walter	37	17/09/18	575	971
	Zetzsche	Hans-Jürgen	34	05/10/15	28, 10	20, 4, 560, 591
k	Ziehm	Ernst	33	20/07/14		78, 232
p	Ziesmer	Reimar	37	23/11/17	98, 38	145, 236, 591
	Zimmermann	Eberhard	37	27/10/16	130	351, 548
k	Zimmermann	Gero	29	28/06/10	124	401
k	Zimmermann	Heinrich	33	27/01/07		136
k	Zinke	Armin	33	30/07/08		1229
	Zippel	Rudolf		12/09/14		2540 ?
k	von Zitzewitz	Alexander	34	23/03/16		706
	Zoller	Herbert	38	19/05/19	569	3, 315
	Zorn	Rudolf	37	20/07/17	456	29, 419, 382, 650
	Zschech	Peter	36	01/10/18		505
	Zurmühlen	Bernhard	34	23/02/09	331	600
	Zwarg	Heinz	37	22/11/17	97	416, 276, 3528

Appendix 3: **U-boats and their Commanders**

Each entry gives the number of the boat followed by its class; and the names of successive commanders, with dates during wartime.

U1 IIA
KK Ewerth, KL Gelhaar, KL Loof, KL Grosse, KK J. Deecke 10/38-4/40

U2 IIA
KK Michahelles, KK Liebe, KL Rosenbaum 3/39-7/40, OL Heidtmann 7/40-8/40, KL von Wilamowitz-Moellendorff 8/40-10/41, OL Kölzer 10/41-5/42, OL Schwaff 5/42-11/42, Herglott 11/42-12/43, OL. Schwarzkopf 12/43-4/44

U3 IIA
KK Meckel, KK Heinricke, KL Rosenbaum, KL Schepke 10/38-1/40, KL Schreiber 1/40-7/40, KL Franzke 7/40-11/40, KL von Bülow 11/40- 7/41, OL Trojer 7/41-3/42, OL Zander 3/42-9/42, OL Zoller 10/42- 5/43, OL Hartmann 5/43-6/44, OL Neumeister 6/44-8/44

U4 IIA
KK Weingaertner, KL von Kloth-Heydenfeldt 10/38-1/40, OL Hinsch 1/40-6/40, KL Schultze 6/40-7/40, OL Zetzschke 7/40-2/41, OL Bernbeck 2/41-12/41, OL Leimkühler 12/41-6/42, OL Marienfeld 6/42-1/43, LT Düppe 1/43-5/43, OL Sander 5/43-8/43, OL Mumm 8/43-5/44, LT Rieger 5/44-7/44

U5 IIA
KK Dau, KK Glattes, KL Kutschmann 1/38-12/39, KL Lehmann- Willenbrock 12/39-8/40, OL Bothe 8/40-1/42, OL Friedrich 1/42- 3/42, OL Mohs 3/42-9/42, OL Pressel 9/42-11/42, LT Jestel 4/44-7/44

U6 IIA
KK Mathes, KL Heidel, KL Matz 12/38-11/39, OL Michalowski 11/39- 12/39, OL Harms 12/39-1/40, OL Schnee 1/40-6/40, KL Peters 6/40- 7/40, OL Liebe 7/40-3/41, KL Bobst 3/41-9/42, LT Brünninghaus 9/42-10/42, OL Niethmann 10/42-6/43, OL König 6/43-4/44, LT Jestel 4/44-7/44

U7 IIB
KK Freiwald, OL Salman 5/39-11/39, OL Heidel for short period 7- 8/39, KL Schrott 11/39-10/40, OL Reeder 10/40-1/41, OL Brüller 1/41-2/41, OL Reeder 2/41-3/41, OL Kuhlmann 3/41-5/41, OLSchmid 5/41-1/42, OL Koitschka 1/42-10/42, OL Schrenk 10/42-1/44, OL Loeschke 1/44-2/44

U8 IIB
KL Grosse, KL Peters 6/38-9/39, KL Stiebler 9-10/39, KL Lehmann-Willenbrock 10-11/39, KL Michel 12/39-5/40, KL Kentrat 5-9/40, OL Kell 9-12/40, KL Heinsohn 12/40-5/41, KL Borcherdt 5/41, OL Steinhaus 6-7/41, OL Deckert 8/41-5/42, OL Hoffmann 6/42-3/43, OL Werner 3/43-5/44, OL Iversen 5-11/44, OL Kriegshammer 11/44-3/45

U9 IIB
KK Looff, KL Mathes 10/37-9/39, OL Schulte 9-12/39, OL Lüth 12/39-6/40, KL Kaufmann 6-10/40, KL Deecke 10/40-6/41, KL Schmidt-Weichert 7/41-4/42, KL Schmidt-Weichert 10/42-9/43, OL Klapdor 9/43-8/44, KL Petersen 4-6/44

U10 IIB
KK Scheringer, KK Weingaertner, KK Schler, KK Schulz until 10/39, OL Lorentz 10/39-1/40, OL Preuss 1-6/40, KL Mützelburg 6-11/40, KL von Rabenau 11/40-6/41, OL Ruwiedel 6/41-11/41, OL Karpf 11/41- 6/42, OL Coester 6/42-2/43, OL Strenger 2/43-2/44, OL Ahlers 2- 8/44

U11 IIB
KS Rösing, KL Schütze -9/43, KL Peters 9/39-2/43, OL Stolzenburg 3/43-7/44, OL Dobenecker 7-12/44

U12 IIB
KK von Schmidt, FK Pauckstadt, KL von der Ropp 10/37-10/39

U13 IIB
KK von Stockhausen, KL Daublebsky von Eichhain 10/37-11/39, KL Scheringer 11-12/39, OL Lüth 12/39, OL Schulte 12/39-5/40

U14 IIB
FK Oehrn, KL Purkhold, KL Wellner -10/39, OL Wohlfahrt 10/39-5/40, KL Bigalk 6-8/40, OL Heidtmann 8-9/40, KL Könenkamp 9/40-5/41, OL Przikling 5/41-2/42, OL Köhntopp 7/42-7/43, OL Bortfeldt 7/43- 7/44, OL Dierks 7/44-3/45

U15 IIB
KK von Schmidt, KL Buchholz 10/37-10/39, KL Frahm 10/39-1/40

U16 IIB
KK Beduhn, KL Behrens, KL Weingaertner 7/37-10/39, KL Wellner 10/39

U17 IIB
KL Fresdorf, KL Wollschläger, KL von Reiche 10/39, KL Jeppener-Haltenhoff 9-10/39, KL Stiebler 10-11/39, KL Behrens 11/39-7/40, OL Collmann 7-12/40, KL Schultze 12/40-10/41, OL Heydemann 10/41-5/42, LT Sitek 5/42-3/43, OL Schmidt 3/43-5/44, OL Bartsch 5-12/44, OL Baumgärtel 12/44-2/45

U18 IIB
FK Pauckstadt, KL Bauer 9/37-11/39, OL Mengersen 11/39-9/40, KL Linder 9-12/40, KL Vogelsang 12/40-5/41, OL von Rosenberg- Gruszcynski 5/41-5/42, OL Wissmann 5-8/42, OL Fleige 12/42-8/44, OL Batsch, OL Arendt 5-6/44

U19 IIB
KS Schütze, KL Meckel 10/37-11/39, KL Müller-Arnecke 11/39-1/40, KL Schepke 1-4/40, KL Prellberg 5-7/40, KL Lohmeyer 7-10/40, KL Kaufmann 10-11/40, KL Schendel 11/40-6/41, OL Litterscheid 6/41- 2/42, OL Gaude 2/42-10/43, OL Ohlenburg 10/43-9/44, OL Verpoorten 9/44

U20 IIB
FK Eckermann, KL Moehle 10/37-1/40, KL von Klot-Heydenfeld 1- 4/40, OL Driver 4-5/40, OL Zetzsche 5-6/40, KL Paulshen 6-11/40, KL Schauenburg 11/40-5/41, OL Sträter 5-12/41, OL Nölke 12/41-

4/42, OL Schöler 5-9/42 and 5-10/43, OL Grafen 11/43-9/44

U21 IIB
KL Frauenheim -1/40, KL Stiebler 1-8/40, OL Heidtmann 8-12/40, KL Lohse 12/40-5/41, OL Herbschleb 5/41-1/42, OL Döhler 1-9/42, LT Geisler 9/42-1/43, OL Kugelberg 1/43-5/44, OL Schwarzkopf 5-8/44

U22 IIB
FK Grosse, KL Winter 10/37-10/39, KL Jenisch 10/39-4/40

U23 IIB
KL Kretschmer 10/37-4/40, KL Beduhn 3-5/40, OL Driver 5-9/40, OL Reichenbach-Klinke 10/40-3/41, OL Brüller 3-9/41, OL Gräf 9/41- 3/42, KL Wahlen 3-10/42 and 6/43-6/44 OL Arendt 6-9/44

U24 IIB
KL Behrens 10/37-10/39, KL Jeppener-Haltenhoff 10-11/39, OL Heilmann 11/39-8/40, OL Borchert 8/40-3/41, OL Hennig 3-8/41, OL Rodler von Roithberg 8/41-5/42, OL Petersen 10-11/42, OL Schöler 11/42-4/43, KL Petersen 4/43-4/44, OL Landt-Hayen 4-7/44, OL Lenzmann 7-8/44

U25 IA
FK Scheer, GA von Friedeburg, KA Godt, KK Lott, KK von Schmidt, OL Michel -9/39, KK Schütze 10/39-5/40, KL Beduhn 5-8/40

U26 IA
KS Hartmann, FK Schomburg 11/38-8/39, KK Ewerth 9/39-1/40, KL Scheringer 1-7/40

U27 VIIA
KS Ibbeken, KK Looff (?), KL Franz -10/37-9/39

U28 VIIA
FK Ambrosius, KL Kuhnke 4/39-11/40, OL Guggenberger 11/40-2/41, OL Ratsch 2-6/41, OL Eckhardt 6/41-7/41, OL Marbach 7-11/42, OL Christiansen 12/42-7/43, OL Krempl 7-12/43, OL Sachse 12/43-3/44

U29 VIIA
FK Fischer, KL Schuhart 4/39-1/41, OL Lassen 1-9/41, OL Hasenschar 9/41-5/42, OL Marbach 5-6/42, OL Zorn 11/42-8/43, OL Aust 8-11/43, OL Graf von und zu Arco-Zinneberg 12/43-4/44

U30 VIIA
FK Cohausz, KL Lemp 11/38-9/40, KK Prützmann 9/40-4/41, OL Loeser 4/41, OL Baberg 4/41-3/42, OL Bauer 3-10/42, LT Saar 10- 12/42, OL Fischer 5-12/43, OL Fabricius 12/43-12/44, OL Schimmel 1/45

U31 VIIA
KK Dau, KL Habekost 11/36-3/40, KL Prellberg 7-11/40

U32 VIIA
KK Lott 4-8/37, KK Büchel 8/37-2/40, KL Jenisch 2-10/40

U33 VIIA
FK Junker, KS Freiwald, KL von Dresky 11/38-2/40

U34 VIIA
FK Sobe, FK Grosse, KL Jürs, FK Pauckstadt, KL Rollmann 10/38- 9/40, OL Meyer 9/40-5/41, OL Schultz 5-11/41, OL Remus 12/41- 6/42, OL Fenski 6/42-2/43, LT Aust 3-8/43

U35 VIIA
FK Ewerth, KL Lott 9/38-11/39

U36 VIIA
KA Michahelles, KL Fröhlich 2-12/39

U37 IXA
KL Schuch 8/38-9/39, KK Hartmann 9/39-5/40, KL Oehrn 5-10/40, KL Clausen 11/40-4/41, OL Folkers 4-11/41, OL Janssen 11/41-6/42, OL Lauzemis 7/42-1/43, OL Kelling 1-11/43, OL Gerlach 11/43-1/44, OL Seiler 2-11/44, KL von Wenden 12/44-5.45

U38 IXA
KL Liebe 10/38-7/41, KK Schuch 7/41-1/42, OL Keller 1/42-1/43, OL Laubert 1-8/43, OL von Möllendorf 8-12/43, OL Kühn 1-4/44, KK Peters 4/44-5/45

U39 IXA
KL Glattes 12/38-9/39

U40 IXA
KL von Schmidt 2-9/39, KL Barten 9-10/39

U41 IXA
KL Mugler 4/39-2/40

U42 IXA
KL Dau 7-10/39

U43 IXA
KL Ambrosius 8/39-10/40, KL Lüth 11/40-4/42, OL Schwantke 4/42- 7/43

U44 IXA
KL Mathes 11/39-3/40

U45 VIIB
KL Gelhaar 6/38-10/39

U46 VIIB
KL Sohler 11/38-5/40, KL Endrass 5/40-9/41, OL Grau 9-11/41, OL von Puttkammer 11/41-3/42, OL Neubert 4-5/42, OL von Witzendorff 5/42, LT Saar 6-7/42, OL Knecht 8/42-5/43, OL Jewinski 5-10/43

U47 VIIB
KK Prien 12/38-3/41

U48 VIIB
KL Schultze 4/39-5/40, KK Rösing 5-8/40, KL Bleichrodt 8-12/40, KL Schultze 12/40-7/41, OL Atzinger 8/41-9/42, OL Todenhagen 9/42- 10/43

U49 VIIB
KL von Gossler 8/39-4/40

U50 VIIB
KL Bauer 12/39-4/40

U51   VIIB
KL Heinicke 8/38-8/39, KL Knorr 8/39-8/40

U52   VIIB
KL Barten 2-9/39, KL Salman 11/39-6/41, KL von Rabenau 6-7/41, OL Freyberg-Eisenberg 7/41-1/42, OL Mumm 1-7/42, OL Rossmann 7/42- 3/43, OL Racky 4-10/43

U53   VIIB
OL Knorr 6-8/39, KL Heinicke 8-12/39, OL Schonder 12/39-1/40, KK Grosse 1-2/40

U54   VIIB
KL Michel 9-11/39, KL Kutschmann 12/39-2/40

U55   VIIB
KL Heidel 11/39-1/40

U56   IIC
KL Zahn 11/38-1/40, OL Harms 1-10/40, KL Pfeifer 10/40-4/41, OL Römer 4/41-1/42, OL Grave 1-11/42, OL Deiring 11/42-2/44, OL Sausmikat 2-6/44, LT Miede 7/44-2/45, OL Sauerbier 2-4/45

U57   IIC
KL Korth 12/38-6/40, OL Topp 6-9/40, OL Eisele 11/41-5/43, OL Zenker 5/43-7/44, OL Kühl 8/44-4/45

U58   IIC
KL Kuppisch 2/39-6/40, OL Schonder 6-11/40, OL Rahmlow 11/40- 4/41, OL Hamm 4-9/41, OL Barber 11-8/42, OL Schöneboom 8- 11/42, OL Willner 11/42-2/44, OL Rix 2-7/44, OL Schulz 7/44-4/45

U59   IIC
KL Jürst 3/39-7/40, KL Matz 7-11/40, KL von Forstner 11/40-4/41, OL Gretschel 11/41-2/42, OL Poser 2-7/42, OL Sammler 7/42-6/43, OL Schley 6/43-7/44, LT Walter 7/44-4/45

U60   IIC
KL Schewe 7/39-8/40, OL Schnee 8-11/40, OL Wallas 11/40-9/41, LT Pressel 9/41-4/42, OL Mohs 4-8/42, OL Pressel 8-9/42, OL Mohs 10- 12/42, OL Kregelin 12/42-2/44, OL Giesewetter 2/44-3/45

U61   IIC
KL Oesten 8/39-8/40, KL Stiebler 8-11/40, OL Mattke 11/40-5/41, OL Lange 5/41-1/42, OL Geider 1-11/42, OL Ley 11/42-9/43, OL Schultze 9/43-11/44, LT Zapf 12/44-3/45

U62   IIC
KL Michalowski 12/39-11/40, OL Forster 12/40-9/41, OL Wintermeyer 9-11/41, KL Mehl 11/41, OL Schünemann 11/41-4/42, OL Slevogt 7/43-11/44, LT Augustin 11/44-3/45

U63   IIC
OL Lorentz 1-2/40

U64   IXB
KL Schultz 12/39-4/40

U65   IXB
KK von Stockhausen 2/40-3/41, KL Hoppe 3-4/41

U66   IXB
KL Zapp 1/41-6/42, KL Markworth 6/42-9/43, OL Seehausen 9/43- 5/44

U67   IXB
KL Bleichrodt 1-5/41, OL Pfeffer 6/41, KL Müller-Stöckheim 7/41- 7/43

U68   IXB
KK Merten 2/41-1/43, OL Lauzemis 1-6/43, OL Seehausen 7/43, OL Lauzemis 7/43-4/44

U69   VIIC
KL Metzler 11/40-8/41, KL Zahn 8/41-3/42, KL Gräf 3/42-2/43

U70   VIIC
KL Matz 11/40-3/41

U71   VIIC
KL Flachsenberg 12/40-6/42, OL Rodler von Roithberg 6/42-7/43, OL Christiansen 7/43-6/44, OL Ranzau 6/44-2/45

U72   VIIC
KK Neumann 1-8/41, OL Köster 8-12/41, KL Mehl 12/42-5/43, OL Scheibe 5-11/42, OL Sander 12/43-5/44, OL Mayer 5/44-3/45

U73   VIIB
KL Rosenbaum 9/40-9/42, OL Deckert 10/42-12/43

U74   VIIB
KL Kentrat 10/40-3/42, OL Friedrich 3-5/42

U75   VIIB
KL Ringelmann 12/40-12/41

U76   VIIB
OL von Hippel 12/40-4/41

U77   VIIC
KL Schonder 1/41-9/42, OL Hartmann 9/42-3/43

U78   VIIC
KL Dumrese 2-7/41, OL Makowski 7/41`-2/41, KL Dietrich 2-7/42, KL Ziehm 7-11/42, KL Sommer 11/42-5/43, OL Eisele 5/43-11/44, OL Hübsch 11/44-4/45

U79   VIIC
KL Kaufmann 3-12/41

U80   VIIC
OL Staats 4-10/41, OL Benker 10/41-5/42, OL Curio 5-11/42, OL Isermeyer 11/42-10/43, OL Keerl 12/43-11/44

U81   VIIC
KL Guggenberger 4/41-12/42, OL Krieg 12/42-1/44

U82   VIIC
KK Rollmann 5/41-2/42

U83   VIIB
KL Kraus 2/41-10/42, OL Sträter 12/41-1/42, OL Wörishoffer 10/42-3/43

U84   VIIB
KL Uphoff 4/41-8/43

U85   VIIB
OL Greger 6/41-4/42

U86   VIIB
KL Schug 7/41-11/43

U87   VIIB
KL Berger 8/41-3/43

U88   VIIC
KL Bohmann 10/41-9/42

U89   VIIC
KK Lohmann 11/41-5/43

U90   VIIC
KL Oldörp 12/41-7/42

U91   VIIC
KL Walkerling 1/42-4/43, KL Hungerhausen 4/43-2/44

U92   VIIC
KL Oelrich 3/42-8/43, KL Queck 8/43-6/44, KL Brauel 6-10/44

U93   VIIC
KL Korth 7/40-9/41, OL Kapitzky 8-9/41, OL Elfe 9/41-1/42

U94   VIIC
KL Kuppisch 8/40-9/41, OL Ites 9/41-8/42

U95   VIIC
KL Schreiber 8/40-11/41

U96   VIIC
KL Lehmann-Willenbrock 9/40-4/42, OL Hellriegel 3/42-3/43, OL Peters 3-10/43, In dockyard, OL Willner 2-7/44, OL Rix 7/44-2/45

U97   VIIC
KL Heilmann 9/40-5/42, OL Bürgel 5-8/42, KL Trox 2-6/43

U98   VIIC
KL Gysae 10/40-3/42, KL Schulte 4-6/41 while Gysae was absent, KK Schulze 3-11/42, OL Eichmann 11/42

U99   VIIB
KK Kretschmer 4/40-3/41

U100   VIIB
KL Schepke 5/40-3/41

U101   VIIB
KL Frauenheim 4-11/40, KL Mengersen 11/40-12/41, OL Marbach 12/41-1/42, OL Rothe 2-5/42, OL von Witzendorff 6-9/42, OL Münster 9/42-10/43

U102   VIIB
KL Klot-Heydenfeld 4-6/40

U103   IXB
KK Schütze 7/40-8/41, KL Winter 8/41-7/42, KL Janssen 7/42-1/44, OL Schunck 3-4/45

U104   IXB
KL Jürst 8-11/40

U105   IXB
KL Schewe 9/40-1/42, KK Schuch 1-10/42, KL Nissen 10/42-6/43

U106   IXB
KL Oesten 9/40-10/41, Rasch 10/41-3/43, OL Damerow 6-8/43

U107   IXB
KK Hessler 10/40-11/41, KL Gelhaus 11/41-6/43, KL Simmermacher 7/43-8/44, LT Fritz 8/44

U108   IXB
KK Scholtz 10/40-10/42, OL Hilsensitz 10/42, KK Wolfram 10/42- 10/43, OL Brünig 10/43-4/44

U109   IXB
KK Fischer 10/40-6/41, KL Bleichrodt 6/41-2/43, OL Schramm 2- 5/43

U110   IXB
KL Lemp 11/40-10/41

U111   IXB
KL Kleinschmidt 12/40-10/41

U112 - U115   XI
Large submarine cruisers due to have been built at Deschimag in Bremen but the building contracts were never issued.

U116   XB
KK von Schmidt 7/41-9/42, OL Grimme 9-10/42

U117   XB
KK Neumann 10/41-8/43

U118   XB
KK Czygan 12/41-6/43

U119   XB
KL Zech 4/42-4/43, KL von Kameke 4-6/43

U120   IIB
OL Bauer 4-11/40, OL Heyda 11/40-5/41, OL Körner 5/41-2/42, OL Fiedler 2-9/42, LT Rademacher 9/42-5/43, OL Sauerbier 7/43-9/44, OL Bensel 9/44-5/45

U121   IIB
KL Schroeter 5/40-3/41, KL Harms 10-11/40, KL von Schlippenbach 3-7/41, KL Hetschko 7/41-3/42, OL von Witzendorff 3-4/42, OL Westphalen 5/42-2/43, OL Hülsenbeck 2/43-2/44, OL Horst 2/44-5/45

U122   IXB
KL Looff 3-6/40

U123   IXB
KL Moehle 5/40-5/41, KL Hardegen 5/41-7/42, OL von Schroeter 8/42-6/44

U124   IXB
KL Schulz 6/40-9/41, KL Mohr 9/41-4/43

U125   IXC
KL Kuhnke 3/41-1/42, KL Folkers 1/42-5/43

U126   IXC
KL Bauer 3/41-3-43, OL Kietz 3-7/43

U127   IXC
KL Hansmann 4-12/41

U128   IXC
KL Heyse 5/41-2/42, KL Steinert 2-5/43

U129   IXC
KL Clausen 5/41-5/42, KK Witt 5/42-7/43, OL von Harpe 7/43-7/44

U130   IXC
KK Kals 6/41-1/43, OL Keller 2-4/42

U131   IXC
KK Baumann 7-12/41

U132   VIIC
KL Vogelsang 5/41-11/42

U133   VIIC
KL Hesse 7/41-2/42, OL Mohr 2-4/42

U134   VIIC
KL Schendel 7/41-3/43, KL Brosin 3-8/43

U135   VIIC
KL Practorius 8/41-11/42, OL Schütt 11/42-6/43, OL Luther 6-7/43

U136   VIIC
KL Zimmermann 8/41-7/42

U137   VIIC
KL Wohlfarth 6-12/40, OL Massmann 12/40-12/41, OL Brünning 12/41-8/42, OL Gemeiner 8/42-12/43, OL Schimmel 12/43-1/45, OL Fischer 1-2/45, OL Dierks 3-5/45

U138   IID
OL Lüth 6-10/40, KL Lohmeyer 10-12/40, OL Gramitzky 1-6/41

U139   IID
KL Bartels 5-12/40, OL Elfe 12/40-10/41, OL Fenn 10/41-5/42, OL Lauzemis 6-7/42, KL Sommer 7-10/42, OL Böttcher 10/42-9/43, LT Korndörfer 9-12/43, OL Lube 12/43-7/44, OL Kimmelmann 7/44-5/45

U140 IID
OL Hinsch 8/40-4/41, OL Hellriegel 4/41-1/42, OL Popp 1-8/42, OL Markert 8/42-7/44, OL Zeissler 7-11/44, OL Schefling 11/44-5/45

U141 IID
OL Schultze 8/40-3/41, OL Schüler 3-11/41, OL Krüger 11/41-6/42, OL Möller 6/42-2/43, OL Rauch 2-7/43, OL Luttmann 7/43-11/44, OL Hoffmann 11/44-5/45

U142 IID
OL Clausen 9-10/40, KL Kettner 10/40-10/41, LT Lindke 10/41- 3/42, OL Bertelsmann 3-9/42, OL Krieg 9-12/42, OL Laudahn 12/42- 6/44, OL Schauroth 3/44-2/45, OL Baumgärtel 2-5/45

U143 IID
KL Mengersen 9-11/40, OL Möhlmann 11/40-3/41, KL von Rosenstiel 3-5/41, OL Gelhaus 5-11/41, OL Manseck 11/41-4/42, OL Groth 4- 12/42, OL Schwager 12/42-2/43, OL Vogel 2/43-5/44, OL Kasparek 5/44-6/45

U144 IID
OL von Hippel 10-11/40, KL von Mittelstaedt 11/40-8/41

U145 IID
OL Driver 10-12/40, KL Franzius 12/40-10/41, OL Schomburg 10- 11/41, OL Ziesmer 11/41-12/42, OL Hübschen 12/42-3/44, OL Hübsch 3-11/44, OL Görner 11/44-6/45

U146 IID
KL Hoffmann 10/40-4/41, OL Ites 4-8/41, LT Hülsenbeck 8-10/41, LT Grimme 10/41-6/42, OL Gemeiner 6-7/42, OL Nissen 9-10.42, OL Hilsenitz 11/42-7/43, OL Waldschmidt 7/43-12/44, OL Wüst 12/44- 4/45, OL Schauroth 4-5/45

U147 IID
KL Hardegen 12/40-5/41, OL Wetjen 5-6/41

U148 IID
OL Radke 12/40-9/41, OL Mohr 9/41-2/42, OL Franke 2-10/42, OL Brüninghaus 10/42-3/43, OL von Möllendorff 3-8/43, OL Schäffer 12/43-12/44, OL Tammen 12/44-5/45

U149 IID
KL Höltring 11/40-8/41, KL Borchers 11/41-7/42, OL von Hammerstein-Equord 7/42-5/44, OL Plohr 5/44-5/45

U150 IID
OL Kelling 11/40-8/42, OL Schultz 10/42-5/44, OL Ranzau 5-6/44, OL von Ahlefeld 7-12/44, OL Anschütz 1-4/45, OL Kriegshammer 4-5/45

U151 IID
KL Oestermann 1-7/41, OL Janssen 7-11/41, OL Eichmann 11/41- 9/42, OL Just 9/42-5/43, OL Utischill 5/43-9/44, OL Graf von Arco 9/44-5/45

U152 IID
KL Cremer 1-7/41, OL Benker 7-9/41, OL Hildebrandt 9/41-8/42, OL Geisler 8-9/42, OL Nonn 9/42, OL Bergemann 7/43-10/44, OL Thiel 10/44-5/45

U153 IXC
KK Reichmann 7/41-7/42

U154 IXC
KK Kölle 8/41-9/42, KK Schuch 10/42-2/43, OL Kusch 2/43-1/44, OL Gemeiner 1-7/44

U155 IXC
KK Piening 8/41-2/44, OL Rudolph 3-8/44, LT von Friedeburg 8- 10/44, OL Rudolph 10-12/44, KL Witte 1-3/45, OL Altmeier 3-5/45

U156 IXC
KK Hartenstein 9/41-3/43

U157 IXC
KK Henne 9/41-6/42

U158 IXC
KL Rostin 9/41-6/42

U159 IXC
KL Witte 10/41-6/43, OL Beckmann 6-7/43

U160 IXC
KL Lassen 10/41-6/43, OL von Pommer-Esche 6-7/43

U161 IXC
KL Witt 7-12/41, KL Achilles 1/42-9/43

U162 IXC
FK Wattenberg 9/41-9/42

U163 IXC
KK Engelmann 10/41-3/43

U164 IXC
KK Fechner 11/41-1/43

U165 IXC
KK Hoffmann 2-9/42

U166 IXC
OL Kuhlmann 3-8/42

U167 IXC
KL Neubert 7/42-2/43, KK Sturm 2-4/43

U168 IXC
KL Pich 9/42-10/44

U169 IXC
OL Bauer 11/42-3/43

U170 IXC
KL Pfeffer 1/43-7/44, OL Hauber 7/44-5/45

U171 IXC
KL Pfeffer 10/41-10/42

U173 IXC
FK Beucke 11/41-9/42, OL Schweichel 9-11/42

U174 IXC
FK Thilo 11/41-9/42, OL Grandefeld 3-4/43

U175 IXC
KL Bruns 12/41-4/43

U176 IXC
KK Dierksen 12/41-5/43

U177 IXD2
KL Schulze 3/42, KK Gysae 4/42-11/43, KK Buchholz 11/43-2/44

U178 IXD2
KS Ibbeken 2/42-2/43, KK Dommes 2-11/43, KL Spahr 11/43-8/44

U179 IXD2
KK Sobe 3-10/42

U180 IXD1
FK Musenberg 5/42-1/44, OL Lange 10-11/43, OL Riesen 4-8/44

U181 IXD2
KK Lüth 5/42-10/43, KS Freiwald 11/43-end

U182 IXD2
KL Clausen 6/42-5/43

U183 IXC/40
KK Schäfer 4/42-11/43, KL Schneewind 11/43-4/45

U184 IXC/40
KL Dangschat 5-11/42

U185 IXC/40
KL Maus 6/42-8/43

U186 IXC/40
KL Hesemann 7/42-5/43

U187 IXC/40
KL Münnich 7/42-2/43

U188 IXC/40
KL Lüdden 2/42-8/44

U189 IXC/40
KL Kurrer 8/42-4/43

U190 IXC/40
KL Wintermeyer 9/42-9/44, OL Reith 9/44-5/45

U191 IXC/40
KL Fiehn 10/42-4/43

U192 IXC/40
OL Happe 11/42-5/43

U193 IXC/40
KK Pauckstadt 12/42-3/44, OL Abel 3-4/44

U194 IXC/40
KL Hesse 1-6/43

U195 IXD1
KK Buchholz 9/42-10/43, OL Steinfeldt 10/43-5/45

U196 IXD2
KK Kentrat 9/42-9/44, OL Striegler 9-11/44

U197 IXD2
KL Bartels 10/42-8/43

U198 IXD2
KS Hartmann 11/42-1/44, OL Heusinger von Waldegg 1-8/44

U199 IXD2
KL Kraus 11/42-7/43

U200 IXD2
KL Schonder 12/42-6/43

U201 VIIC
KL Schnee 1/41-7/42, OL Rosenberg 7/42-2/43

U202 VIIC
KL Linder 3/41-9/42, KL Poser 9/42-6/43

U203 VIIC
KL Mützelburg 2/41-9/42, OL Seidel 9/42, KL Kottmann 9/42-4/43

U204 VIIC
KL Kell 3/41-10/41

U205 VIIC
KL Reschke 5/41-10/42, OL Bürgel 10/42-2/43

U206 VIIC
KL Opitz 5-11/41

U207 VIIC
OL Meyer 6-9/41

U208 VIIC
OL Schlieper 7-12/41

U209 VIIC
KL Brodda 10/41-5/43

U210 VIIC
KL Lemcke 2-8/42

U211 VIIC
KL Hause 3/42-11/43

U212 VIIC
KL Vogler 4/42-7/44

U213 VIID
OL von Varendorff 8/41-7/42

U214 VIID
KL Reeder 11/41-5/43, OL Fischer Graf von Treuberg 5-7/43, KL Stock 7/43-7/44, OL Conrad 7/44

U215 VIID
KL Hoeckner 11/41-7/42

U216 VIID
KL Schultz 12/41-10/42

U217 VIID
KL Reichenbach-Klinke 1/42-6/43

U218 VIID
KL Becker 1/42-9/44, KL Stock 9/44-5/45

U219 XB
KK Burghagen 12/42-5/45

U220 XB
OL Barber 3-10/43

U221 VIIC
KL Trojer 5/42-9/43

U222 VIIC
KL von Jessen 5-9/42

U223 VIIC
KL Wächter 6/42-1/44, OL Gerlach 1-3/44

U224 VIIC
OL Kosbadt 6/42-1/43

U225 VIIC
OL Leimkühler 7/42-2/43

U226 VIIC
KL Borchers 8/42-8/43, OL Gänge 8-11/43

U227 VIIC
KL Kuntze 8/42-4/43

U228 VIIC
KL Christophersen 9/42-9/44, KL Engel 9-10/44

U229 VIIC
OL Schetelig 10/42 - 9/43

U230 VIIC
KL Siegmann 10/42-8/44, OL Eberbach 8/44

U231 VIIC
KL Wenzel 11/43-1/44

U232 VIIC
KL Ziehm 11/42-7/43

U233 XB
KL Steen 9/43-7/44
U234 XB
KL Fehler 3/44-end

U235 VIIC
OL von Möllendorff 12/42-1/43, OL Becker 1-5/43, OL Kummetz 10/43-3/45, KL Huisgen 4/45

U236 VIIC
OL Ziesmer 1-5/43, OL Harmann 9/43-7/44, OL Mumm 7/44-5/45

U237   VIIC
KL Nordheimer 1-5/43, KL König 10/43-9/44, OL van Stipriaan 9- 10/44, KL Menard 10/44-4/45

U238   VIIC
OL Hepp 2/43-2/44

U239   VIIC
OL Vöge 3/43-7/44

U240   VIIC
OL Link 4/43-5/44

U241   VIIC
OL Werr 7/43-5/44

U242   VIIC
OL Pencke 8/43-2/45, OL Riedel 2-4/45

U243   VIIC
KL Märtens 10/43-7/44

U244   VIIC
KL Fischer 10/43-4/45, OL Mackeprang 4-5/45

U245   VIIC
KK Schumann-Hindenberg 12/43-5/45

U246   VIIC
KL Raabe 1/44-3/45

U247   VIIC
OL Matschulat 10/43-9/44

U248   VIIC
OL Emde 11/43-10/44, OL Loos 11/44-1/45

U249   VIIC
OL Lindschau 10/43-7/44, KL Kock 7/44-5/45

U250   VIIC
KL Schmidt 12/43-7/44

U251   VIIC
KL Timm 9/41-9/43, OL Säck 11/43-4/45, OL Sauerbier 4/45

U252   VIIC
KL Schiebusch 10-12/41, KL Lerchen 12/41-4/42

U253   VIIC
KL Friedrichs 10/42-9/42

U254   VIIC
KL Gilardone 11/41-12/42, KL Loewe 9-10/42

U255   VIIC
KL Reche 11/41-6/43, OL Harms 6/43-8/44, LT Brischke 8-9/44, OL Heinrich 3-5/45

U256   VIIC
KL Loewe 12/41-11/42, OL Brauel 8/43-8/44, KL Giladrone for passage from Lorient to Brest, KK Lehmann-Willenbrock 9-10/44

U257   VIIC
KL Rahe 1/42-2/44

U258   VIIC
KL von Mässenhausen 2-10/42, OL Koch 11/42-3/43 KL von Mässenhausen 3-5/43

U259   VIIC
KL Köpke 2-11/42

U260   VIIC
KL Purkhold 3/42-4/44, OL Becker 4/44-3/45

U261   VIIC
KL Lange 3-9/42

U262   VIIC
KL Schiebusch 4-10/42, KL Franke 10/42-2/44, OL Wieduwilt 2- 11/44, KL Laudahn 11/44-4/45

U263   VIIC
KL Nölke 5/42-1/44

U264   VIIC
KL Looks 5.42-2/44

U265   VIIC
OL Auffhammer 6/42-2/43

U266   VIIC
OL Leinemann 6-9/42, KL von Jessen 9/42-5/43

U267   VIIC
KL Tinschert 7/42-7/44, OL von Witzendorff 8-11/43, OL Knieper 7/44-5/45

U268   VIIC
OL Heydemann 7/42-2/43

U269   VIIC
KL Harlfinger 8/42-3/44, KL Hansen 6-9/43, OL Uhl 4-6/44

U270   VIIC
KL Otto 9/42-7/44, OL Schreiber 7-8/44

U271   VIIC
KL Barleben 9/42-1/44

U272   VIIC
OL Hepp 10-11/42

U273   VIIC
OL Engel 10/42-3/43, OL Rossmann 3-5/43

U274   VIIC
OL Jordan 11/42-10/43

U275   VIIC
OL Bork 11/42-7/44, OL Wehrkamp 7/44-3/45

U276   VIIC
OL Thimme 12/42-10/43, KL Borchers 10/43-7/44, OL Zwarg 7-9/44

U277   VIIC
KL Lübsen 12/42-5/44

U278   VIIC
KL Franze 1/43-5/45
  U279   VIIC
KL Finke 2-10/43

U280   VIIC
OL Hungerhausen 2-11/43

U281   VIIC
KL von Davidson 2/43-5/45

U282   VIIC
OL Müller 3-10/43

U283   VIIC
OL Scholz 3-8/43, OL Ney 8/43-2/44

U284   VIIC
OL Scholz 4-12/43

U285   VIIC
OL Otto 5/43-4/44, KL Bornhaupt 4/44-5/45

U286   VIIC
OL Dietrich 6/43-4/45

U287   VIIC
OL Meyer 9/43-5/45

U288   VIIC
OL Meyer 6/43-4/44

U289   VIIC
KL Hellwig 7/43-5/44

U290   VIIC
KL Strenger 7-12/43, OL Herglotz 12/43-4/45, OL Maum 4-5/45

U291   VIIC
OL Keerl 8-11/43, OL Stege 11/43-6/44, OL Neumeister 7/44-5/45

U292   VIIC
OL Schmidt 8/43-5/44

U293   VIIC
KL Klingspor 9/43-5/45

U294   VIIC
OL Schütt 10/43-5/45

U295   VIIC
KL Wieboldt 10/43-5/45

U296   VIIC
KL Rasch 11/43-3/45

U297   VIIC
OL Aldegarmann 11/43-12/44

U298   VIIC
 OL Hohmann 12/43-7/44, OL Gerken 7/44-5/45

U299   VIIC
OL Heinrich 12/43-12/44, OL Emde 12/44-5/45

U300   VIIC
OL Hein 12/43-2/45

U301   VIIC
KL Körner 5/42-1/43

U302   VIIC
KL Sickel 6/42-4/44

U303   VIIC
KL Heine 7/42-5/43

U304   VIIC
OL Koch 8/42-5/43

U305   VIIC
KL Bahr 9/42-1/44
U306   VIIC
KL von Trotha 10/42-10/43

U307   VIIC
OL Herrle 11/41-12/44, OL Krüger 12/44-4/45

U308   VIIC
OL Mühlenpfort 12/42-6/43

U309   VIIC
OL Mahrholz 1/43-9/44, OL Loeder 9/44-2/45

U310   VIIC
OL Friedland 2-9/43, OL Ley 9/43-5/45

U311   VIIC
OL Zander 3/43-4/44

U312   VIIC
KL Nicolay 4/43-12/44, OL Herrle 12/44-2/45, OL von Gaza 2-5/45
U313   VIIC
KL Schweiger 5/43-5/45

U314   VIIC
KL Basse 6/43-1/44

U315   VIIC
OL Zoller 7/43-5/45

U316   VIIC
OL Stuckmann 8/43-5/44, OL König 5/44-5/45

U317   VIIC
OL Rahlf 10/43-6/44

U318   VIIC
OL Will 11/43-5/45

U319   VIIC
OL Clemens 12/43-7/44

U320   VIIC
OL Breinlinger 12/43-7/44, OL Emmrich 7/44-5/45

U321   VIIC
KL Drews 1-8/44, OL Berends 8/44-4/45

U322   VIIC
OL Wysk 2-11/44

U323   VIIC
OL Bokelberg 3-7/44, KL Pregel 7/44-2/45, OL Dobinsky 2-5/45

U324   VIIC
OL Edelhoff 4/44-5/45 Joachim Sauerbier was due to have taken command, but he was killed before the switch could be made.

U325   VIIC
OL Dohrn 5/44-4/45

U326   VIIC
KL Matthes 6/44-4/45

U327   VIIC
KL Lemcke 7/44-2/45

U328   VIIC
OL Lawrence 9-12/44, OL Scholle 2-5/45

U329   VIIC
Probably not appointed

U330   VIIC
Not laid down

U331   VIIC
KL von Tiesenhausen 3/41-11/42

U332   VIIC
KL Liebe 6/41-1/43, OL Hüttemann 1-5/43

U333   VIIC
OL Schwaff 10/42-5/43, KL Cremer 5/43-7/44, KL Fiedler 7/44

U334   VIIC
KL Siemon 10/41-4/43, OL Ehrich 4-6/43

U335   VIIC
KL Pelkner 12/41-8/42

U336   VIIC
KL Hunger 2/42-10/43

U337   VIIC
OL Ruwiedel 5/42-1/43

U338   VIIC
KL Kinzel 6/42-9/43

U339   VIIC
OL Basse 8/42-5/43, OL Remus 5/43-2/45

U340   VIIC
OL Klaus 10/42-11/43

U341   VIIC
OL Epp 11/42-9/43

U342   VIIC
OL Hossenfelder 1/43-4/44

U343   VIIC
OL Rahn 2/43-3/44

U344   VIIC
KL Pietsch 3/43-8/44

U345   VIIC
OL Knackfuss 5-12/43

U346   VIIC
OL Leisten 6-9/43

U347   VIIC
OL de Buhr 7/43-7/44

U348   VIIC
OL Schunck 8/43-3/45, OL Seeger 6-7/44
while Schunck was absent

U349   VIIC
OL Lottner 9-12/43, OL Dähne 12/43-
5/45

U350   VIIC
OL Niester 10/43-3/45

U351   VIIC
OL Hause 6-12/41, OL Roisenberg 12/41-
8/42, OL Zimmermann 8/42- 5/43, OL
Roth 5-9/43, OL Wicke
12/43-6/44, OL Schley 7/44-3/45, OL
Strehl 3-5/45

U352   VIIC
KL Rathke 8/41-5/42

U353   VIIC
OL Römer 3-10/42

U354   VIIC
KL Herbschleb 4/42-2/44, KL Sthamer 2-
8/44

U355   VIIC
KL La Baume 10/41-4/44

U356   VIIC
KL Wallas 12/41-11/42, OL Ruppelt 11-
12/42

U357   VIIC
KL Kellner 6-12/42

U358   VIIC
KL Manke 8/42-3/44

U359   VIIC
OL Föster 10/42-7/43
U360   VIIC
OL Bühring 11/42-5/43, KL Becker 5.43-
4/44

U361   VIIC
KL Seidel 12/42-7/44

U362   VIIC
OL Franz 2/43-9/44

U363   VIIC
OL Wilzer 3-8/43, KL Nees 9/43-5/45

U364   VIIC
OL Sass 5/43-1/44

U365   VIIC
KL Wedemeyer 6/43-12/44, OL
Todenhagen 12/44

U366   VIIC
OL Langenberg 7/43-3/44

U367   VIIC
OL Becker 1-3/44, OL Stegemann 3/44-
3/45

U368   VIIC
OL Schaiper 1/44-1/45, OL Giesewetter
1-5/45

U369   VIIC
KL Schaafhausen 10/43-4/45, OL
Schunck 4-5/45

U370   VIIC
OL Nielsen 11/43-5/45

U371   VIIC
KL Driver 3/41-4/42, KL Neumann 4-
5/42, KL <ehl 5/42-3/44, OL Fenski 3-
5/44

U372   VIIC
KL Neumann 4/41-842

U373   VIIC
KL Loeser 5/41-9/43, OL von Lehsten
10/43-6/44

U374   VIIC
OL von Fischel 6/41-1/42

U375   VIIC
KL Könenkamp 7/41-7/43

U376   VIIC
KL Marks 8/41-4/43

U377   VIIC
KL Köhler 10/41-8/43, OL Kluth 8/43-
1/44

U378   VIIC
KL Hoschatt 10/41-10/42, KL Mäder
10/42-10/43

U379   VIIC
KL Kettner 11/41-8/42

U380   VIIC
KL Röther 12/41-11/43, KL Brandi 1-4/44

U381   VIIC
KL Graf von Pückler und Limburg 2/42-
5/43

U382   VIIC
KL Juli 4/42-5/43, OL Koch 5-11/43, OL
Zorn 11/43-7/44,OL Gerke 5-7/44 while
Zorn was absent, OL Schimmel 1-3/45

U383   VIIC
KL Kremser 6-42-8/43

U384   VIIC
OL von Rosenberg-Gruszczynsli 7/42-
3/43

U385   VIIC
KL Valentiner 8/42-8/44

U386   VIIC
OL Kandler 10/42-6/43, OL Albrecht
6/43-2/44

U387   VIIC
KK Büchler 11/42-12/44

U388   VIIC
OL Sues 12/42-6/43

U389   VIIC
KL Heilmann 2-10/43

U390   VIIC
OL Geissler 3/43-7/44

U391   VIIC
OL Dültgen 4-12/43

U392   VIIC
OL Schümann 5/43-3/44
U393   VIIC
OL Rademacher 7/43-9/44, OL Zenker
9/44-1/45, OL Seeger 1-3/45, OL Herrle 4-
5/45

U394   VIIC
KL Borger 8/43-9/44, OL.Unterhorst 8-
9/43 while Borger was absent

U395   VIIC
Damaged during an air raid and not completed

U396   VIIC
KL Unterhorst 10/43-3/45, KL Siemon 3-
4/45

U397   VIIC
OL Kallipke 11/43-7/44, OL Stege 9/44-
4/45, KL Groth 4-5/45

U398   VIIC
KK Reckhoff 12/43-11/44, OL Cranz
11/44-4/45

U399   VIIC
OL van Meeteren 1-7/44, OL Buhse 7/44-
3/45
U400   VIIC
KL Creutz 3-10/44

U401   VIIC
KL Zimmermann 4-8/41

U402   VIIC
KK Freiherr von Forstner 5/41-10/43

U403   VIIC
KL Clausen 6/41-6/43

U404   VIIC
KK von Bülow 8/41-7/43, OL Schönberg
7/43

U405   VIIC
KK Hopman 9/41-11/43

U406   VIIC
KL Dietrichs 10/41-2/44

U407   VIIC
KL Brüller 12/41-1/44, OL Korndörfer 1-
9/44, OL Kolbus 9/44

U408   VIIC
KL von Hymmen 11/41-11/42

U409   VIIC
OL Massmann 1/42-7/43

U410   VIIC
KK Sturm 2/42-2/43, OL Fenski 2/43-
3/44

U411   VIIC
OL Litterscheid 3-10/42, KL Spindlegger
10-11/42

U412   VIIC
KL Jahrmärker 4-10/42

U413   VIIC
KL Poel 6/42-4/44, OL Sachse 4-8/44

U414   VIIC
OL Huth 7/42-5/43

U415   VIIC
KL Neide 8/42-4/44, OL Werner 4-7/44

U416   VIIC
OL ,Reich 11/42-4/43, OL Zorn 10-11/43,
KL Zwarg 11/43-5/44, OL Riegler 7-
12/44

U417   VIIC
OL Schreiner 9/42-6/43

U418   VIIC
OL Lange 10/42-6/43

U419   VIIC
OL Giersberg 11/42-10/43

U420   VIIC
OL Reese 12/42-10/43

U421   VIIC
OL Kolbus 1/43-4/44

U422   VIIC
OL Poeschel 2-10/43

U423   VIIC
OL Methner 3-9/43, OL Kelling 9-10/43,
OL Hackländer 10/43-6/44

U424   VIIC
OL Lüders 4/43-2/44

U425   VIIC
KL Bentzien 4/43-2/45

U426   VIIC
KL Reich 5/43-1/44

U427   VIIC
OL Graf von Gudenus 6/43-5/45

U428   VIIC
OL Münster 9/43-5/44, OL Hanitsch
5/44-5/45

U429   VIIC
OL Racky 9/43-5/44, OL Kuttkat 10/44-
3/45

U430   VIIC
LT Nachtigall 9/43-1/44, OL Hammer
1/44-3/45

U431   VIIC
KL Dommes 4/41-12/42, OL
Schöneboom 12/42-10/43

U432   VIIC
KL Schultze 4/41-1/43, KL Eckhardt 1-
3/43

U433   VIIC
OL Ey 5-11/41

U434   VIIC
KL Heyda 6-12/41

U435   VIIC
KL Strelow 8/41-7/43

U436   VIIC
KL Seibicke 9/41-6/43

U437   VIIC
KL Schulz 10/41-12/42, KL Lamby 12/42-
10/44

U438   VIIC
KL Franzius 11/41-3/43, KL Heinsohn 3-
5/43

U439   VIIC
KL Sporn 12/41-2/43, OL von
Tippelskirch 2-5/43

U440 VIIC
KL Geissler 1/42-5/43, OL Schwaff 5/43

U441   VIIC
KL Hartmann (Klaus) 2-5/43, KL von
Hartmann (Götz) 5-8/43, KL Hartmann
(Klaus) 8/43-6/44

U442   VIIC
KK Hesse 3/42-2/43

U443   VIIC
OL von Puttkammer 4/42-2/43

U444   VIIC
OL Langfeld 5/42-3/43

U445   VIIC
OL Fenn 5/42-1/44, OL Fischler Graf von
Treuberg 1-8/44

U446   VIIC
OL Richard 6-9/42

U447   VIIC
OL Bothe 7/42-5/43

U448   VIIC
OL Dauter 8/42-4/44

U449   VIIC
OL Otto 8/42-6/43

U450   VIIC
OL Böhme 9/42-3/44

U451   VIIC
KL Hoffmann 5-12/41

U452   VIIC
KL March 5-9/41

U453   VIIC
KL Hetschko 6-7/41, KL von
Schlippenbach 7/41-12/43, OL Lührs
12/43-5/44

U454   VIIC
KL Hackländer 7/41-8/43

U455   VIIC
KL Giessler 8/41-12/42, KL Scheibe
12/42-4/44

U456   VIIC
KL Teichert 9/41-5/43

U457   VIIC
KK Brandenburg 11/41-9/42

U458   VIIC
KL Diggins 12/41-8/43

U459   XIV
KK von Wilamowitz-Möllendorf 11/42-
7/43

U460   XIV
KL Schäfer 12/41-8/42, KL Schnoor 8/42-
10/43

U461   XIV
OL Bernbeck 1-4/42, KK Stiebler 4/42-
7/43

U462   XIV
OL Vowe 3/42-7/43

U463   XIV
KK Wolfbauer 4/42-5/43

U464   XIV
KL Harms 4-8/42

U465   VIIC
KL Wolf 5/42-5/43

U466   VIIC
KL Thäter 6/42-8/44

U467   VIIC
KL Kummer 7/42-5/43

U468   VIIC
OL Schamong 8/42-8/43

U469   VIIC
OL Claussen 10/42-3/43

U470   VIIC
OL Grave 1-10/43

U471   VIIC
KL Kloevekorn 5/43-8/44

U472   VIIC
OL von Forstner 5/43-3/44

U473   VIIC
KL Sternberg 6/43-5/44

U474   VIIC
Damaged during an air raid before being
completed and then scrapped

U475   VIIC
KL Stoeffler 7/43-5/45

U476   VIIC
OL Niethmann 7/43-5/44

U477   VIIC
OL Jenssen 8/43-6/44

U478   VIIC
OL Rademacher 9/43-6/44

U479   VIIC
OL Sons 10/43-12/44

U480   VIIC
OL Förster 10/43-2/45

U481   VIIC
OL Pick 11/43-3/44, KL Andersen 3/44-
5/45

U482   VIIC
KL Graf von Matuschka 12/43-1/45

U483   VIIC
KL von Morstein 12/43-5/45

U484   VIIC
KK Schaefer 1-9/44

U485   VIIC
KL Lutz 2/44-5/45

U486   VIIC
OL Meyer 3/44-4/45

U487   XIV
OL Metz 12/42-7/43

U488   XIV
OL Bartke 2/43-2/44, OL Studt 2-4/44

U489   XIV
OL Schmandt 3-8/43

U490   XIV
OL Gerlach 3/43-6/44

U491 - U500   XIV
Due to have been built in Kiel but building contract cancelled and probably not
even started,
certainly not finished

U501   IXC/40
KK Förster 4-9/41

U502   IXC/40
KL von Rosenstiel 5/41-7/42

U503   IXC/40
KL Gericke 7/41-3/42

U504   IXC/40
KK Poske 7/41-1/43, KL Luis 1-7/43

U505   IXC/40
KK Loewe 8/41-9/42, KL Zschech 9/42-
10/43, OL Meyer 10-11/43, OL Lange
11/43-6/44

U506   IXC/40
KL Würdemann 9/41-7/43

U507   IXC/40
KK Schacht 10/41-1/43

U508   IXC/40
KL Staats 10/41-11/43

U509   IXC/40
KK Wolff 11/41-10/42, KL Witte 10/42-
7/43

U510   IXC/40
FK Neitzel 11/41-5/43, KL Eick 5/43-5/45

U511   IXC/40
KL Steinhoff 12/41-12/42, KL
Schneewind 12/42-9/43

U512   IXC/40
KL Schultze 12/41-10/42

U513   IXC/40
KK Rüggeberg 1/42-5/43, KL
Guggenberger 5-7/43

U514   IXC/40
KL Auffermann 1/42-7/43

U515   IXC/40
KL Henke 2/42-4/44

U516   IXC/40
KK Wiebe 3/42-6/43, KL Kuppisch 6/43,
KL Tillessen 7/43-12/43, OL Petran 12/44-
5/45

U517   IXC/40
KL Hartwig 3-11/42

U518   IXC/40
FK Brachmann 4-8/42, KL Wissmann 8/42-
1/44, OL Offermann 1/44- 4/45

U519   IXC/40
KL Eppen 5/42-2/43

U520   IXC/40
KL Schwartzkopff 5-10/42

U521   IXC/40
KL Bargsten 6/42-6/43

U522   IXC/40
KL Schneider 6/42-2/43

U523   IXC/40
KL Pietsch 6/42-8/43

U524   IXC/40
KL Freiherr von Steinaecker 7/42-3/43

U525   IXC/40
KL Drewitz 7/42-8/43

U526   IXC/40
KL Möglich 8/42-4/43

U527   IXC/40
KL Uhlig 9/42-7/43

U528   IXC/40
OL von Rabenau 12/42-5/43

U529   IXC/40
KL Fraatz 9/42-2/43

U530   IXC/40
KL Lange 10/42-1/45, OL Wermuth 1-5/45

U531   IXC/40
KL Neckel 10/42-5/43

U532   IXC/40
FK Junker 11/42-5/45

U533   IXC/40
KL Henning   11/42-10/43

U534   IXC/40
KL Nollau 10/42-5/45

U535   IXC/40
KL Ellmenreich 12/42-7/43

U536   IXC/40
KL Schauenburg 1-11/43

U537   IXC/40
KL Schrewe 1/43-11/44

U538   IXC/40
KL Gossler 2-11/43

U539   IXC/40
KL Lauterbach-Emden 2/43-5/45

U540   IXC/40
KL Kasch 3-10/43

U541   IXC/40
KL Petersen 3/43-5/45

U542   IXC/40
OL Coester 4-11/43

U543   IXC/40
KL Hellriegel 4/43-7/44

U544   IXC/40
KL Mattke 5/43-1/44

U545   IXC/40
KL Mannesmann 5/43-2/44

U546   IXC/40
KL Just 6/43-4/45

U547   IXC/40
FK Sturm 6/43-4/44, OL Niemeyer 4-
12/44

U548   IXC/40
OL Zimmermann 6/43-2/45, KL Pfeffer 8-
11/44 while Zimmermann was absent,
OL Krempl 2-4/45

U549   IXC/40
KL Krankenhagen 7/43-5/44

U550   IXC/40
KL Hänert 7/43-4/44

U551   VIIC
KL Schrott 11/40-4/41

U552   VIIC
KK Topp 12/40-8/42, KL Popp 9/42-
7/44, OL Lube 7/44-5/45

U553   VIIC
KK Thurmann 12/40-1/43

U554   VIIC
KL Lohmann 1-4/41, OL Stein 6/41-
3/42, OL von Trotha 3-9/42, KL Siebold
11/42-9/44, OL Hartmann 6/44, KL Rave
10/44-3/45, OL Remus 3-5/45

U555   VIIC
KL Horrer 1-8/41, KL von Hartmann
8/42-2/42, OL Rendtel 2-8/42, KL Saar 8-
10/42, OL Erdmann 11/42-11/43, OL
Fritz   12/43-5/45

U556   VIIC
KL Wohlfarth 2-6/41

U557   VIIC
KL Paulsen 2-12/41

U558   VIIC
KL Krech 2/41-7/43

U559   VIIC
KL Heidtmann 2/41-10/42

U560   VIIC
OL Zetsche 3-8/41, OL Cordes 8/41-
7/42, KL von Rappard 7/42- 8/43, OL
Wicke 8-12/43, OL Jacobs 12/43-5/45

U561   VIIC
KL Bartels 3/41-7/42, KL Schomburg
7/42-7/43, OL Henning 7/43

U562   VIIC
OL Collmann 3-9/41, KL Hamm
9/41-2/43

U563   VIIC
OL Bargsten 3/41-3/42, KL von
Hartmann 4/42-5/43, OL Borchardt 5/43

U564   VIIC
KK Suhren 4/41-10/42, OL Fiedler
10/42-6/43

U565   VIIC
OL Jebsen 4/41-4/42, KL Franken 4/42-
10/43, KL Henning 10/43- 9/44

U566   VIIC
KL Borchert 4/41-7/42, OL Remus 7/42-
1/43, KL Hornkohl 1-10/43

U567   VIIC
KL Fahr 4-10/41, KL Endrass 4-12/41

U568   VIIC
KL Preuss 5/41-5/42

U569 VIIC
KL Hinsch 5/41-2/43, OL Johannsen 2-5/43

U570 VIIC
KL Rahmlow 5-8/41

U571 VIIC
KL Möhlmann 5/41-5/43, OL Lüssow 5/43-1/44

U572 VIIC
KL Hirsacker 5/41-12/42, OL Kummetat 12/42-8/43

U573 VIIC
KL Heinsohn 6/41-5/42

U574 VIIC
OL Gengelbach 6-12/41

U575 VIIC
KL Heydemann 6/41-7/43, OL Boehner 9/43-3/44

U576 VIIC
KL Heinicke 6/41-7/42

U577 VIIC
KL Schauenburg 9/41-1/42

U578 VIIC
KK Rehwinkel 7/41-8/42

U579 VIIC
KL Lohmann 7-10/41, OL Ruppelt 5-10/42, OL Linder 10/42-9/44, OL Schwarzenberg 9-44-5/45

U580 VIIC
OL Kuhlmann 7-11/41

U581 VIIC
KL Pfeifer

U582 VIIC
KL Schulte 8/41-10/42

U583 VIIC
KL Ratsch 8-11/41

U584 VIIC
KL Deecke 8/41-10/43

U585 VIIC
KL Lohse 8/41-3/42

U586 VIIC
KL von der Esch 9/41-9/43, OL Götze 10/43-7/44

U587 VIIC
KL Borcherdt 9/41-4/42

U588 VIIC
KL Vogel 9/41-7/42

U589 VIIC
KL Horrer 9/41-9/42

U590 VIIC
KL Müller-Edzards 10/41-6/43, OL Krüer 6-7/43

U591 VIIC
KL Zetsche 10/41-6/43, OL Ziesmer 6-7/43

U592 VIIC
KL Borm 10/41-7/43, OL Jaschke 9/43-1/44

U593 VIIC
KL Kelbing 10/41-12/43

U594 VIIC
KL Hoffmann 10/41-7/42, KL Mumm 7/42-6/43

U595 VIIC
KL Quaet-Faslem 11/41-11/43

U596 VIIC
KL Jahn 11/41-7/43, OL Nonn 8/43-7/44, OL Kolbus 7-9/44

U597 VIIC
KL Bobst 11/41-10/42

U598 VIIC
KL Holtorf 11/41-7/43

U599 VIIC
KL Breithaupt 12/41-10/42

U600 VIIC
KL Zurmühlen 12/41-11/43

U601 VIIC
KL Grau 12/41-11/43, OL Hansen 11/43-2/44

U602 VIIC
KL Schüler 12/41-4/43

U603 VIIC
KL Kölzer 1-9/42, OL Bertelsmann 9/42-5/43, OL Baltz 5/43-1/44, KL Bertelsmann 1-3/44

U604 VIIC
KL Höltring 1/42-8/43

U605 VIIC
KL Schütze 1-11/42

U606 VIIC
OL Klatt 1-10/42, OL Döhler 10/42-2/43

U607 VIIC
KL Mengersen 1/42-5/43, OL Jeschonnek 6-7/43

U608 VIIC
KL Struckmeier 2/42-1/44, OL Reisener 1-8/44

U609 VIIC
KL Rudloff 2/42-2/43

U610 VIIC
KL Freiherr von Freyberg-Eisenberg-Allmendingen 2/42-10/43

U611 VIIC
KL von Jacobs 2-12/42

U612 VIIC
KL Siegmann 3-8/42, OL Petersen 5/43-2/44, OL Dick 2/44-5/45

U613 VIIC
KL Köppe 3/42-7/43

U614 VIIC
KL Sträter 3/42-7/43

U615 VIIC
KL Kapitzky 3/42-8/43

U616 VIIC
OL Spindlegger 4-10/42, OL Koitschka 10/42-5/44

U617 VIIC
KL Brandi 4/42-9/43

U618 VIIC
OL Faust 5-8/44

U619 VIIC
OL Makowski 4-10/42

U620 VIIC
KL Stein 4/42-2/43

U621 VIIC
KL Schünemann 5-12/42, OL Kruschka 12/42-5/44, OL Stuckmann 5- 8/44

U622 VIIC
KL Queck 5/42-7/43

U623 VIIC
OL Schröder 5/42-2/43

U624 VIIC
KL Graf von Soden-Frauenhofen 5/42-2/43

U625 VIIC
KL Benker 6/42-3/44, OL Sureth 1/44, OL Straub 1-3/44

U626 VIIC
LT Bade 6-12/42

U627 VIIC
KL Kindelbacher 6-10/42

U628 VIIC
KL Hasenschar 6/42-7/43

U629 VIIC
OL Bugs 7/42-6/44

U630 VIIC
OL Winkler 7/42-5/43

U631 VIIC
OL Krüger 7/42-10/43

U632 VIIC
KL Karpf 7/42-3/43

U633 VIIC
OL Müller 7/42-3/43

U634 VIIC
OL Brosin 8/42-2/43, OL Dahlhaus 2-8/43

U635 VIIC
OL Eckelmann 8/42-4/43

U636 VIIC
KL Hildebrandt 8/42-2/44, OL Schendel 2/44-4/45

U637 VIIC
KL Dietrich 8/42-2/43, KL Zedelius 2/43-7/44, OL Fabricius 7-9/44, KL Riekeberg 10/44-4/45, OL Weber 4-5/45

U638 VIIC
OL Staudinger 9-12/42, KL Bernbeck 12/42-3/43, KL Staudinger 3- 5/43

U639 VIIC
OL Wichmann 9/42-8/43

U640 VIIC
OL Nagel 9/42-5/43

U641 VIIC
KL Rendtel 9/42-1/44

U642 VIIC
KL Brünning 10/42-7/44

U643 VIIC
KL Speidel 10/42-10/43

U644 VIIC
OL Jensen 10/42-4/43

U645 VIIC
OL Ferro 10/42-12/43

U646 VIIC
OL Wulff 10/42-5/43

U647 VIIC
KL Hertin 11/42-8/43

U648 VIIC
OL Stahl 11/42-8/43

U649 VIIC
OL Tiesler 11/42-2/43

U650 VIIC
OL von Witzendorff 10/42-7/44, KL Tinschert 8-1043, OL Zorn 7/44- 1/45

U651 VIIC
KL Lohmeyer 2-6/41

U652 VIIC
OL Fraatz 4/41-6/42

U653 VIIC
KL Feiler 5/41-9/43, OL Kandler 10/43-3/44

U654 VIIC
KK Hesse 9-11/41, OL Forster 11/41-8/42

U655 VIIC
KL Dumrese 8/41-3/42

U656 VIIC
KL Kröning 9/41-3/42

U657 VIIC
OL Radke 10-12/41, KL Göllnitz 12/41-5/43

U658 VIIC
KL Senkel 11/41-10/42

U659 VIIC
KL Stock 12/41-10/42

U660 VIIC
KL Baur 1-11/42

U661 VIIC
Ol von Lilienfeld 2-10/42

U662 VIIC
KK Hermann 4/42-2/43, KL Müller 3-7/43

U663 VIIC
KL Schmid 5/42-5/43

U664 VIIC
OL Graef 6/42-8/43

U665 VIIC
OL Haupt 7/42-3/43

U666 VIIC
KL Engel 8/42-12/43, OL Wilberg 12/43-2/44

U667 VIIC
KL Schroeteler 10/42-7/44, OL Wilberg 12/43-2/44

U668 VIIC
KL von Eickstedt 11/42-4/45, KL Henning 4-5/45

U669 VIIC
OL Köhl 12/42-9/43

U670 VIIC
OL Hyronimus 1-8/43

U671 VIIC
OL Hewecker 3-5/43, OL Hegewald 5/43-8/44

U672 VIIC
OL Lawaetz 4/43-7/44

U673 VIIC
KL Haelbich 5-10/43, OL Sauer 10/43-7/44, OL Gerke 8-10/44

U674 VIIC
OL Muhs 6/43-5/44

U675 VIIC
OL Sammler 7/43-5/44

U676 VIIC
KL Sass 8/43-2/45

U677 VIIC
OL Weber 9/43-7/44, OL Ady 8/44-4/45

U678   VIIC
OL Hyronimus 10/43-7/44

U679   VIIC
OL Breckwoldt 11/43-10/44, OL Aust
10/44-1/45

U680   VIIC
OL Ulber 12/43-5/45

U681   VIIC
OL Bach 2-8/44, OL Gebauer 8/44-3/45

U682   VIIC
OL Thinemann 4/44-3/45

U683   VIIC
KL Keller 7/41-7/42

U684 - U700 building contracts cancelled

U701   VIIC
KL Degen 7/41-7/42

U702   VIIC
KL von Rabenau 9/41-4/42

U703   VIIC
KL Bielefeld 10/41-7/43, OL Brünner
7/43-9/44

U704   VIIC
KL Kessler 11/41-4/43, OL Hagenau
4/43-6/44, OL Ady 6-8/44, OL
Schwarzkopf 8-12/44, OL Nolte
12/44-3/45

U705   VIIC
KL Horn 12/41-9/42

U706   VIIC
KL von Zitzewitz 3/42-8/43

U707   VIIC
OL Gretschel 9/42-11/43

U708   VIIC
OL Heintze 7/42-6/43, OL Andersen
6/43-2/44, OL Kühn 5/44-5/45

U709   VIIC
OL Weber 8/42-12/43, OL Ites 12/43-
3/44

U710   VIIC
OL von Carlowitz 9/42-4/43
U711   VIIC
KL Lange 9/42-5/45

U712   VIIC
OL Pietschmann 11/42-12/43, OL Koch
12/43-6/44, OL Freiherr von Ketelhodt
7/44-5/45

U713   VIIC
OL Gosejakob 12/42-2/44

U714   VIIC
KL Schwebcke 2/43-3/45

U715   VIIC
KL Röttger 3/43-6/44

U716   VIIC
OL Dunkelberg 4/43-1/45, OL Thimme 1-
5/45

U717   VIIC
OL von Rothkirch und Panthen 5/43-
5/45

U718   VIIC
OL Wieduwilt 6-11/43

U719   VIIC
OL Steffens 7/43-6/44

U720   VIIC
OL Schüler 9/43-12/44, OL Boldt 5-
11/44, OL Wendelberger 11/44- 5/45

U721   VIIC
OL Wollschläger 9/43-12/44, OL Fabricius
12/44-5/45

U722   VIIC
OL Reimers 12/43-3/45

U723 - U730 VIIC
Building contracts cancelled

U731   VIIC
OL Techand 10/42-11/43, OL Graf Keller
12/43-5/44

U732   VIIC
OL Carlsen 10/42-10/43

U733   VIIC
OL von Trotha 11/42/5/43, OL Hellmann
12/43-4/45, OL Hammer 4- 5/45

U734   VIIC
OL Blauert 12/42-2/44

U735   VIIC
OL Börner 12/42-12/44

U736   VIIC
OL Reff 1/43-8/44

U737   VIIC
LT Poeschel 1-2/43, KL Brasack 2/43-
11/44, OL Greus 11-12/44

U738   VIIC
OL Hoffmann 2/43-2/44

U739   VIIC
OL Mangold 3/43-2/45, OL Kosnick 3-
5/45

U740   VIIC
KL Stark 4/43-6/44

U741   VIIC
OL Palmgren 4/43-8/44

U742   VIIC
KL Schwassmann 5/43-7/44

U743   VIIC
OL Kandzior 5/43-9/44

U744   VIIC
OL Blischke 6/43-3/44

U745   VIIC
KL von Trotha 6/43-2/45

U746   VIIC
LT Kaschke 10/43-1/44, OL Lottner 1/44-
5/45

U747   VIIC
OL Jewinski 10/43-5/44, OL Zahnow
5/44-4/45

U748   VIIC
OL Roth 9/43-9/44, OL Knecht 9-11/44,
OL Dingler 4-5/45

U749   VIIC
OL Fischler Graf von Treuberg 9-12/43,
OL Fischer 12/43-11/44, OL Huisgen
12/44-4/45

U750   VIIC
OL von Bitter 9/43-8/44, OL Grawert
8/44-5/45

U751   VIIC
KL Bigalk 1/41-9/42

U752   VIIC
KL Schroeter 5/41-5/43

U753   VIIC
KK Manhardt von Mannstein 6/41-5/43

U754   VIIC
KL Oestermann 8/41-7/42

U755   VIIC
KL Göing 11/41-5/43

U756   VIIC
KL Harney 12/41-5/43

U757   VIIC
KL Deetz 2/42-1/44

U758   VIIC
KL Manseck 5/42-3/44, OL Feindt 4/44-
3/45

U759   VIIC
KL Friedrich 8/42-7/43

U760   VIIC
OL Blum 10/42-9/43

U761   VIIC
OL Geider 12/42-2/44

U762   VIIC
KL Hille 1-12/43, OL Pietschmann 12/43-
2/44

U763   VIIC
KL Cordes 3/43-10/44, LT Braun 8-10/44,
OL Schröter 11/44-1/45

U764   VIIC
OL von Bremen 5/43-5/45

U765   VIIC
OL Wendt 6/43-5/44

U766   VIIC
OL Wilke 7/43-8/44

U767   VIIC
OL Dankleff 9/43-6/44

U768   VIIC
OL Buttjer 10-11/43

U769 & U770
Destroyed during an air raid and not
completed

U771   VIIC
OL Block 11/43-11/44

U772   VIIC
KL Rademacher 12/43-12/44

U773   VIIC
OL Lange 1-4/44, OL Baldus 4/44-5/45

U774   VIIC
OL Buttjer 2-10/44, KL Sausmikat 10/44-
4/45

U775   VIIC
OL Tachenmacher 3/44-5/45

U776   VIIC
KL Martin 4/44-5/45

U777   VIIC
OL Ruperti 5-10/44

U778   VIIC
KL Jürs 7/44-5/45

U779   VIIC
OL Stegmann

U780 - U790 VIIC
Not laid down

U791   XVIIA   ex-V300
Scrapped before being completed

U792   XVIIA
Experimental boat: OL Heitz 11/43-
10/44, OL Duis 10/44-5/45

U793   XVIIA
Experimental boat: OL Schauenburg
4/44-1/45, OL Schmidt 1-5/45

U794   XVIIA
Experimental boat: OL Klug 11/43-9/44,
OL Becker 9/44-5/45

U795   XVIIA
Experimental boat: OL Selle 4/44-5/45

U796 & U797 XVIII
Similar to Type XXI but with closed circuit Walter turbine. Not laid down

U798   XVIIK
Building contract cancelled

U799 & U800 XVIIK
Not laid down

U801   IXC/40
KL Brans 3/43-3/44

U802   IXC/40
KL Steinhaus 6-12/43, KL Schmoeckel
12/43-5/45

U803   IXC/40
KL Schimpff 9/43-4/44

U804   IXC/40
OL Meyer 12/43-4/45

U805   IXC/40
KK Bernardelli 2/44-5/45

U806   IXC/40
KL Hornbostel 4/44-5/45

U807 - U820 IXC/40
Building contracts not finished, probably
not laid down, certainly never finished

U821   VIIC
OL Fabricius 10-11/43, OL Fischer 11-
12/43, OL Knackfuss 1-6/44

U822   VIIC
OL Elsinghorst 7/44-5/45

U823 & U824 VIIC
Building contracts cancelled

U825   VIIC
OL Stoelker 5/44-5/45

U826   VIIC
KL Lübcke 5/44-5/45

U827   VIIC
KL Hunck 5/44-4/45, KL Baberg 4-5/45

U828   VIIC
OL John 6/44-5/45

U829 - U840 VIIC
Building contracts cancelled

U841   IXC
KL Bender 2-10/43

U842   IXC
KK Heller 3-11/43

U843   IXC
KL Herwartz 3/43-4/45

U844   IXC
OL Möller 4-10/43

U845   IXC
KK Behrens 5-7/43, KL Hoffmann 7-
10/43, KK Weber 10/43-3/44

U846   IXC
OL Hashagen 5/43-5/44

U847   IXD2
KL Guggenberger 1-2/43, KL Metzler 2-
7/43, KL Kuppisch 7-8/43

U848   IXD2
KK Rollmann 2-11/43

U849   IXD2
KL Schultze 3-10/43

U850   IXD2
FK Ewerth 4-12/43

U851   IXD2
KK Weingaertner 5/43-3/44

U852   IXD2
KL Eck 6/43-5/44

U853   IXC
KL Sommer 6/43-7/44, OL Wermuth 7-8/44, OL Frömsdorf

U854   IXC
KL Weiher 7/43-2/44

U855   IXC
KL Sürenhagen 8/43-4/44, OL Ohlsen 4-9/44

U856   IXC
OL Wittenberg 8/43-4/44

U857   IXC
KL Premauer 9/43-4/45

U858   IXC
KL Bode 9/43-5/45

U859   IXD2
KL Jebsen 7/43-9/44

U860   IXD2
 FK Büchel 8/43-6/44

U861   IXD2
KK Oesten 9/43-5/45

U862   IXD2
KK Timm 10/43-5/45

U863   IXD2
KL von der Esch 11/43-9/44

U864   IXD2
KL Hahndorff ?, KK Wolfram 12/43-2/45

U865   IXD2
OL Stellmacher 10/43-9/44

U866   IXC
KK Pommerehne 11/43-12/44, OL Rogowsky 12/44-3/45

U867   IXC
KS Mühlendahl 12/43-9/44

U868   IXC
KL Rauch 12/43-7/44, OL Turre 7/44-5/45

U869   IXC
KL Neuerburg 1/44-2/45

U870   IXC
KK Hechler 2/44-3/45

U871   IXD2
KL Ganzer 1-9/44

U872   IXD2
KL Grau 2-7/44

U873   IXD2
KL Steinhoff 3/44-5/45

U874   IXD2
OL Petersen 4/44-5/45

U875   IXD2
KL Preuss 4/44-5/45

U876   IXD2
KL Bahn 5/44-5/45

U877   IXC
KL Findeisen 3-12/44

U878   IXC
KL Rodig 4/44-4/45

U879   IXC
KL Manchen 4/44-4/45

U880   IXC
KL Schötzau 5/44-4/45

U881   IXC
KL Frischke 5/44-5/45

U882   IXC
Not laid down

U883   IXD2
OL Uebel 3/45-5/45

U884   IXD2
KL Lüders - boat was destoyed during an air raid before being completed

U885 & U886   IXD2
Boats destroyed during air raids before being completed

U887 & U888 IXD2
Building contracts cancelled

U889   IXC
KL Braeucker 8/44-5/45

U890 - U900
Building contracts cancelled

U901   VIIC
KL Schrenk 4-5/45

U902   VIIC
Building contract cancelled

U903   VIIC
OL Hellmann 9-12/43, OL Fränzel 12/43-4/45, KL Tinschert 4-5/45

U904   VIIC
OL Fritz 9-11/43, OL Erdmann 12/43-6/44, OL Stührmann 6/44-5/45

U905   VIIC
OL Brüllau 3-5/44, OL Schwarting 6/44-3/45

U906   VIIC
Commissioned 15/7/44 in Hamburg and destoyed during an air raid 31/12/44. Commander ?

U907   VIIC
OL Cabolet 5/44-5/45

U908 - U920   VIIC
These boats were not built or some of them destroyed during air raids before they could be commissioned.

U921   VIIC
OL Leu 5/43-5/44, OL Werner 6-9/44

U922   VIIC
 OL Graf von und zu Arco-Zinneberg 8-11/43, OL Aust 11/43-1-/44, OL Käselau 10/44-5/45

U923   VIIC
OL Frömmer 10/43-2/45

U924   VIIC
OL Schild 11/43-5/45

U925   VIIC
OL Knocke 12/43-9/44

U926   VIIC
OL von Wenden 2-7/44, OL Roost 8/44-2/45, OL Rehren 2-5/45

U927   VIIC
KL Ebert 6/44-2/45

U928   VIIC
KL Stähler 7/44-5/45

U929   VIIC
OL Schulz 9/44-5/45

U930   VIIC
OL Mohr 12/44-5/45

U931 - U950 VIIC
Building contracts cancelled

U951   VIIC
KL Pressel 12/42-7/43

U952   VIIC
KL Curio 12/42-8/44

U953   VIIC
OL Marbach 12/42-9/44, OL Werner 9/44-3/45, OL Steinbrink 3-5/45

U954   VIIC
KL Loewe 12/42-5/43

U955   VIIC
OL Baden 12/42-6/44

U956   VIIC
KL Mohs 1/43-5/45

U957   VIIC
OL Saar 1/43-3/44, OL Schaar 3-10/44

U958   VIIC
KL Groth 1/43-4/45, OL Stege 4-5/45

U959   VIIC
OL Duppel 1-7/43, OL Weitz 7/43-5/44

U960   VIIC
 OL Heinrich 1/43-5/44

U961   VIIC
OL Fischer 2/43-3/44

U962   VIIC
OL Liesberg 2/43-4/44

U963   VIIC
OL Boddenberg 2/43-12/44, OL Wentz 12/44-3/45

U964   VIIC
OL Hummerjohann 2-10/43

U965   VIIC
KL Ohling 2/43-6/44, OL Unverzagt 6/44-3/45

U966   VIIC
OL Wolf 4-11/43

U967   VIIC
OL Loeder 3/43-3/44, FK Brandi 4-7/44, OL Eberbach 7-8/44

U968   VIIC
OL Westphalen 3/43-5/45

U969   VIIC
OL Dobbert 3/43-5/45

U970   VIIC
KL Ketels 3/43-6/44

U971   VIIC
OL Zeplien 4/43-6/44

U972   VIIC
OL König 4/43-1/44

U973   VIIC
OL Paepenmöller 4/43-3/44

U974   VIIC
OL Zaubitzer 4-11/43, OL Wolff 11/43-4/44

U975   VIIC
OL Bersbach 4-11/43, OL Frerks 11/43-3/44, OL Jeschke 3-7/44, OL Koch 7/44-4/45, KL Brauel 4-5/45

U976   VIIC
KL Tiesler 5/43-3/44

U977   VIIC
KL Leilich 5/43-3/45, OL Schäffer 3/45-5/45,

U978   VIIC
KL Pulst 5/43-5/45

U979   VIIC
KL Meermeier 5/43-5/45

U980   VIIC
KL Dahms 5/43-6/44

U981   VIIC
OL Sitek 6/43-6/44, OL Keller 6-8/44

U982   VIIC
OL Grochowiak 6/43-4/44, OL Schwirley 4-7/44, OL Hartmann 7/44- 4/45

U983   VIIC
OL Reimers 6-9/43

U984   VIIC
OL Siedler 6/43-8/44

U985   VIIC
KL Kessler 6/43-4/44, KL Wolff 4-11/44

U986   VIIC
OL Kaiser 7/43-4/44

U987   VIIC
OL Schreyer 7/43-6/44

U988   VIIC
OL Dobberstein 7/43-6/44

U989   VIIC
KL Rodler von Roithberg 7/43-2/45

U990   VIIC
KL Nordheimer 7/43-5/44

U991   VIIC
KL Balke 7/43-5/45

U992   VIIC
OL Falke 8/43-5/45

U993   VIIC
OL Hilbig 8/43-9/44, OL Steinmetz 9-10/44

U994   VIIC
OL Ackermann 9/43-3/44, OL Melzer 4/44-5/45

U995   VIIC
KL Köhntopp 9/43-10/44, OL Hess 10/44-5/45

U996   VIIC
Destroyed during an air raid before being completed

U997   VIIC
KL Lehmann 9/43-5/45

U998   VIIC
KL Fiedler 10/43-6/44

U999   VIIC
OL Hansen 10/43-7/44, OL Peters 7-11/44, OL Heibges 11/44-5/45

U1000   VIIC
OL Müller 11/43-9/44

U1001   VIIC
KL Blaudow 11/43-4/45

U1002   VIIC
OL Schubart 11/43-7/44, OL Boos 7/44-
5/45

U1003   VIIC
OL Strübing 12/43-3/45

U1004   VIIC
OL Schimmelpfennig 12/43-1/45, OL
Hinz 1-5/45

U1005   VIIC
OL Methner 12/43-7/44, OL Lauth 7/44-
5/45

U1006   VIIC
OL Voigt 1-10/44

U1007   VIIC
KL Hornkohl 1-7/44, OL Wicke 7/44-
3/45, KL von Witzendorff 3-5/45

U1008   VIIC
OL Todenhagen 2-11/44, OL Gessner
11/44-5/45

U1009   VIIC
OL Hilgendorf 2/44-5/45, OL Zehle
11/44-5/45 while Hilgendorf was absent

U1010   VIIC
OL Bitter 2-7/44, KL Strauch 7/44-5/45

U1011 & U1012   VIIC
Destroyed during air raids before being
completed

U1013   VIIC
OL Linck 3/44

U1014   VIIC
OL Glaser 3/44-2/45

U1015   VIIC
OL Boos 3-5/44

U1016   VIIC
OL Ehrhardt 4/44-2/45

U1017   VIIC
OL Riecken 4/44-4/45

U1018   VIIC
KL Faber 4-12/44, KL Burmeister 12/44-
2/45

U1019   VIIC
OL Rinck 5/44-5/45

U1020   VIIC
OL Eberlein 5/44-1/45

U1021   VIIC
OL Holpert 5/44-3/45

U1022   VIIC
KL Ernst 6/44-5/45

U1023   VIIC
OL Strenger 6/44-3/45, KL Schroeteler
3/43-5/45

U1024   VIIC
KL Gutteck 6/44-4/45

U1025   VIIC
OL Pick 4-5/45

U1026 - U1050   VIIC
It seems unlikely that any of these boats
were commissioned; a few were nearing
completion but
the majority were not even laid down

U1051   VIIC
OL von Holleben 3/44-1/45

U1052   VIIC
OL Weidner 1-7/44, OL Scholz 7/44-5/45

U1053   VIIC
OL Lange 2/44-2/45

U1054   VIIC
KL Riekeberg 3-9/44

U1055   VIIC
OL Meyer 4/44-5/45

U1056   VIIC
OL Schwarz 4/44-1/45, OL Schröder 1-
5/45

U1057   VIIC
OL Lüth 5/44-5/45

U1058   VIIC
OL Bruder 6/44-5/45

U1059   VIIF
OL Brünninghaus 5-9/43, OL Leupold
10/43-3/44

U1060   VIIF
OL Brammer 5/43-10/44

U1061   VIIF
OL Hinrichs 8/43-3/45, OL Jäger 3-5/45

U1062   VIIF
OL Albrecht 6/43-9/44

U1063   VIIC
KL Stephan 7/44-4/45

U1064   VIIC
KK Schneidewind 7/44-5/45

U1065   VIIC
OL Panitz 9/44-4/45

U1066 - U1100
The majority of these boats were not
even laid down and none of them were
completed

U1101   VIIC/41
OL Dübler 11/43-5/45
U1102   VIIC/41
OL Schwarting 2-4/44, OL Sell 8/44-5/45

U1103   VIIC/41
KL Bunmgards 1-7/44, OL Sausmikat 7-
10/44, OL Schmidt 10-11/44, OL Ivarsen
11/44-2/45, KL Eisele 2-5/45

U1104   VIIC/41
Ol Perleberg 3/44-5/45

U1105   VIIC/41
OL Schwarz 6/44-5/45

U1106   VIIC/41
OL Bartke 7/44-3/45

U1107   VIIC/41
KL Parduhn 8/44-4/45

U1108   VIIC/41
OL Wiegand 10/44-5/45

U1109   VIIC/41
OL van Riesen 9/44-5/45

U1110   VIIC/41
OL Bach 9/44-5/45

U1111 - U1130 VIIC/41
Not laid down

U1131   VIIC/41
OL Fiebig 5/44-5/45

U1132   VIIC/41
OL Koch 6/44-5/45

U1133 - U1160
Not laid down

U1161   VIIC
OL Raabe 9/43-1/45, KL Schwalbach 1-
5/45

U1162   VIIC/41
OL Sachse 9-12/43, OL Krempl 1/44-
1/45, KL Euler 1-4/45, KL Ketels 4-5/45

U1163   VIIC/41
OL Balduhn 10/43-5/45

U1164   VIIC/41
KL Schlömer 10/43-6/44, KL Wengel 6-
7/44

U1165   VIIC/41
OL Homann 11/43-5/45

U1166   VIIC/41
OL Wagner 12/43-4/44, OL Ballert 4-7/44

U1167   VIIC/41
KL Roeder-Pesch 12/43-8/44, OL
Bortfeldt 8/44-3/45

U1168   VIIC/41
OL Grasse 1-7/44, KL Umlauf 7/44-5/45

U1169   VIIC/41
OL Goldbeck 2/44-4/45

U1170   VIIC/41
KL Justi 3/44-5/45

U1171   VIIC/41
OL Nachtigall 3-7/44, OL Koopmann
7/44-5/45

U1172   VIIC/41
OL Kuhlmann 4/44-1/45

U1173 - U1190
Not laid down

U1191   VIIC/41
OL Grau 9/43-6/44

U1192   VIIC/41
OL Zeissler 9/43-7/44, OL Jewinski 7-
12/44, OL Meenen 12/44-5/45

U1193   VIIC/41
OL Guse 10/43-5/45

U1194   VIIC/41
OL Nolte 10/43-10/44, OL Laudahn 10-
11/44, OL Zeissler 11/44- 5/45

U1195   VIIC/41
OL Schröter 11/43-10/44, KL Cordes
11/44-4/45

U1196   VIIC/41
OL Brand 11/43-2/44, OL Ballert 2/44-
5/45

U1197   VIIC/41
OL Baum 12/43-3/44, OL Lau 3/44-4/45

U1198   VIIC/41
OL Peters 12/43-5/45

U1199   VIIC/41
KL Nollmann 12/43-1/45

U1200   VIIC/41
OL Mangels 1-11/44

U1201   VIIC/41
OL Ebert 1-6/44, OL Ahlers 7-10/44, OL
Merkle 10/44-5/45

U1202   VIIC/41
KL Thomsen 1/44-4/45

U1203   VIIC/41
OL Steinbrink 2-7/44, OL Seeger 7/44-
5/45

U1204   VIIC/41
OL Jestel 8/44-5/45

U1205   VIIC/41
OL Zander 3/44-5/45

U1206   VIIC/41
OL Fritze 3-7/44, KL Schlitt 7/44-4/45

U1207   VIIC/41
OL Lindemann 3/44-5/45

U1208   VIIC/41
KK Hagene 4/44-2/45

U1209   VIIC/41
OL Hülsenbeck 4-12/44

U1210   VIIC/41
KL Gabert 4/44-5/45, OL Süss ?

U1211 - U1220
Not laid down

U1221   IXC/40
OL Kölzer 8/43-1/44, OL Ackermann
1/44-4/45

U1222   IXC/40
KL Bielfeld 9/43-7/44

U1224   IXC/40
KL Preuss 10/43-2/44

U1225   IXC/40
OL Sauerberg 11/43-6/44

U1226   IXC/40
OL Claussen 11/43-10/44

U1227   IXC/40
OL Altmeier 12/43-4/45

U1228   IXC/40
OL Marienfeld 12/43-5/45

U1229   IXC/40
KK Zinke 1-8/44

U1230   IXC/40
KL Hilbig 1/44-5/45

U1231   IXC/40
KS Lessing 2/44-3/45, OL Wicke 3-5/45

U1232   IXC/40
KS Dobratz 3/44-4/45, OL Roth 3-4/45

U1233   IXC/40
KK Kuhn 3/44-4/45, OL Niemeyer 4-
5/45

U1234   IXC/40
KL Thurman 4-5/44, OL Wrode 10/44-
5/45

U1235   IXC/40
KL Barsch 5/44-4/45

U1236 - U1270
Not laid down

U1271   VIIC/41
OL Kniepping 1/44-4/45, OL Thinemann
4-5/45

U1272   VIIC/41
OL Meentzen 1-7/44, OL Schattenburg
7/44-5/45

U1273   VIIC/41
OL Voswinkel 2-7/44, KL Knollmann
7/44-2/45

U1274   VIIC/41
OL Kuscher 3-7/44, OL Fitting 7/44-4/45

U1275   VIIC/41
OL Niss 3-7/44, OL Frohberg 7/44-5/45

U1276   VIIC/41
OL Wendt 4/44-4/45

U1277   VIIC/41
KL Stever 5/44-5/45

U1278   VIIC/41
KL Müller-Bethke 5/44-2/45

U1279   VIIC/41
OL Falke 7/44-2/45

U1280 - U1300
Not laid down

U1301   VIIC/41
OL Feufel 2-7/44, KL Lenkeit 7/44-5/45

U1302   VIIC/41
KL Herwartz 5/44-3/45

U1303   VIIC/41
OL Baum 4/44-4/45, OL Herglotz 4-5/45

U1304   VIIC/41
OL Süss 9/44-5/45

U1305   VIIC/41
OL Christiansen 9/44-5/45

U1306   VIIC/41
OL Kiessling 12/44-5/45

U1307   VIIC/41
OL Buscher 11/44-5/45

U1308   VIIC/41
?

U1309 - U1404
Not laid down

U1405   XVIIB
OL Rex 12/44-5/45

U1406   XVIIB
OL Klug 2-5/45

U1407   XVIIB
OL Heitz 3-5/45

U1408 - U2320
Some of these boats were not laid down, others of Type Hecht are lacking in details

U2321   XXIII
OL Barschkis 6/44-5/45

U2322   XXIII
OL Heckel 7/44-5/45

U2323   XXIII
OL Angermann 7/44

U2324   XXIII
OL Hass 7/44-2/45, KL von Rappard 3-5/45

U2325   XXIII
OL Schüler 8/44-4/45, OL Eckel 4-5/45

U2326   XXIII
OL Jobst 8/44-5/45

U2327   XXIII
OL Mürl 8/44-2/45, OL Müller 2-3/45, OL Pahl 3-4/45, OL Schulz 4- 5/45

U2328   XXIII
OL Scholle 8-11/44, OL Lawrence 12/44-5/45

U2329   XXIII
OL Schlott 9/44-5/45

U2330   XXIII
OL Beckmann 9/44-5/45

U2331   XXIII
OL Pahl 9-10/44

U2332   XXIII
OL Bornkessel 11/44-4/45, OL Junker 4-5/45

U2333   XXIII
OL Baumann 12/44-5/45

U2334   XXIII
OL Angermann 9/44-5/45

U2335   XXIII
OL Benthin 9/44-5/45

U2336   XXIII
OL Vockel 9/44-3/45, KL Klusmeier 4-5/45

U2337   XXIII
OL Behnisch 10/44-5/45

U2338   XXIII
OL Kaiser 10/44-5/45

U2339   XXIII
OL Woermann 11/44-5/45

U2340   XXIII
KL Klusmeier 10/44-3/45

U2341   XXIII
OL Böhm 10/44-5/45

U2342   XXIII
OL Schad von Mittelbiberach 11-12/44

U2343   XXIII
OL Fuhlendorf 11/44-4/45, KL Gause 4-5/45

U2344   XXIII
OL Ellerlage 11/44-2/45

U2345   XXIII
OL Steffen 11/44-5/45

U2346   XXIII
OL von der Höh 11/44-5/45

U2347   XXIII
OL Ulbing 12/44-5/45

U2348   XXIII
OL Goschzig 12/44-5/45

U2349   XXIII
OL Müller 12/44-5/45

U2350   XXIII
OL Schauer 12/44-5/45

U2351   XXIII
OL Brückner 12/44-4/45

U2352   XXIII
OL Budzyn 1-5/45

U2353   XXIII
OL Hillmann 1-5/45

U2354   XXIII
OL Wex 1-5/45

U2355   XXIII
OL Franke 1-5/45

U2356   XXIII
OL Hartel 1-5/45

U2357   XXIII
OL Heinrich 1-5/45

U2358   XXIII
OL Breun 1-5/45

U2359   XXIII
OL Bischoff 1-5/45

U2360   XXIII
OL Schrobach 1-5/45

U2361   XXIII
OL von Hennig 2-5/45

U2362   XXIII
OL Czekowski 2-5/45

U2363   XXIII
OL Frahm 2-5/45

U2364   XXIII
OL Hengen 2-4/45, KL Remus 4-5/45

U2365   XXIII
OL Korfmann 3-5/45, OL Christiansen 5/45

U2366   XXIII
OL Jäckel 3-5/45

U2367   XXIII
OL Schröder 3-5/45

U2368   XXIII
OL Ufermann 4-5/45

U2369   XXIII
OL Schulz 3-4/45, OL Pahl 4-5/45

U2370   XXIII
OL Bornkessel 4-5/45

U2371   XXIII
OL Kühne 4-5/45

U2372 - U2500
It appears that none of these boats were completed; some were not even laid down

U2374   XXIII
OL Waldschmidt, but boat not commissioned

U2375 - U2500
None of these boats were commissioned, although some had almost been completed

U2501   XXI
OL Hübschen 6-11/44

U2502   XXI
KL Mannesmann 7/44-4/45, KL Hornkohl 4/45, KL Franke 4-5/45

U2503   XXI
OL Tiesler 8-10/44, KL Becker 10-11/44, KL Wächter 11/44-5/45

U2504   XXI
OL Günther 8-11/44

U2505   XXI
OL Düppe 11/44-5/45

U2506   XXI
KL von Schroeter 8/44-5/45

U2507   XXI
KL Siegmann 9/44-5/45

U2508   XXI
OL Christiansen 9/44-5/45

U2509   XXI
KK Schendel 9/44-4/45

U2510   XXI
OL Hermann 9/44-5/45

U2511   XXI
KK Schnee 9/44-5/45

U2512   XXI
KL Nordheimer 10/44-5/45

U2513   XXI
KL Bungards 10/44-4/45, KK Topp 4-5/45

U2514   XXI
KL Wahlen 10/44-4/45

U2515   XXI
OL Linder 10/44-2/45

U2516   XXI
OL Kallipke 10/44-4/45

U2517   XXI
OL Hansen 10/44-5/45

U2518   XXI
KL Weidner 11/44-5/45

U2519   XXI
KK Cremer 11/44-2/45

U2520   XXI
OL Schubart 10/44-5/45

U2521   XXI
OL Methner 10/44-5/45

U2522   XXI
KL Queck 11/44-5/45

U2523   XXI
KL Ketels 12/44-1/45

U2524   XXI
KL von Witzendorff 1-5/45

U2525   XXI
KL Otto 12/44-5/45

U2526   XXI
OL Hohmann 12/44-5/45

U2527   XXI
OL Götze 12/44-5/45

U2528   XXI
KL Curio 12/44-5/45

U2529   XXI
OL Feufel 2-4/45, KL Kalipke 4-5/45

U2530   XXI
KL Bokelberg 12/44-2/45

U2531   XXI
KL Niss 1-5/45

U2532   XXI
No commander appointed; boat badly damaged during an air raid before completion

U2533   XXI
OL Günther 1-5/45

U2534   XXI
KL Drews 1/45

U2535   XXI
KL Bitter 1-5/45

U2536   XXI
OL Vöge 2-5/45

U2537   XXI
OL Doppert 3-4/45

U2538   XXI
OL Klapdor 2-5/45

U2539   XXI
OL Jewinski 2-4/45, OL Johann 4-5/45

U2540   XXI
OL Schultze 2-5/45

U2541   XXI
OL Stellmann 3-4/45, KL Wahlen 4-5/45

U2542   XXI
OL Hübschen 3-4/45

U2543   XXI
OL Stolzenburg 3-5/45

U2544   XXI
OL Meinlschmidt 4-5/45

U2545   XXI
OL Freiherr von Müffling 3-5/45

U2546   XXI
OL Dobbert 4-5/45

U2547   XXI
OL Richter, but boat not commissioned

U2548   XXI
OL Utischill 3-5/45

U2551   XXI
KL Schaar 4-5/45

U2552   XXI
KL Rudolf 4-5/45

U3001   XXI
OL Vogel 7-11/44, KL Peters 4-5/45
U3002   XXI
KL Manseck 8-9/44, FK Kaiser 10/44-5/45

U3003   XXI
OL Kregelin 8/44-4/45

U3004   XXI
KL Thurmann 6-44-2/45, KL Peschel 4-4/45

U3005   XXI
KL Hinrichs 1-5/45

U3006   XXI
OL Geisler 10-12/44, OL Linder 11/44-1/45, OL Fischer 1-5/45

U3007   XXI
KL Manseck 10/44-2/45

U3008   XXI
KL Schlömer 10/44-2/45, KL Manseck 3-5/45

U3009   XXI
KL Schimpf 11/44-5/45

U3010   XXI
OL Ebert 11/44-3/45, KK Topp 3-4/45, KL Bungards 4-5/45

U3011   XXI
KL Tinschert 12/44-4/45, OL Fränzel 4-5/45

U3012   XXI
KL Kloevekorn 12/44-5/45

U3013   XXI
KL Simmermacher 11/44-5/45

U3014   XXI
KL Marbach 12/44-5/45

U3015   XXI
KL Grau 12/44-5/45

U3016   XXI
OL Meentzen 1-5/45

U3017   XXI
OL Lindschau 1-5/45

U3018   XXI
OL Breinlinger 1-5/45

U3019   XXI
OL Racky 12/44-5/45

U3020   XXI
OL Mäueler 12/44-5/45

U3021   XXI
OL van Meeteren 1-5/45

U3022   XXI
KL Weber 1-5/45

U3023   XXI
OL Harms 1-5/45

U3024   XXI
OL Blaich 1-5/45

U3025   XXI
KL Vogel 1-5/45

U3026   XXI
OL Drescher 1-5/45

U3027   XXI
KL Mehne 1-5/45

U3028   XXI
KL Christophersen 1-5/45

U3029   XXI
KL Lamby 2-5/45

U3030   XXI
OL Luttmann 2-5/45

U3031   XXI
OL Sach 2-5/45

U3032   XXI
OL Slevogt 2-5/45

U3033   XXI
OL Callsen 2-5/45

U3034   XXI
OL Prehn 3-5/45
U3035   XXI
OL Gerke 3-5/45

U3037   XXI
KK Emmermann 3-4/45, KL Janssen 4-5/45

U3038   XXI
OL Brünig 3-4/45

U3039   XXI
KL Ruperti 3-5/45

U3040   XXI
OL Robbert 3-5/45

U3041   XXI
OL Vieth 3-4/45, KL Hornkohl 4-5/45

U3042   XXI
KL Petersen, but boat not commissioned

U3044   XXI
KL Jaek 3-4/45, KL von Lehsten 4-5/45

U3045   XXI
OL Peters, but boat not commissioned

U3049   XXI
OL Geisler, but boat not commissioned

U3050   XXI
OL Reimann, but boat not commissioned

U3051   XXI
KL Beck, but boat not commissioned

U3501   XXI
OL Münster 7-10/44

U3502   XXI
OL Schultz 8/44-5/45

U3503   XXI
OL Deiring 9/44-5/45

U3504   XXI
KL Siebold 9/44-5/45

U3505   XXI
OL Willner 10/44-4/45

U3506   XXI
KL Thäter 10/44-5/45

U3507   XXI
OL Niethmann 10/44-3/45, OL Schley 3-5/45

U3508   XXI
KL von Lehsten 11/44-3/45

U3509   XXI
KL Franke 3-4/45

U3510   XXI
OL Schwirley 11/44-5/45

U3511   XXI
OL Grasse 11/44-1/45, KL Ketels 1-3/45, KL Schrenk 4-5/45

U3512   XXI
KL Hornkohl 11/44-4/45

U3513   XXI
OL Nachtigall 12/44-5/45

U3514   XXI
OL Fritze 12/44-5/45

U3515   XXI
OL Kuscher 12/44-5/45

U3516   XXI
KL Wengel 12/44-3/45, OL Grote 3-5/45

U3517   XXI
KL Münster 12/44-4/45

U3518   XXI
KL Brünning 12/44-3/45

U3519   XXI
KL von Harpe 1-3/45

U3520   XXI
KL Ballert 1/45

U3521   XXI
OL Keller 1-5/45

U3522   XXI
OL Lenzmann 1-5/45

U3523   XXI
OL Müller 1-5/45

U3524   XXI
KK Witt 1-5/45

U3525   XXI
KL Gaude 1-4/45, KL Kranich -5/45

U3526   XXI
OL Hilbig 3-5/45

U3527   XXI
KL Kronenbitter 3-5/45

U3528   XXI
KL Zwarg 3-5/45

U3529   XXI
OL Schmidt 3-5/45

U3530   XXI
KL Brauel 3-4/45

U4701   XXIII
OL Wiechmann 1-5/45

U4702   XXIII
OL Seeliger 1-5/45

U4703   XXIII
OL Scholz 1-5/45

U4704   XXIII
OL Franceschki 3-5/45

U4705   XXIII
OL Landt-Hayen 2-5/45

U4706   XXIII
OL Schneider 2-5/45

U4707   XXIII
OL Leder 2-5/45

U4709   XXIII
OL Berkemann 3-5/45

U4710   XXIII
OL von Friedeburg 5/45

U4711   XXIII
OL Endler 3-5/45

U4712   XXIII
OL Rohlfing 4-5/45, KL Fleige 5/45

UA
(U-Ausland) Oceangoing boat originally built for Turkey.
KL Cohausz 9/39-11/40, KK Eckermann 11/40-1/42, KK Cohausz 2- 5/42, OL Schnoor 5-8/42, KK Schäfter 10/42-3/43, von Arco- Zinneberg 4/44-3/45, without a commander 3/45-5/45

UB
HM Submarine *Seal*, captured 30/11/40, FK Mahn 11/40-7/41

UC1
Ex-Norwegian B5, captured 1940, KL Kiesewetter 11/40-5/41, KL Lange 6/41-3/42

UC2
Ex-Norwegian B6, captured 1940, OL Wollschläger 11/41-11/43

UD1
Ex-O8, H6, captured in Holland 1940, KK Rigele 11/40-5/41, KL Schäfer 5-11/41, KL Venier 11/41-12/42, KL Ketelsen 12/42-5/43, OL Weidner 5-11/43

UD2
Ex-O12, captured in Holland 1940, KK Venier 1/43-4/44, OL Scholz 4-7/44

UD3
Ex-O25, captured in Holland 1940, KK Rigele 6-7/41, KK Kölle 8/41- 9/42, OL Seeger

UD4
Ex-O26, captured in Holland 1940, Brümmer-Patzig 1-10/41, KK Singule 11/41-4/42, OL Bernbeck 4-10/42, KK Schäfer 4/43-11/44, KL Bart 11/44-3/45, no commander after 3/45

UD5
Ex-O27, captured in Holland 1940, KL Mahn 11/41-1/43, KL von Kameke 1-4/43, KL Scheltz 4/43-5/45

UF2
Ex-*LaFavorite*, captured in France 1940, KK Lange 11/42-10/43, OL Gehrken 10/43-7/44

UIT21
Ex-Italian *Guiseppe Finzi*, OL Steinfeld 10/43-4/44

UIT22
Ex-Italian *Alpine Bagnolini*, OL Wunderlich 10/43-4/44

UIT23
Ex-Italian *Reginaldo Giuliani*, KK Schäfer 12/43-1/44, OL Striegler 2/44

UIT24
Ex-Italian *Commandante Capellini*, OL Pahls 12/43-5/45

UIT25
Ex-Italian *Luigi Torelli*, OL Striegler 12/43-9/44, KL Schrein 9- 11/44, OL Meier 11/44-5/45

Appendix 4: **Service Life of Individual U-Boats**

This chart shows (perhaps not at a glance, but at least with the help of a ruler) which boats were in service on any day of the Second World War. Columns indicating the months of the war run across the page, and the initial of each month is printed at the top and bottom.

The date when the boat was commissioned is shown at the left hand end of its "life line", the left hand digit of the commissioning day being printed in the month column when that boat was commissioned.

The day when it was sunk, or otherwise ceased to be a threat to the Allies, is printed with the right hand digit in the relevant month column. Thus - see chart - e.g. U65 was commissioned on 15 February 1940, and sunk on 28 April 1941; and U107 was commissioned on 8 October 1940, and sunk on 18 August 1944.

This chart is, of course, frustrated by a small number of boats which were sunk so quickly that there is not enough space to write the numbers on their life line. In such cases the full date has been inserted to draw attention to the fact that the numbers are out of alignment –

e.g., U63's week-long career in February 1940, from the 18th to the 25th of that month

Boats which do not have a sinking date, but whose life line reaches May 1945, survived the war. The Instrument of Surrender was signed by the German delegation headed by Admiral Hans-Georg von Friedeburg at 1830 hours on 4 May 1945 to come into effect at 0800 hours (British Double Summer Time) on Saturday 5 May. A few boats still at sea have the day shown when they came into port rather than when they surrendered at sea. Some boats were attacked and sunk after the ceasefire came into force, in which case the sinking date has been added. The majority of boats without dates at the end of their life lines were in German waters around 5 May.

This chart was produced by manually typing each line and I apologise for any mistakes. For some entries, frustratingly, several different dates have been recorded. Generally U-boat Archive figures have been quoted, and later modifications by Axel Niestle, Bob Coppock, Paul Kemp and the author have been included.

```
----  19391940       1941         1942          1943          1944          1945
      SONDJFMAMJJASONDJFMAMJJASONDJFMAMJJASONDJFMAMJJASONDJFMAMJJASONDJFMAM
      ----|-----------|------------|------------|------------|------------|----
  U1  ++++++15
  U2  ++++++++++++++++++++++++++++++++++++++++++++++++++++++++++++++++++8
  U3  +++++++++++++++++++++++++++++++++++++++++++++++++++++++++++++++++++++1
  U4  +++++++++++++++++++++++++++++++++++++++++++++++++++++++++++++++++++++1
  U5  +++++++++++++++++++++++++++++++++++++++++++++++++19
  U6  ++++++++++++++++++++++++++++++++++++++++++++++++++++++++++++++++++++7
  U7  +++++++++++++++++++++++++++++++++++++++++++++++++++++++++++++18
  U8  ++++++++++++++++++++++++++++++++++++++++++++++++++++++++++++++++++++++2
  U9  +++++++++++++++++++++++++++++++++++++++++++++++++++++++++++++20
 U10  +++++++++++++++++++++++++++++++++++++++++++++++++++++++++++1
 U11  +++++++++++++++++++++++++++++++++++++++++++++++++++++++++++++++++++++++3
 U12  +8
 U13  ++++++++31
 U14  +++++++++++++++++++++++++++++++++++++++++++++++++++++++++++++++++++++++2
 U15  +++31
 U16  24
 U17  +++++++++++++++++++++++++++++++++++++++++++++++++++++++++++++++++++++++2
 U18  +++++++++++++++++++++++++++++++++++++++++++++++++++++++++++++++++++25
 U19  ++++++++++++++++++++++++++++++++++++++++++++++++++++++++++++++++++11
 U20  +++++++++++++++++++++++++++++++++++++++++++++++++++++++++++++++++10
 U21  +++++279+++++++++++++++++++++++++++++++++++++++++++++++++++++++++5
 U22  ++++++?
 U23  +++++++++++++++++++++++++++++++++++++++++++++++++++++++++++++++++10
 U24  +++++++++++++++++++++++++++++++++++++++++++++++++++++++++++++++++25
 U25  +++++++++++3
 U26  ++++++++++1
 U27  20*  (20/9/39)
 U28  ++++++++++++++++++++++++++++++++++++++++++++++++++++++++17

      ----|-----------|------------|------------|------------|------------|----
      SONDJFMAMJJASONDJFMAMJJASONDJFMAMJJASONDJFMAMJJASONDJFMAMJJASONDJFMAM
----  19391940       1941         1942          1943          1944          1945
```

```
---- 19391940        1941         1942         1943         1944         1945
     SONDJFMAMJJASONDJFMAMJJASONDJFMAMJJASONDJFMAMJJASONDJFMAMJJASONDJFMAM
     ----|-----------|-----------|-----------|-----------|-----------|----
 U29 +++++++++++++++++++++++++++++++++++++++++++++++++++++++17
 U30 ++++++++++++++++++++++++++++++++++++++++++++++++++++++++++++++++++++++
 U31 +++++11     +++2
 U32 ++++++++++++30
 U33 ++++12
 U34 ++++++++++++++++++++++++++++++++++++++++++++++++++5
 U35 +29
 U36 +++4
 U37 +++++++++++++++++++++++++++++++++++++++++++++++++++++++++++++++++++++8
 U38 +++++++++++++++++++++++++++++++++++++++++++++++++++++++++++++++++++++5
 U39 14*
 U40 13
 U41 +++++5
 U42 13
 U43 +++++++++++++++++++++++++++++++++++++++++++++++++30
 U44 +++++20
 U45 14
 U46 ++++++++++++++++++++++++++++++++++++++++++++++++++++++
 U47 ++++++++++++++++++?
 U48 +++++++++++++++++++++++++++++++++++++++++++++++++++++
 U49 ++++++15
 U50 ++++++10
 U51 ++++++++++20
 U52 +++++++++++++++++++++++++++++++++++++++++++++++++
 U53 ++++23
 U54 +++++?
 U55    21+++++++++++30
 U56 +++++++++++++++++++++++++++++++++++++++++++++++++++++++++++++++++++28
 U57 ++++++++++++3
 U58 ++++++++++++++++++++++++++++++++++++++++++++++++++++++++++++++++++++++
 U59 ++++++++++++++++++++++++++++++++++++++++++++++++++++++++++++++++++++++
 U60 ++++++++++++++++++++++++++++++++++++++++++++++++++++++++++++++++++++++
 U61 ++++++++++++++++++++++++++++++++++++++++++++++++++++++++++++++++++
 U62    21++++++++++++++++++++++++++++++++++++++++++++++++++++++++++++++++
 U63    1825/2/40
 U64    16+13
 U65     15+++++++++++28
 U66         2++++++++++++++++++++++++++++++++++++++++++++6
 U67         22+++++++++++++++++++++++++16
 U68         11++++++++++++++++++++++++++++++++++10
 U69         2+++++++++++++++++++++++++17
 U70         23++7
 U71          14++++++++++++++++++++++++++++++++++++++++++++++
 U72          4+++++++++++++++++++++++++++++++++++++++++++++++++30
 U73        30+++++++++++++++++++++++++++++++++++++++16
 U74        31+++++++++++++++2
 U75          19+++++++++28
 U76          3+++5
 U77          18++++++++++++++++++++++++18
 U78          15++++++++++++++++++++++++++++++++++++++++++++++16
 U79          13++++++23
 U80           8++++++++++++++++++++++++++++++++++++++++++++28
 U81           26++++++++++++++++++++++++++++++++++9
 U82          14+++++++7
 U83           8++++++++++++++++++++++++++9
 U84          29+++++++++++++++++++++++++24
 U85          7++++++++14
 U86           8+++++++++++++++++++++++++++29
 U87           19+++++++++++++++++4
 U88           15++++++++12
 U89           19++++++++++++++14
 U90           20+++24

     ----|-----------|-----------|-----------|-----------|-----------|----
     SONDJFMAMJJASONDJFMAMJJASONDJFMAMJJASONDJFMAMJJASONDJFMAMJJASONDJFMAM
---- 19391940        1941         1942         1943         1944         1945
```

```
---- 19391940      1941        1942        1943        1944        1945
     SONDJFMAMJJASONDJFMAMJJASONDJFMAMJJASONDJFMAMJJASONDJFMAMJJASONDJFMAM
     ----|-----------|-----------|-----------|-----------|-----------|----
U91                          28+++++++++++++++++++++++25
U92                          3++++++++++++++++++++++++++++++++4
U93             30++++++++++++++15
U94          10++++++++++++++++++++++28
U95          31+++++++++++++28
U96           14+++++++++++++++++++++++++++++++++++++++++++++++++++++++++
U97          28++++++++++++++++++++++++++++++++++16
U98           12++++++++++++++++++++++19
U99        18++++++++17
U100       30+++++++17
U101       11+++++++++++++++++++++++++++++++++++++++++++++21
U102       2730/6/40
U103          5+++++++++++++++++++++++++++++++++++++++++++
U104          19+?
U105           10++++++++++++++++++++++++++++++++++2
U106           24++++++++++++++++++++++++++++++++2
U107             8+++++++++++++++++++++++++++++++++++++++++++++++++18
U108           22+++++++++++++++++++++++++++++++++++++++++++11
U109            5++++++++++++++++++++++++++++++++5
U110           21++++9
U111           19+++++++++4
U116                    26+++++++++++++?
U117                   25+++++++++++++++++++++7
U118                   6+++++++++++++++12
U119                    2+++++++++++++24
U120          20+++++++++++++++++++++++++++++++++++++++++++++++++++++++++++
U121          20+++++++++++++++++++++++++++++++++++++++++++++++++++++++++++
U122          30+?
U123          30+++++++++++++++++++++++++++++++++++++++++++++++++17
U124           11+++++++++++++++++++++++++++++++++2
U125                3+++++++++++++++++++++++++6
U126                22++++++++++++++++++++++++3
U127              24+++++15
U128               12++++++++++++++++++++17
U129                21++++++++++++++++++++++++++++++++++++4
U130               11+++++++++++++++++12
U131               1+++17
U132               29++++++++++++++++5
U133                5++++++14
U134               26+++++++++++24
U135                16+++++++++++++++++15
U136                30++++++++11
U137          15++++++++++++++++++++++++++++++++++++++++++++++++++++++++++
U138          27++++++++++18
U139            24++++++++++++++++++++++++++++++++++++++++++++++++++++++++
U140           7+++++++++++++++++++++++++++++++++++++++++++++++++++++++++++
U141           21++++++++++++++++++++++++++++++++++++++++++++++++++++++++++
U142          4++++++++++++++++++++++++++++++++++++++++++++++++++++++++++++
U143           18+++++++++++++++++++++++++++++++++++++++++++++++++++++++++++
U144           2++++++++++9
U145           16++++++++++++++++++++++++++++++++++++++++++++++++++++++++++
U146           30++++++++++++++++++++++++++++++++++++++++++++++++++++++++++
U147       11++++++++++++++2
U148            18+++++++++++++++++++++++++++++++++++++++++++++++++++++++++
U149           13+++++++++++++++++++++++++++++++++++++++++++++++++++++++++++
U150           27+++++++++++++++++++++++++++++++++++++++++++++++++++++++++++
U151           15+++++++++++++++++++++++++++++++++++++++++++++++++++++++++++
U152           29+++++++++++++++++++++++++++++++++++++++++++++++++++++++++++
U153                19+++++++++13
U154             2+++++++++++++++++++++++++++++++++++++++3
U155             23+++++++++++++++++++++++++++++++++++++++++++++++
U156            4++++++++++++++++8

     ----|-----------|-----------|-----------|-----------|-----------|----
     SONDJFMAMJJASONDJFMAMJJASONDJFMAMJJASONDJFMAMJJASONDJFMAMJJASONDJFMAM
---- 19391940      1941        1942        1943        1944        1945
```

```
 ----  19391940         1941           1942           1943           1944           1945
       SONDJFMAMJJASONDJFMAMJJASONDJFMAMJJASONDJFMAMJJASONDJFMAMJJASONDJFMAMJJASONDJFMAM
       ----|-----------|-----------|-----------|-----------|-----------|-----------|----
 U157                      15++++++13
 U158                      25+++++30
 U159                       4++++++++++++++++++++15
 U160                       16+++++++++++++++++14
 U161                    18++++++++++++++++++++++++27
 U162                      9++++++++++3
 U163                       21+++++++++++++13
 U164                       28++++++++++++6
 U165                         3++++27
 U166                        23+++1
 U167                          4+++++++++6
 U168                            10++++++++++++++++++++++++6
 U169                            16+27
 U170                              19++++++++++++++++++++++++++++++
 U171                     25++++++++++9
 U172                       5++++++++++++++++++++++++12
 U173                      15+++++++++16
 U174                      26++++++++++++++27
 U175                       5+++++++++++++17
 U176                       15++++++++++++++15
 U177                        14++++++++++++++++++++6
 U178                        14+++++++++++++++20
 U179                       7++++++8
 U180                         16++++++++++++++++++++++++22
 U181                          9++++++++++++++++++++++++++++++++++++
 U182                        30+++++++++16
 U183                          1+++++++++++++++++++++++++++++++++++++23
 U184                       29+++20
 U185                        13++++++++++++24
 U186                        10+++++++13
 U187                       23+++++4
 U188                         5++++++++++++++++++++20
 U189                        15+++++24
 U190                          24+++++++++++++++++++++++++++++++++14
 U191                        20+++23
 U192                        16++++5
 U193                         10+++++++++++++28
 U194                        8+++24
 U195                         5+++++++++++++++++++++++++++++++++++++
 U196                         11++++++++++++++++++++++?
 U197                         10+++++++20
 U198                          3++++++++++++++++++++12
 U199                         28+++++31
 U200                         22+++24
 U201                     25++++++++++++++++++++++17
 U202                      22++++++++++++++++++++++++2
 U203                     18++++++++++++++++++++++++25
 U204                     8+++++19
 U205                      3++++++++++++++++++++17
 U206                     17+++30
 U207                     7+11
 U208                     5++++7
 U209                       11+++++++++++++++++?
 U210                        21++++6
 U211                          7++++++++++++++++++19
 U212                          25++++++++++++++++++++++++21
 U213                     30+++++++++31
 U214                          1++++++++++++++++++++++++++++++++26
 U215                      22++++++3
 U216                      15+++++++20
 U217                        31++++++++++++++5
 U218                         24++++++++++++++++++++++++++++++++++++++++
       ----|-----------|-----------|-----------|-----------|-----------|-----------|----
       SONDJFMAMJJASONDJFMAMJJASONDJFMAMJJASONDJFMAMJJASONDJFMAMJJASONDJFMAMJJASONDJFMAM
 ----  19391940         1941           1942           1943           1944           1945
```

```
---- 19391940      1941        1942        1943        1944        1945
     SONDJFMAMJJASONDJFMAMJJASONDJFMAMJJASONDJFMAMJJASONDJFMAMJJASONDJFMAM
     ----|-----------|-----------|-----------|-----------|-----------|----
U219                                      12++++++++++++++++++++++++++++++
U220                                     27++++27
U221                               9+++++++++++++27
U222                             23++2
U223                               6+++++++++++++++++30
U224                             20++++13
U225                            11++++21
U226                              1++++++++++++++6
U227                             22+++++30
U228                                12++++++++++++++++++++++++++4
U229                             3+++++++++22
U230                              24++++++++++++++++++21
U231                             14+++++++++++13
U232                             28++++++8
U233                                       22+++++++++6
U234                                                 2++++++++++++16
U235                              19++14  }All  three boats
U236                              9++14   }raised and used
U237                              30+14   }non-operationally
U238                              20+++++++++9
U239                             13+++++++++++++24
U240                              3++++++++++16
U241                               3++++++++18
U242                                      14+++++++++++++++++30
U243                                      2++++++++8
U244                                       9++++++++++++++++++++
U245                                         18+++++++++++++++
U246                                        11+++++++++++29
U247                                     23+++++++++1
U248                                       6+++++++++++16
U249                                        20+++++++++++++++
U250                                       12++++30
U251                      20++++++++++++++++++++++++++++++++++++++++++19
U252                             4++++14
U253                            21++++++++23
U254                             8++++++++++++8
U255                      29+++++++++++++++++++++++++++++++++++++++++++++
U256                             18++++++++++++++++++23 used as Flak trap
U257                            14++++++++++++++++++++24
U258                            4+++++++++++++21
U259                            18++++++15
U260                             14+++++++++++++++++++++++++++++++++++++12
U261                            28+++15
U262                             15++++++++++++++++++++++++++++++++++?
U263                             6+++++++++++++++++20
U264                             22++++++++++++++++++19
U265                            6+++++++3
U266                             24++++++++14
U267                              11++++++++++++++++++++++++++++++++++++
U268                            29++++19
U269                             16+++++++++++++++++27
U270                             5+++++++++++++++++++++12
U271                             23+++++++++++++28
U272                            712*
U273                            21++++19
U274                             7+++++++++23
U275                             25++++++++++++++++++++++++++++++10
U276                             9++++++++++++++++++29
U277                             21++++++++++++++1
U278                             16+++++++++++++++++++++++++++++++++
U279                             2++++++4
U280                             13++++++16

     ----|-----------|-----------|-----------|-----------|-----------|----
     SONDJFMAMJJASONDJFMAMJJASONDJFMAMJJASONDJFMAMJJASONDJFMAMJJASONDJFMAM
     ---- 19391940      1941        1942        1943        1944        1945
```

```
---- 19391940      1941         1942         1943         1944         1945
     SONDJFMAMJJASONDJFMAMJJASONDJFMAMJJASONDJFMAMJJASONDJFMAMJJASONDJFMAM
     ----|-----------|-----------|-----------|-----------|-----------|----
U281                                                     27+++++++++++++++++++++++++
U282                                          13++++29
U283                                          31++++++++11
U284                                          14+++++21
U285                                             15++++++++++++++++++++15
U286                                              5+++++++++++++++++++29
U287                                                 22++++++++++++++++16
U288                                           26+++++++++4
U289                                           10+++++++31
U290                                              24+++++++++++++++++++++
U291                                               4+++++++++++++++++++++
U292                                           25++++++27
U293                                                8++++++++++++++++++++
U294                                                 6++++++++++++++++++
U295                                              20+++++++++++++++++++
U296                                              3++++++++++++++22
U297                                             17+++++++++++6
U298                                               1++++++++++++++++++
U299                                              15+++++++++++++++++
U300                                               29+++++++++++22
U301                             9++++++21
U302                             16+++++++++++++++++++6
U303                            7++++++++21
U304                           5+++++++28
U305                             17++++++++++++++17
U306                            21+++++++++31
U307                               18+++++++++++++++++++++++++++29
U308                            23+++++4
U309                               27++++++++++++++++++++++16
U310                                24+++++++++++++++++++++++++
U311                              23++++++++++22
U312                                21++++++++++++++++++++++++++
U313                               20++++++++++++++++++++++++
U314                              10++++30
U315                               10++++++++++++++++++++
U316                                5+++++++++++++++++++2
U317                              23+++++26
U318                                13++++++++++++++++
U319                              4+++++15
U320                                30++++++++++++++++7
U321                               20++++++++++++2
U322                               5+++++++25
U323                                2+++++++++++++
U324                                5++++++++++++
U325                                 6+++++++++30
U326                                 6+++++++++?
U327                                 18++++27
U328                                 19+++++++
U329                                  ?+++30
U331                     31++++++++++++++++++17
U332                       7+++++++++++++++++++29
U333                        25+++++++++++++++++++++++++++++++31
U334                        9++++++++++++++++++14
U335                          17++++++3
U336                         14+++++++++++++++++++4
U337                          6++++++15
U338                           25+++++++++++++20
U339                            25++++++++++++++++++++++++++++++++
U340                           16++++++++++++1
U341                           28+++++++19
U342                            12++++++++++++17
U343                            18+++++++++++10
U344                            26++++++++++++++22
     ----|-----------|-----------|-----------|-----------|-----------|----
     SONDJFMAMJJASONDJFMAMJJASONDJFMAMJJASONDJFMAMJJASONDJFMAMJJASONDJFMAM
---- 19391940      1941         1942         1943         1944         1945
```

```
----  19391940        1941          1942          1943          1944          1945
      SOND J FMAM J JASOND J FMAM J JASOND J FMAM J JASOND J FMAM J JASOND J FMAM J JASOND J FMAM
      ----|-----------|-----------|-----------|-----------|-----------|----

U345                                            4+++++13
U346                                            7+20
U347                                            7++++++++++17
U348                                              10+++++++++++++++30
U349                                                8++++++++++++++++++++
U350                                               7+++++++++++++++30
U351                      20++++++++++++++++++++++++++++++++++++++++++++++++++
U352                         28+++++++9
U353                           31++++16
U354                              22+++++++++++++++++++++++++24
U355                           29+++++++++++++++++++++++++++++1
U356                         20+++++++++27
U357                            18+++26
U358                               15++++++++++++++++1
U359                                5+++++++28
U360                                12++++++++++++++2
U361                                 18++++++++++++++++17
U362                                   4+++++++++++++++++5
U363                                   18+++++++++++++++++++++++++
U364                                 3++++++30
U365                                   8++++++++++++++++13
U366                                  16+++++++5
U367                                     27+++++++++++++++15
U368                                       7++++++++++++++++
U369                                     15++++++++++++++++++
U370                                     19+++++++++++++++++
U371                     15++++++++++++++++++++++++++++++++++++++++++++4
U372                    19++++++++++++++4
U373                      22+++++++++++++++++++++++++++++++++++++++8
U374                     21++++12
U375                     19++++++++++++++++++++30
U376                      21++++++++++++++++10
U377                        2+++++++++++++++++++++++++++15
U378                       30++++++++++++++++++++++20
U379                      29+++++++8
U380                       22+++++++++++++++++++++++++13
U381                        25+++++++++++++19
U382                          25++++++++++++++++++++++++++++++++++12
U383                           6+++++++++++++1
U384                          18+++++19
U385                           29+++++++++++++++++++++11
U386                           10+++++++++++++19
U387                            24++++++++++++++++++++++9
U388                           31+++20
U389                            6+++++++5
U390                             13++++++++++++++5
U391                            24+++++13
U392                            29+++++++16
U393                               3+++++++++++++++++++++4
U394                             7++++++++++++2
U396                                  16+++++++++++++++23
U397                                   20++++++++++++++++++
U398                                    18+++++++++++++++?
U399                                     22+++++++++++26
U400                                      18++++++17
U401          10++3
U402                     21+++++++++++++++++++++++++++13
U403                     25++++++++++++++++++++++++17         .
U404                   6++++++++++++++++++++++28
U405                     17+++++++++++++++++++++++1
U406                     22++++++++++++++++++++++++++++18
U407                      18+++++++++++++++++++++++++++++++++++19
U408                    19+++++++++5
      ----|-----------|-----------|-----------|-----------|-----------|----
      SOND J FMAM J JASOND J FMAM J JASOND J FMAM J JASOND J FMAM J JASOND J FMAM J JASOND J FMAM
----  19391940        1941          1942          1943          1944          1945
```

```
---- 19391940        1941         1942         1943         1944         1945
     SONDJFMAMJJASONDJFMAMJJASONDJFMAMJJASONDJFMAMJJASONDJFMAMJJASONDJFMAM
     ----|-----------|-----------|-----------|-----------|-----------|----

U409                           21+++++++++++++++16
U410                           23++++++++++++++++++++++11
U411                         18+++++28
U412                         29+++22
U413                             3++++++++++++++++++++++++20
U414                           1++++++++25
U415                               5++++++++++++++++++++++14
U416                             4++30        4++++++++++++12
U417                           26++++++11
U418                           21+++++++1
U419                             18+++++++++8
U420                             16++++++++17
U421                               13++++++++++++29
U422                             10+++++++4
U423                               3+++++++++++++17
U424                             7+++++++++11
U425                               21++++++++++++++++++++17
U426                             12++++++8
U427                                 2+++++++++++++++++++++++++
U428                                 26+++++++++++++++++++++++
U429                               14++++++++++++++++++?
U430                                 4+++++++++++++++++30
U431                       5++++++++++++++++++++++++++++++21
U432                     26+++++++++++++++++++11
U433                     24+++16
U434                     21+++18
U435                       30++++++++++++++++++++++9
U436                       27+++++++++++++++++26
U437                       25+++++++++++++++++++++++++++++++++++4
U438                       22++++++++++++++++6
U439                       20++++++++++++++3
U440                       24++++++++++++++31
U441                         21+++++++++++++++++++++++18
U442                         21++++++++12
U443                       18+++++++23
U444                       9++++++++11
U445                         30+++++++++++++++++++++++24
U446                       2021
U447                           11++++++++7
U448                             1++++++++++++++++++14
U449                           22+++++++24
U450                             12++++++++++++++++10
U451                   3+++++21
U452                   2925
U453                       26++++++++++++++++++++++++++++++++++++21
U454                       24++++++++++++++++++++++1
U455                       21++++++++++++++++++++++++++++++6
U456                       18++++++++++++++++++13
U457                       5++++++++16
U458                           12++++++++++++++++22
U459                         15+++++++++++++++++27
U460                         24++++++++++++++++++4
U461                       30+++++++++++++++30
U462                         5++++++++++++++30
U463                         2+++++++++++15
U464                         30+20
U465                         20+++++++++++5
U466                           17+++++++++++++++++++++++++++19
U467                           15+++++++29
U468                           12+++++++++11
U469                           7+++25
U470                             7+++++++16

     ----|-----------|-----------|-----------|-----------|-----------|----
     SONDJFMAMJJASONDJFMAMJJASONDJFMAMJJASONDJFMAMJJASONDJFMAMJJASONDJFMAM
---- 19391940        1941         1942         1943         1944         1945
```

```
----  19391940      1941         1942         1943         1944         1945
      SONDJFMAMJJASONDJFMAMJJASONDJFMAMJJASONDJFMAMJJASONDJFMAMJJASONDJFMAM
      ----|-----------|-----------|-----------|-----------|-----------|----
U468                                    12+++++++++11
U469                                    7+++25
U470                                       7+++++++16
U471                                          5+++++++++++++6
U472                                       26+++++++++4
U473                                        16+++++++++5
U475                                            7++++++++++++++++++++3
U476                                        28+++++++24
U477                                          18+++++++++3
U478                                           8+++++++30
U479                                             27+++++++++++12
U480                                             6+++++++++++++24
U481                                               10+++++++++++++++++
U482                                              1+++++++++++16
U483                                               22+++++++++++++++
U484                                                19++++++9
U485                                                 23+++++++++++++8
U486                                                   22++++++++++12
U487                                    21++++13
U488                                      1++++++++++++26
U489                                     8++++4
U490                                       27+++++++++++11
U501          30++10
U502          31+++++++++++++5
U503           10+++++15
U504           30++++++++++++++++++++++30
U505            26++++++++++++++++++++++++++++++++4
U506           15++++++++++++++++++12
U507           8+++++++++++++13
U508           20++++++++++++++++++12
U509           4++++++++++++++++15
U510           25+++++++++++++++++++++++++++++++++++++++8
U511           12++++++++++++++++++16
U512           20++++++++2
U513            10+++++++++++++++19
U514            24+++++++++++++++8
U515             21+++++++++++++++++++++++9
U516             10++++++++++++++++++++++++++++++++++++++++14
U517             21+++++21
U518             25++++++++++++++++++++++++++++++++++++22
U519            7++++++++10
U520            19++30
U521             3+++++++++++2
U522            11+++++23
U523            25++++++++++++25
U524            8++++++22
U525            30++++++++++11
U526            12++++++14
U527            2+++++++++23
U528            16+++++11
U529            30++15
U530             14+++++++++++++++10/7/45 La Plata
U531            28+++++6
U532             11++++++++++++++++++++++++++++++++++++10
U533            25+++++++++16
U534             23+++++++++++++++++++++++++++++++++5
U535            23+++++5
U536            13+++++++20
U537             27+++++++++++++++++++9
U538            10++++++21
U539             24+++++++++++++++++++++++++++++++
U540            10++++18

      ----|-----------|-----------|-----------|-----------|-----------|----
      SONDJFMAMJJASONDJFMAMJJASONDJFMAMJJASONDJFMAMJJASONDJFMAMJJASONDJFMAM
----  19391940      1941         1942         1943         1944         1945
```

```
---- 19391940        1941          1942          1943          1944          1945
     SONDJFMAMJJASONDJFMAMJJASONDJFMAMJJASONDJFMAMJJASONDJFMAMJJASONDJFMAM
     ----|------------|------------|------------|------------|------------|----
U541                                          24+++++++++++++++++++++++++++
U542                                          7+++++28
U543                                          21+++++++++++++2
U544                                          5++++++17
U545                                          19+++++11
U546                                            2+++++++++++++++++++++++24
U547                                            16++++++++++++++31
U548                                            30+++++++++++++++?
U549                                             10+++++++29
U550                                             28++++++16
U551              7++23
U552            4+++++++++++++++++++++++++++++++++++++++++++++++++++++++2
U553            23+++++++++++++++++++++28
U554             15+++++++++++++++++++++++++++++++++++++++++++++++++++++3
U555             30++++++++++++++++++++++++++++++++++++++++++++++++++++?
U556              6++27
U557             13+++++++16
U558             20+++++++++++++++++++++++++++++20
U559             27+++++++++++++++++30
U560               6+++++++++++++++++++++++++++++++++++++++++++++++++++++3
U561              13++++++++++++++++++++++++12
U562              20+++++++++++++++++++19
U563              27+++++++++++++++++++++31
U564              3+++++++++++++++++++++++14
U565              10+++++++++++++++++++++++++++++++++++++++24
U566              19+++++++++++++++++++++++++24
U567             24++++21
U568              1++++++++++28
U569              8+++++++++++++++++++22
U570             1527
U571              22+++++++++++++++++++++++++++++28
U572              29+++++++++++++++++++++++++3
U573              5+++++++++29
U574              12+++19
U575              19+++++++++++++++++13
U576              24++++++++++15
U577              3+++++9
U578              10++++++++++10
U579             17+?         ?+++++++++++++++++++++++++++++++++++++++++5
U580             24+11
U581             31+++++2
U582              7+++++++++++++5
U583             1415
U584              21++++++++++++++++++++++̂+31
U585             28++++29
U586                4++++++++++++++++++++++++++++++++++++5
U587             11+++27
U588             18++++++++31
U589             25+++++++++12
U590               2++++++++++++++++++9
U591               9++++++++++++++++++30
U592               16+++++++++++++++++++++++31
U593               23++++++++++++++++++++++13
U594               30++++++++++++++++++7
U595              6++++++++++14
U596               13++++++++++++++++++++++++++++++++15
U597               20++++++++12
U598               27+++++++++++++++++26
U599               4++++++++24
U600               11+++++++++++++++++++++25
U601               18+++++++++++++++++++++++25
U602               29+++++++++++++23
U603               2++++++++++++++++++++++++1
     ----|------------|------------|------------|------------|------------|----
     SONDJFMAMJJASONDJFMAMJJASONDJFMAMJJASONDJFMAMJJASONDJFMAMJJASONDJFMAM
---- 19391940        1941          1942          1943          1944          1945
```

```
----  19391940        1941          1942          1943          1944          1945
      SONDJFMAMJJASONDJFMAMJJASONDJFMAMJJASONDJFMAMJJASONDJFMAMJJASONDJFMAM
      ----|-----------|-----------|-----------|-----------|-----------|----
U604                            8+++++++++++++++++11
U605                            15+++++++13
U606                            22+++++++++22
U607                            29++++++++++++++13
U608                              5++++++++++++++++++++++++++++10
U609                            12++++++++++7
U610                              19++++++++++++++++++8
U611                            26+++++++10
U612                          5+++24
U613                              12+++++++++++++23
U614                              19++++++++++++29
U615                            26++++++++++++++6
U616                                2++++++++++++++++++++++++14
U617                                9+++++++++++++12
U618                                16++++++++++++++++++++++++++14
U619                            23++++5
U620                            30+++++++14
U621                                7++++++++++++++++++++++++++++18
U622                              14++++++++++++24
U623                            21+++++21
U624                            28+++++++7
U625                                4+++++++++++++++++10
U626                              11+++15
U627                              18+27
U628                              25+++++++++++3
U629                                7+++++++++++++++++++++8
U630                              9+++++++++4
U631                                16++++++++++++18
U632                              23+++++++6
U633                              30++++++7
U634                                6++++++++++30
U635                              13++++++6
U636                                20+++++++++++++++++++++++++++++21
U637                                27++++++++++++++++++++++++++++26
U638                              3+++++++5
U639                              10++++++++26
U640                              17+++++17
U641                              24+++++++++++++19
U642                                1+++++++++++++++++++5
U643                              8+++++++++++8
U644                              15++++7
U645                              22++++++++++++24
U646                              29++++17
U647                              5+++++++?3
U648                              12+++++++++23
U649                              1924
U650                              26++++++++++++++++++++++++?7
U651         12+29
U652         3+++++++++++++2
U653         25+++++++++++++++++++++++++++++++++++15
U654           5+++++++++++22
U655           11++++24
U656           17++++1
U657             8++++++++++++++++14
U658             5++++++++++30
U659             9++++++++++++++++3
U660             8++++++++++12
U661             12+++++15
U662               9+++++++++++++21
U663               14++++++++++7
U664               17+++++++++++9
U665             22+++++22
U666               26+++++++++++++++10
      ----|-----------|-----------|-----------|-----------|-----------|----
      SONDJFMAMJJASONDJFMAMJJASONDJFMAMJJASONDJFMAMJJASONDJFMAMJJASONDJFMAM
----  19391940        1941          1942          1943          1944          1945
```

```
----  19391940       1941         1942         1943         1944         1945
      SONDJFMAMJJASONDJFMAMJJASONDJFMAMJJASONDJFMAMJJASONDJFMAMJJASONDJFMAM
      ----|-----------|-----------|-----------|-----------|-----------|----
U667                                          20+++++++++++++++++++25
U668                                          16+++++++++++++++++++++++++++++
U669                                          12+++++++7
U670                                          26++++20
U671                                              3+++++++++++++++++4
U672                                            6++++++++++++++18
U673                                              8++++++++++++++++24
U674                                             15++++++++++2
U675                                             14++++++++24
U676                                              6++++++++++++++++19
U677                                                 20++++++++++++++++++8
U678                                                 25++++++++6
U679                                                 29+++++++++++10
U680                                                  23+++++++++++++++++
U681                                                  3++++++++++++11
U682                                                    17+++++29
U683                                                    30++++++++12
U701            16+++++++++++7
U702            3++++++4
U703             16++++++++++++++++++++++++++++++++++++++++++?
U704              18++++++++++++++++++++++++++++++++++++++++++++++++++3
U705            30+++++++3
U706               16+++++++++++++++++2
U707                  1++++++++++++++++9
U708                  24++++++++++++++++++++++++++++++++++++++++++++3
U709                  12+++++++++++++++++++1
U710                  2+++++24
U711                  26++++++++++++++++++++++++++++++++++++++++++++5
U712                   5++++++++++++++++++++++++++++++++++++++++++++
U713                  29+++++++++++24
U714                    10+++++++++++++++++++++++14
U715                    17+++++++++++12
U716                    14++++++++++++++++++++++++++++
U717                     19+++++++++++++++++++++++++
U718                    25++18
U719                    17+++++++++26
U720                      17+++++++++++++++++++++
U721                      22++++++++++++++++++++++
U722                        15+++++++++++++27
U731              3+++++++++++++++++++15
U732              24++++++++++31
U733              14++++++++++++++++++++++++++++++++++++++4
U734              5++++++++++++++9
U735              28+++++++++++++++++++++++++28
U736              16+++++++++++++++++6
U737              30++++++++++++++++++++++++19
U738              20++++++++++14
U739                6+++++++++++++++++++++++++++++
U740              27+++++++++++++9
U741                10++++++++++++++15
U742                1+++++++++++++19
U743                15+++++++++++++++9
U744                5++++++++6
U745                  19+++++++++++++++++++6
U746                   4+++++++++++++++++++++++4
U747                   17+++++++++++++++++++++1
U748                   31+++++++++++++++++++++++3
U749                   14+++++++++++++++++++4
U750                    26+++++++++++++++++++++
U751            31+++++++++++++++17
U752            24++++++++++++++++++++++++23
U753            18+++++++++++++++++++++15

      ----|-----------|-----------|-----------|-----------|-----------|----
      SONDJFMAMJJASONDJFMAMJJASONDJFMAMJJASONDJFMAMJJASONDJFMAMJJASONDJFMAM
----  19391940       1941         1942         1943         1944         1945
```

```
---- 19391940      1941         1942         1943         1944         1945
     SONDJFMAMJJASONDJFMAMJJASONDJFMAMJJASONDJFMAMJJASONDJFMAMJJASONDJFMAM
     ----|-----------|-----------|-----------|-----------|-----------|----
U754               28++++++++31
U755             3+++++++++++++++28
U756             30+++++++1
U757               28++++++++++++++++++++++8
U758                 5+++++++++++++++++++++++++++++++++++++11
U759               10++++++++26
U760                15++++++++++8
U761                 3+++++++++++24
U762                30+++++++++++8
U763                    13+++++++++++++++++24
U764                     6+++++++++++++++++++++++
U765                    16++++++++++6
U766                    30++++++++++21
U767                    11++++++18
U768                    1420/11/43
U771                    18+++++++++11
U772                    23++++++++++30
U773                    20+++++++++++++++
U774                    17+++++++++++18
U775                    23++++++++++++++
U776                    13++++++++++20
U777                     9+++15
U778                      7++++++++++
U779                      24+++++++++
U801               24++++++++++17
U802                 12++++++++++++++++++++++11
U803                7+++++27
U804                      4+++++++++++++++++9
U805                      12++++++++++++++14
U806                      29+++++++++++++
U821                    11+++++10
U822                        1+++++++++3
U825                        4+++++++++++++
U826                        11+++++++++11
U827                        25++++++++++4
U828                        17+++++++++3
U841               6++++++17
U842               1+++++++6
U843               24+++++++++++++++++++++++9
U844               7++++16
U845               1++++++++10
U846               29+++++++++++4
U847             23++++27
U848             20+++++++5
U849             11+++++25
U850             17+++++20
U851                21++++++++++3
U852                15++++++++++3
U853                25+++++++++++++++++++++++6
U854               19+++++4
U855                 2++++++++++++++?
U856               19++++++7
U857                      16++++++++++++++++++7
U858                      30++++++++++++++++++14
U859                8++++++++++++23
U860                12+++++++15
U861                 2+++++++++++August 45
U862                 7++++++++++++++++++++
U863                  3++++++++29
U864                     9++++++++++++++9
U865                  25++++++++++?
U866                    17+++++++++++++18

     ----|-----------|-----------|-----------|-----------|-----------|----
     SONDJFMAMJJASONDJFMAMJJASONDJFMAMJJASONDJFMAMJJASONDJFMAMJJASONDJFMAM
---- 19391940      1941         1942         1943         1944         1945
```

```
---- 19391940        1941         1942         1943         1944         1945
     SONDJFMAMJJASONDJFMAMJJASONDJFMAMJJASONDJFMAMJJASONDJFMAMJJASONDJFMAM
     ----|-----------|-----------|-----------|-----------|-----------|----
U867                                                      11++++++19
U868                                                      23++++++++++++++++
U869                                                      26++++++++++28
U870                                                        3++++++++++++30
U871                                                      15+++++26
U872                                                      10+++10
U873                                                        1+++++++++++++16
U874                                                        8+++++++++++++
U875                                                       21++++++++++++
U876                                                        24++++++++++4
U877                                                     24+++++27
U878                                                       14+++++++++10
U879                                                      19+++++++++19
U880                                                      11+++++++++16
U881                                                       27++++++++++6
U883                                                                 27+
U889                                                          4++++++++15
U901                                                     29+++++++++++15
U903                                               4++++++++++++++++++++3
U904                                              25++++++++++++++++++++4
U905                                                      8++++++++++20
U906                                                        15++31
U907                                                       8+++++++++++++
U921                                        30+++++++++++++30
U922                                              1+++++++++++++++++++3
U923                                              4++++++++++++++++9
U925                                             30++++++18
U926                                                     29++++++++++++++
U927                                                        26+++++24
U928                                                       10++++++++++
U929                                                        6+++++++3
U930                                                          6+++++
U951                                       3++++++7
U952                                       10++++++++++++++++++6
U953                                       17++++++++++++++++++++++++++++++
U954                                       23++19
U955                                       31++++++++++++++++7
U956                                        6+++++++++++++++++++++++++++++
U957                                        7+++++++19
U958                                        14+++++?
U959                                        21+++++++++++++2
U960                                        28+++++++++++++19
U961                                         4++++++++++29
U962                                         11+++++++++++8
U963                                         17+++++++++++++++++++++++++++20
U964                                         18+++++16
U965                                         25+++++++++++++++++++++++++27
U966                                          4++++++10
U967                                         11+++++++++++++11
U968                                         18+++++++++++++++++++++++++++
U969                                         24+++++++++++++6
U970                                         25+++++++++++++7
U971                                          1++++++++++++24
U972                                          8++++++++?
U973                                         15+++++++++6
U974                                         22+++++++++19
U975                                         29+++++++++++++++August 45
U976                                          5++++++++25
U977                                          6++++++++++++++++++++++++++
U978                                         12+++++++++++++++++++++++++
U979                                         20+++++++++++++++++++++++3
U980                                         27++++++++++11

     ----|-----------|-----------|-----------|-----------|-----------|----
     SONDJFMAMJJASONDJFMAMJJASONDJFMAMJJASONDJFMAMJJASONDJFMAMJJASONDJFMAM
---- 19391940        1941         1942         1943         1944         1945
```

```
----  19391940      1941         1942         1943         1944         1945
      SONDJFMAMJJASONDJFMAMJJASONDJFMAMJJASONDJFMAMJJASONDJFMAMJJASONDJFMAM
      ----|-----------|-----------|-----------|-----------|-----------|----
U981                                           3++++++++++++12
U982                                           10++++++++++++++++++++++8
U983                                           16+8
U984                                           17+++++++++++20
U985                                           24+++++++++++++23
U986                                           1++++++++17
U987                                           8+++++++++15
U988                                           15++++++++29
U989                                           22+++++++++++++++14
U990                                           28++++++25
U991                                           29++++++++++++++++++++
U992                                            2++++++++++++++++++++
U993                                           19++++++++++++4
U994                                            2+++++++++++++++++++
U995                                           16+++++++++++++++++8
U997                                           23++++++++++++++++++
U998                                            7++++++27
U999                                           21+++++++++++++++++
U1000                                           4+++++++15
U1001                                           18+++++++++++++++8
U1002                                           30+++++++++++++++++
U1003                                            9+++++++++++++23
U1004                                           16+++++++++++++++++
U1005                                           30+++++++++++++++++
U1006                                           11++++++16
U1007                                           18+++++++++++++++2
U1008                                            1+++++++++++++++6
U1009                                           10+++++++++++++10
U1010                                           22+++++++++++14
U1013                                           217/3/44
U1014                                           14++++++++++4
U1015                                           2319/5/44
U1016                                            4+++++++++++++
U1017                                            1+++++++++++29
U1018                                            1+++++++++27
U1019                                            4+++++++++++++
U1020                                           17++++++?
U1021                                           25+++++++30
U1022                                            7++++++++++
U1023                                           15++++++++10
U1024                                           28+++++++12
U1025                                           12++++++++++
U1051                                            4++++++++26
U1052                                           20++++++++++++++
U1053                                           12+++++++++15
U1054                                           25+++16
U1055                                            8+++++++++30
U1056                                           29+++++++++++
U1057                                           20++++++++++
U1058                                           10++++++++++
U1059                                           1++++++++19
U1060                                           15+++++++++++++27
U1061                                           25++++++++++++++++++++
U1062                                           19+++++++++++30
U1063                                            8+++++++15
U1064                                           29+++++++++
U1065                                           23+++++9
U1101                                           10++++++++++++++++++
U1102                                           22++++++++++++++
U1103                                            8+++++++++++++++
U1104                                           15+++++++++++++
U1105                                            3++++++++++

      ----|-----------|-----------|-----------|-----------|-----------|----
      SONDJFMAMJJASONDJFMAMJJASONDJFMAMJJASONDJFMAMJJASONDJFMAMJJASONDJFMAM
----  19391940      1941         1942         1943         1944         1945
```

```
---- 19391940        1941         1942         1943         1944         1945
     SONDJFMAMJJASONDJFMAMJJASONDJFMAMJJASONDJFMAMJJASONDJFMAMJJASONDJFMAM
     ----|-----------|-----------|-----------|-----------|-----------|----
U1106                                                            5++++++29
U1107                                                            8++++++25
U1108                                                                 18+++++
U1109                                                              31++++++++
U1110                                                             24+++++++
U1131                                                         20++++++11
U1132                                                            24+++++++++++
U1161                                                    25++++++++++++++++++++
U1162                                                    15+++++++++++++++++++
U1163                                                      6+++++++++++++++++++
U1164                                                    27++++++23
U1165                                                       17+++++++++++++++++
U1166                                                       8+++++28
U1167                                                     29+++++++++++30
U1168                                                        19+++++++++++++++
U1169                                                        9++++++++++++++++
U1170                                                        1+++++++++++++3
U1171                                                        22+++++++++++++
U1172                                                          20+++++27
U1191                                                   9+++++++25
U1192                                                     23++++++++++++++++++9
U1193                                                       7++++++++++++++++++
U1194                                                       21++++++++++++++++
U1195                                                       4+++++++++++++++6
U1196                                                    18+++++++?
U1197                                                       2+++++++++++++25
U1198                                                       9+++++++++++++++++
U1199                                                       23++++++++++21
U1200                                                      5++++++++11
U1201                                                       13++++++++++++3
U1202                                                     27+++++++++++++10
U1203                                                      10+++++++++++++
U1204                                                       17++++++++++++++
U1205                                                        2+++++++++++++3
U1206                                                       16++++++++++14
U1207                                                      23+++++++++++++
U1208                                                      6++++++++?
U1209                                                      13+++++18
U1210                                                       22+++++++++++3
U1221                                                 11+++++++++++++++++3
U1222                                                 1+++++++++11
U1223                                                     6++++++++++++++++23
U1224                                                  20++++13 Japanese c
U1225                                                 10++++24
U1226                                                 24++++++++28
U1227                                                    8+++++++++++++++9
U1228                                                    22+++++++++++++++++
U1229                                                  13++++20
U1230                                                    26++++++++++++++++
U1231                                                     9+++++++++++++14
U1232                                                     8+++++++++3
U1233                                                     22+++++++++++++
U1234                                                    19sunk17+++++
U1235                                                      17+++++++++15
U1271                                                      12++++++++++++++
U1272                                                      28+++++++++++++++
U1273                                                    16+++++++++17
U1274                                                     1+++++++++++16
U1275                                                      22++++++++++++
U1276                                                     6+++++++++20
U1277                                                        3++++++++++++
U1278                                                      31++++++17

     ----|-----------|-----------|-----------|-----------|-----------|----
     SONDJFMAMJJASONDJFMAMJJASONDJFMAMJJASONDJFMAMJJASONDJFMAMJJASONDJFMAM
---- 19391940        1941         1942         1943         1944         1945
```

	1939	1940	1941	1942	1943	1944	1945
	SOND	JFMAMJJASOND	JFMAMJJASOND	JFMAMJJASOND	JFMAMJJASOND	JFMAMJJASOND	JFMAM
U1279						5++++++	3
U1301						11+++++++++++++	+++
U1302						25+++++++	+7
U1303						5++++++++++++	+++
U1304						6+++++++	+
U1305						13++++++	+
U1306						20+++	+
U1307						17++++	+
U1308						17++	2
	SOND	JFMAMJJASOND	JFMAMJJASOND	JFMAMJJASOND	JFMAMJJASOND	JFMAMJJASOND	JFMAM
	1939	1940	1941	1942	1943	1944	1945

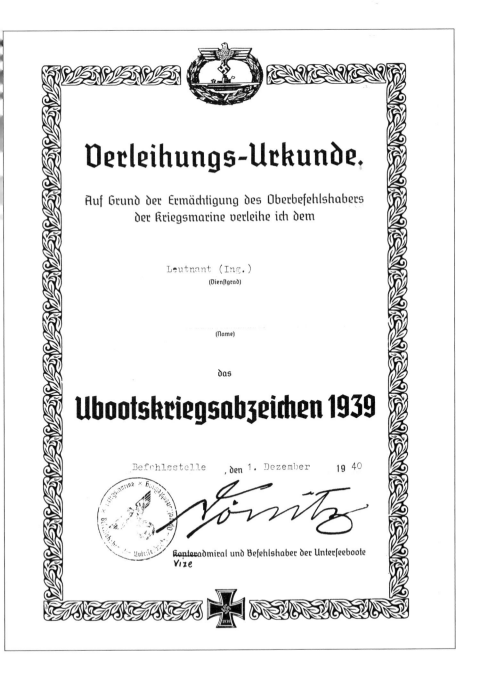

Select Bibliography

Beaver, Paul, *U-boats in the Atlantic*, Patrick Stephens Ltd, Cambridge 1979

Bekker, Cajus, *Flucht über's Meer*, Ullstein, Frankfurt 1959

Brennecke, Jochen, *Jäger-Gejagte*, Koehlers Verlag, Jugendheim 1956

Breyer, Siegfried, *Handbuch für U-Bootkommandanten*, Podzun-Pallas, Wölfersheim-Berstadt 1997

Brustat-Naval, Fritz, *Ali Cremer U333*, Ullstein, Frankfurt am Main 1982

Brustat-Naval, Fritz and Suhren, Teddy, *Nasses Eichenlaub*, Koehlers, Herford 1983

Busch, Harald, *So war der Ubootskrieg*, Deutsche Heimat Verlag, Bielefeld 1954

Busch, Rainer and Röll, Hans-Joachim, *Der U-boot-Krieg 1939-1945, Vol. 1. Die deutschen U-boot Kommandanten*, Koehler/Mittler, Hamburg/Berlin/Bonn 1996

Caram, Ed, *U352 - The Sunken German U-boat in the Graveyard of the Atlantic*, Caram 1987

Compton-Hall, Richard, *The Underwater War 1939-45*, Blandford, Poole 1982

Davis, Brian Leigh and Lyles, Kevin, "U-boat Uniforms", *Military Illustrated* Nos 4, 5 & 7, London 1987

Cremer, Peter, *U-boat Commander,* The Bodley Head, London 1982

Davis, Brian Leigh, *German Uniforms of the Third Reich 1933-1945*, Blandford, Poole 1980

Deutscher Marinebund, *Ubootmuseum U995*, Laboe

Deutsches Marineinstitut, *Marineschule Mürwik*, E.S. Mittler & Sohn, Herford

Dönitz, Karl, *Zehn Jahre und Zwanzig Tage*, Athenäum Verlag, Bonn 1958

Dönitz, Karl, *Mein wechselvolles Leben*, Musterschmidt Verlag, Göttingen 1968

Drummond, John D., *HM U-boat*, W.H. Allen, London 1958

Ellenbeck, Major Dr Hans, *Die Verantwortung des deutschen Offiziers*, Tornisterschrift des Oberkommando der Wehrmacht, Berlin 1941

Frank, Wolfgang, *Die Wölfe und der Admiral*, Gerhard Stalling Verlag, Oldenburg 1953

Frank, Wolfgang, *Enemy Submarine*, William Kimber, London 1954

Frank, Wolfgang, *Prien greift an*, Köhler Verlag, Hamburg 1942

Gadow, R., *Jahrbuch der deutschen Kriegsmarine*, Breitkopf & Härtel, Leipzig 1937-1944

Gasaway, E.B., *Grey Wolf Grey Sea,* Arthur Baker, London 1972

Giese, Fritz, *Die deutsche Marine 1920-45*, Bernard & Graefe, Frankfurt am Main 1956

Giese, Otto and Wise Capt. James E., *Shooting the War*, Naval Institute Press, Annapolis 1994

Gretton, Peter, *Crisis Convoy*, Purnell Book Sevices, London 1974

Gretton, Peter, *Convoy Escort Commander*, Cassel, London 1964

Gröner, Erich, *Die Handelsflotten der Welt*, J.F. Lehmanns Verlag, Munich 1976

Gröner, Erich and Jung, Dieter and Maass, Martin, *Die deutschen Kriegsschiffe 1815-1945*, Vol. 3, Bernard & Graefe Verlag, Koblenz 1985

Güth, Rolf, *Die Marine des deutschen Reiches*, Bernard & Graefe Verlag 1972

Hadley, Michael, *U-boats against Canada*, McGill-Queen's University Press, Kingston and Montreal 1985

Hadley, Michael, *Count Not the Dead*, McGill-Queen's University Press, Kingston and Montreal 1995

Hahn, F., *Guidebook to the Military Historical Training Centre Exhibition of the Marineschule Mürwik*, Marineschule Mürwik Press, Flensburg 1978

Harlinghausen, C. Harald, *Ein Junge geht zur Kriegsmarine*, Wilhelm Köhler Verlag, Minden 1942

Hering, Robert, *Chronik der Crew 37a*, Gärtringen 1987

Herwig, Holger H., *Das Elitekorps des Kaisers*, H. Christian Verlag, Hamburg 1977

Herzog, Bodo, *60 Jahre deutsche Uboote 1906-66*, J.F. Lehmanns Verlag, Munich 1968

Herzog, Bodo, *U-boats in Action 1939-1945*, Podzun Verlag and Ian Allan, Dorheim and Shepperton

Hirschberg, Johannes & Hedwig, *Ein deutscher Seeoffizier*, Hedwig Hirschberg, Wiesbaden 1897

Hirschfeld, Wolfgang, *Feindfahrten*, Neff Verlag, Vienna 1982

Hirschfeld, Wolfgang and Brooks, Geoffrey, *The Story of a U-boat NCO 1940- 1946*, Leo Cooper, London 1996

Hirschfeld, Wolfgang, *Das letzte Boot - Atlantik Farewell*, Universitas Verlag, Munich 1989

Högel, Georg, *Embleme Wappen Mallings deutscher Uboote*, Koehlers Verlagsgesellschaft, Herford 1987

Hoffmann, Rudolf, *50 Jahre Olympia Crew*, Hoffmann, Hamburg 1986 & 1988

Howarth, Stephen and Law, Derek, *The Battle of the Atlantic 1939-1945* (The 50th Anniversary International Naval Conference), Greenhill Books, London 1994

Hutson, Harry C., *Grimsby's Fighting Fleet*, Hutton Press, Beverley 1990

Jones, Geoff, *The Month of the Lost U-boats*, William Kimber, London 1977

Jones, Geoff, *Autumn of the U-boats*, William Kimber, London 1984

Jones, Geoff, *Defeat of the Wolf Packs*, William Kimber, London 1986

Jones, Geoff, *U-boat Aces*, William Kimber, London 1988

Jones, Geoff, *Submarines versus U-boats*, William Kimber 1986

Lüth, Wolfgang and Korth, Claus, *Boot greift wieder an*, Klinghammer, Berlin 1943

Keatts, Henry and Farr, George, *Dive into History - U-boats*, American Merchant Marine Museum Press, New York 1986

Keatts, Henry, *Field Reference to Sunken U-boats*, American Merchant Marine Museum Press, New York 1987

Kemp, Paul, *U-boats Destroyed*, Arms and Armour Press, London 1997

Kieler Lehrthemen, *Geschichte der deutschen Kriegsmarine*, Verlag Alfred Burkhardt, Kiel 1943

Köhl, Fritz and Niestle, Axel, *Vom Original zum Modell - Uboottyp VIIC*, Bernard & Graefe Verlag, Koblenz 1989

Köhl, Fritz and Niestle, Axel, *Vom Original zum Modell - Uboottyp IXC*, Bernard & Graefe Verlag, Koblenz 1990

Köhl, Fritz and Rössler, Eberhard, *The Type XXI U-boat*, Conway Maritime Press, London 1988

Koop, Gerhard and Mulitze, Erich, *Die Marine in Wilhelmshaven*, Bernhard & Graefe Verlag, Koblenz 1987

Kurowski, Franz, *Knight's Cross Holders of the U-boat Service*, Schiffer Publishing Ltd., Pennsylvania 1995

Lohmann, W. and Hildebrand, H.H., *Kriegsmarine 1939-45*, Podzun Verlag, Dorheim 1956-64

Lumsden, R., *A Collector's Guide to Third Reich Militaria*, Ian Allan Ltd, Shepperton 1987

MacIntyre, Donald, *U-boat Killer*, Weidenfeld and Nicolson, London 1956

MacIntyre, Donald, *The Battle of the Atlantic*, Batsford, London 1961

Merten, Karl Friedrich and Baberg, Kurt, *Wir Ubootfahrer sagen 'Nein - So was das nicht'*, J. Reiss Verlag, Grossaitingen 1986

Metzler, Jost, *The Laughing Cow*, William Kimber, London 1955

Ministry of Defence, *The U-boat War in the Atlantic 1939-1945*, HMSO, London 1989 (This is the German view of the war at sea, written shortly after the war by Günter Hessler, Alfred Hoschatt and others)

Moore, Capt. Arthur R., *A Careless Word ... A Needless Sinking*, American Merchant Marine Museum, New York 1988

Mulligan, Timothy P., *Lone Wolf*, Praeger, Connecticut & London, 1993 (about Werner Hencke)

National Archives and Records Administration, *Records Relating to U-boat Warfare 1939-1945*, Washington 1985

Navy Department, *Axis Submarine Manual*, US Naval Intelligence 1942

Oberkommando der marine, *Rangliste der deutschen Kriegsmarine*, Ernst Siegfried Mittler & Sohn, published anually in Berlin until 1944

Oberkommando der Marine, *Bekleidungs und Anzugbestimmungen für die Kriegsmarine*, Verlag Bernard & Graefe, Berlin 1935

Plottke, Herbert, *Fächer Loos! (U172 im Einsatz)*, Podzun-Pallas, Wölfersheim-Berstadt, 1997

Preston, Anthony, *U-Boats*, Bison Books, London 1978

Prochnow, Güter, *Deutsche Kriegsschiffe in zwei Jahrhunderten*, Vol. IV, U- boote, Ernst Gades Verlag, Preetz/Holstein 1969

Range, Clemens, *Ritterkreuzträger der Kriegsmarine*, Motorbuch Verlag, Stuttgart 1974

Robertson, Terrence, *The Golden Horseshoe*, Pan Books, London 1966

Rössler, Eberhard, *Geschichte des deutschen Ubootbaus*, Vols. 1 & 2, Bernard & Graefe Verlag, Koblenz 1986

Rössler, Eberhard, *Die deutschen U-boote und ihre Werften*, Vols. 1 & 2, Bernard & Graefe Verlag, München 1979

Rohwer, Dr. Prof. Jürgen, *Axis Submarine Successes 1939-45*, Patrick Stephens, Cambridge 1983

Rohwer, Dr. Prof. Jürgen, *Uboote - Eine Chronik in Bildern*, Gerhard Stalling Verlag, Oldenburg 1962

Rohwer, Dr. Prof. Jürgen, *U107*, Profile Publications, Windsor 1971

Rohwer, Dr. Prof. Jürgen, *Der Krieg zur See 1939-1945*, Urbes Verlag, Munich 1992

Rohwer, Dr. Prof. Jürgen and Hümmelchen, Gerhard, *Chronology of the War at Sea 1939-1945*, Greenhill Books, London 1992

Ruge, Friedrich, *In vier Marinen*, Bernhard & Graefe Verlag, Munich 1979

Schaeffer, Heinz, *U-boat 977*, William Kimber, London 1952

Schenk, Robert, *What it was like to be a sailor in World War II*, Naval Institute Press (anthology by different authors about duty on all kinds of ships)

Schmoeckel, Helmut, *Menschlichkeit im Seekrieg?*, Mittler & Sohn, Herford 1987

Showell, Jak P. Mallmann, *U-boats under the Swastika*, Ian Allan 1973 (translated as *Uboote gegen England*, Motorbuch Verlag, Stuttgart 1974

Showell, Jak P. Mallmann, *U-boats under the Swastika - 2nd Edition*, Ian Allan 1987

Showell, Jak P. Mallmann, *The German Navy in World War Two*, Arms and Armour Press, London 1979 and 1990 (translated as *Das Buch der deutschen Kriegsmarine*, Motorbuch Verlag, Stuttgart 1982)

Showell, Jak P. Mallmann, *U-boat Command and the Battle of the Atlantic*, Conway Maritime Press, London 1989

Showell, Jak P. Mallmann, "The U-boat which sank itself", *World War II Investigator*, May 1988

Showell, Jak P. Mallmann, newsletter, *Germania International - The German Navy Study Group*, Telford

Sorge, Siegfried, *Der Marineoffizier als Führer und Erzieher*, Mittler und Sohn, Berlin 1943

Stärk, Hans, *Marineunteroffizierschule*, Plön / Holstein 1774

Stern, Robert C., *U-boats in Action*, Squadron/Signal Publications, Michigan 1977

Tarrant, V.E., The *U-boat Offensive*, Arms and Armour Press, London 1989

Verband deutscher Ubootsfahrer, *Schaltung Küste*, Hamburg (journal of the German Submariners' Association, published monthly)

Vincent, C.R., *Consolidated Liberator & Boeing Fortress*, Vol. 2, Canada Wings, Ontario 1975

Vorträge zur Militärgeschichte, Band 2, *Menschenführung in der Marine, Militärgeschichtliches Forschungsamt*, E.S. Mittler und Sohn, Herford 1981

Watts, Anthony J., *Axis Submarines*, MacDonald & Janes, London 1977

Werner, Herbert, *Iron Coffins*, Arthur Baker, London 1970

Westwood, David, *The Type VII U-boat*, Conway Maritime Press, London 1984

Wetzel, Eckard, *U995*, Paschke Verlag, Kiel 1985

Whinney, R., *The U-boat Peril,* Blandford Press, Poole 1986

Williamson, Gordon, *The Iron Cross*, Blandford Press, Poole 1984

Williamson, Gordon, *Knight's Cross of the Iron Cross*, Blandford Press, Poole 1987

Williamson, Gordon and Pavlovic, Darko, *U-boat Crews 1914-45*, Osprey, London 1995

Witthöft, H.J., *Lexikon zur deutschen Marinegeschichte*, Koehlers, Herford 1977 (2 volumes)

Young, George, *The Short Triangle*, Lunenburg County Print, Nova Scotia 1982

Zienert, J., *Unsere Marineuniform*, Helmuth Gerhard Schulz, Hamburg 1970

Fuehrer Conferences on Naval Affairs 1939-1945, Greenhill Books, London 1990

Other sources
Much of this book is based on unpublished material which has been accumulated at the German U-boat Archive at Cuxhaven and the Royal Navy Submarine Museum (HMS *Dolphin*) at Gosport. The most important unpublished documents used for research were:
BdU, Card Index of U-boats and Commanders
BdU, Logbook
Individual boats, Logbooks
Individual boats, U-boat Archive folders of collected information
Lüdde-Neurath, Walter, Collection of files about Dönitz
Merten, Karl-Friedrich, Collection of files about Dönitz
Fels, Maximilian, Dönitz in Nürnberg und Danach, 1966
Royal Navy, Monthly Anti-Submarine Reports published throughout the war.

Helgason, Gudmundur, has published a great deal of information on the Internet, http,//uboat.net. Contact pages, gummi@europe.is